IMPRESSIONISM AND THE SEA

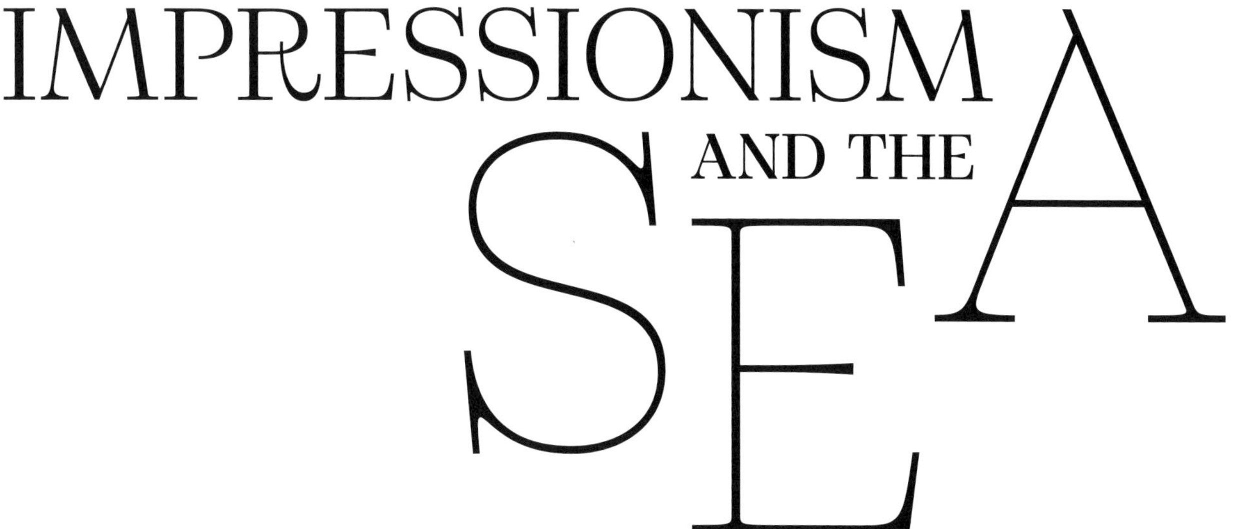

Editorial direction by Cyrille Sciama

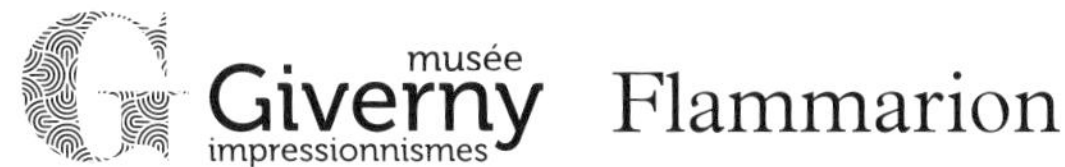

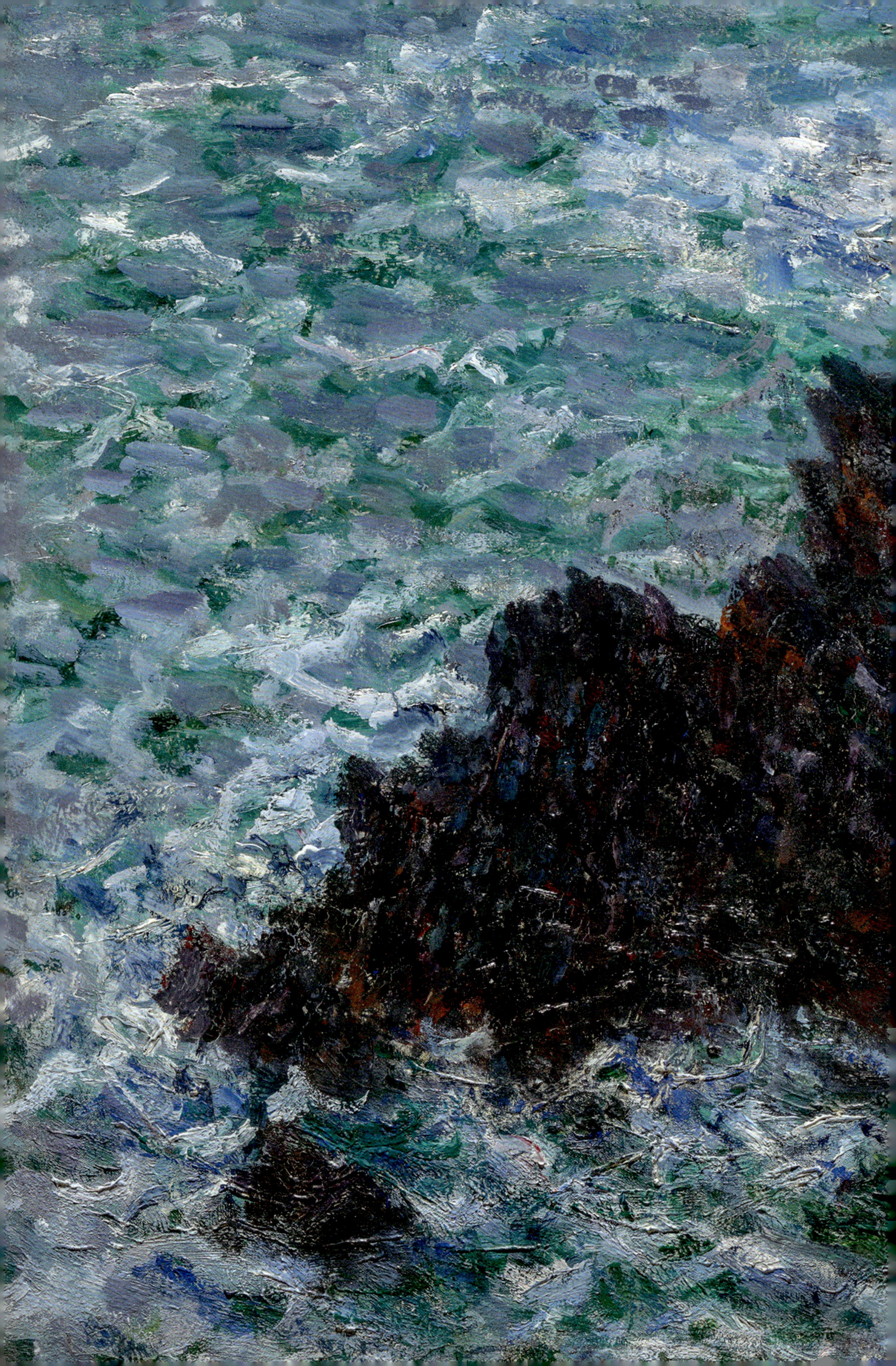

PREFACE

On the 150th anniversary of the first impressionist exhibition in 1874, the Musée des Impressionnismes Giverny is hosting an unprecedented exhibition, *L'Impressionnisme et la mer* (*Impressionism and the Sea*), from March 29 to June 30, 2024, accompanied by this richly illustrated volume. The event and the book benefit from the exceptional support of the Musée d'Orsay and the Normandie Impressionniste 2024 festival.

The theme of impressionism and the sea may seem somewhat banal, but it has, in fact, only been partially examined in previous exhibitions and works, and mostly from the perspective of seaside leisure pursuits; previous studies have amply demonstrated the impressionist penchant for beach scenes, seascapes, and portraits of summer vacationers. This volume sheds a new light on the impressionists' fascination with the sea, exploring works that reflect a different version of maritime life, from portrayals of dockers, fisherman, and laundrywomen, to renderings of the tides, storms, and the effects of light on the rippling waves. The movement—whose very roots lie at the water's edge, with Claude Monet's *Impression, soleil levant* (*Impression, Sunrise*), painted in Le Havre in 1872—encompassed artists with different temperaments and personal concerns, which are reflected in their diverse approaches to this theme. Here, lesser-known works dialogue with famous canvases, creating a fruitful exchange between paintings, drawings, prints, and archival documents.

We wish to thank all of the lenders, and extend our special thanks to the Musée d'Orsay, which has shown enormous generosity in this exceptional anniversary year. Many public and private museums in France and abroad, as well as private collectors, enthusiastically agreed to present their works in this exhibition, and we are extremely grateful to them. The board of trustees and scientific council of the Musée des Impressionnismes Giverny, the Cercle des Mécènes (Patrons' Circle), and Les Amis du Musée (Friends of the Museum) also provided invaluable support. Finally, we express our sincere thanks to the entire museum team, who have organized this ambitious exhibition to great success.

Sébastien Lecornu
President of the Musée des Impressionnismes Giverny
Minister for Armed Forces

Cyrille Sciama
General director and chief curator of the Musée des Impressionnismes Giverny

Claude Monet, *Les Rochers de Belle-Île, la Côte sauvage* (Rocks on Belle-Île, Côte Sauvage), detail, 1886 {cat. 68}.

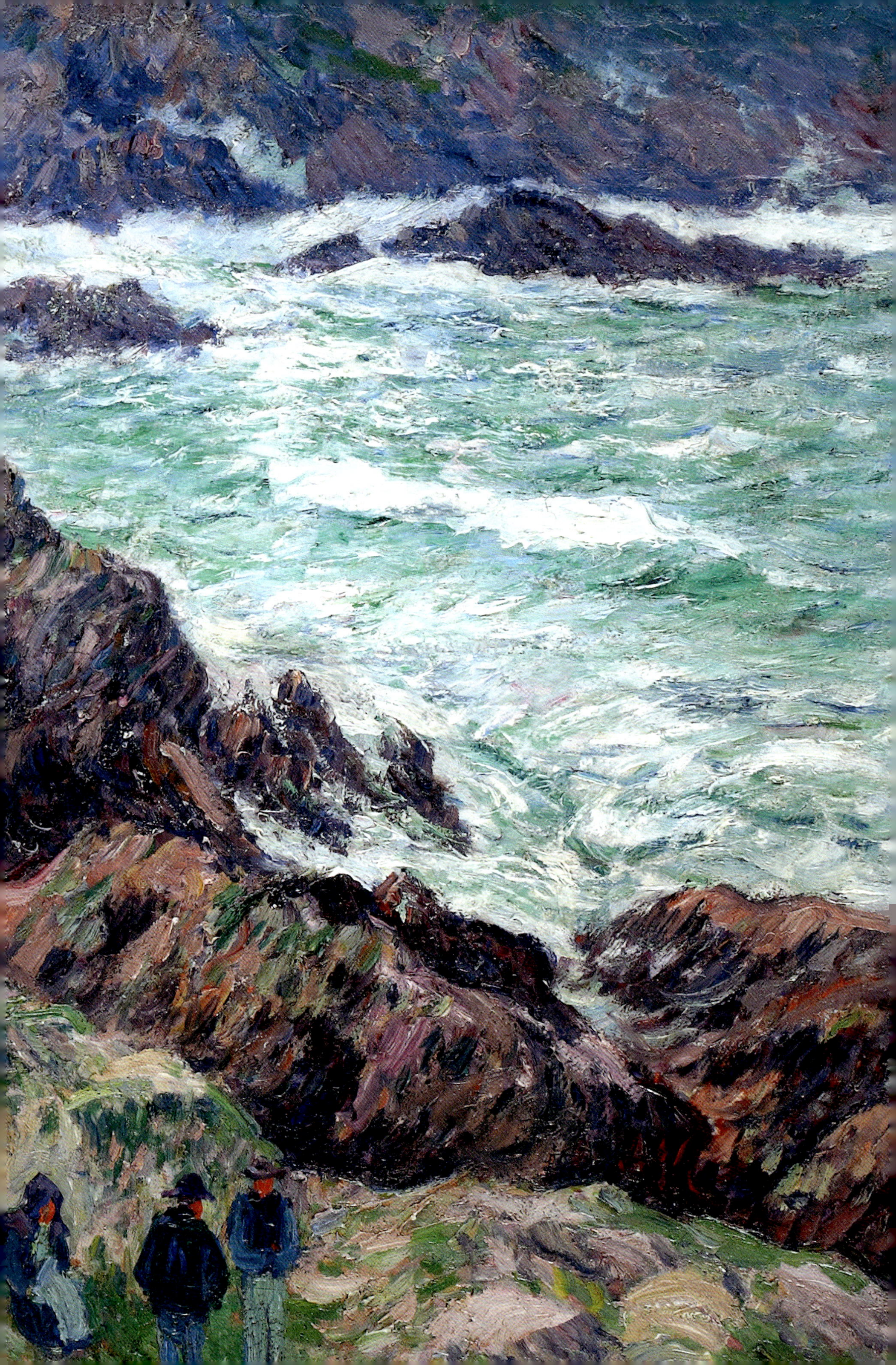

IMPRESSIONIST NORMANDY

If we had to choose a slogan for the fifth year of the Normandie Impressionniste festival, there could be only one: "The spirit of invention!" This is the theme for the 2024 festival, but it is also what best describes impressionism, whose 150th anniversary takes place the same year.

All of the festival's offerings—whether they be historical or contemporary—are rooted in the same spirit. Through the use of new methods, the hybridization of artistic practices, and innovative discourse, every event shares this bold guiding principle that brings together multiple disciplines.

The impressionists were also driven by a spirit of invention, which led them to transform the world of art. It is important to remember that 150 years ago they disrupted popular conventions of the day. Times have changed and so have artistic techniques, but the fundamental driving forces remain: artists must be fully of their time, and the festival must be open to all disciplines—this is the hallmark of postmodernity and ensures that the event will continue to offer added value in the future.

Now in its fifth year, the festival invites the world to celebrate the 150th anniversary of impressionism throughout Normandy, with leading figures from the international contemporary creative world, including David Hockney, Robert Wilson, and Sean Scully, to name but a few.

Another of the festival's defining characteristics is its firm connection to the region; each year, the event is made possible as a result of the collaboration of Normandy's cultural professionals. It unfolds throughout the entire region in spaces dedicated to culture, as well as in unexpected locations, in order to reach as large an audience as possible. The exceptional ability of the region's public authorities to unite their ambitions around this project is to be commended, as are the patrons and partners who continue to support this flagship program of French cultural life.

The festival is contemporary by virtue of the sustainable model it has developed over an intentionally long period, drawing as much as possible on what already exists and favoring inclusivity. In 1874, just one woman participated in the first impressionist exhibition: Berthe Morisot. A century and a half later, 47 percent of the artists in the Normandie Impressionniste events program are women.

Joachim Pissarro
President

Philippe Platel
Director

Philippe Piguet
General curator

Henry Moret, *Gros temps à Doëlan* (Rough weather at Doëlan), detail, n.d. {cat. 67}.

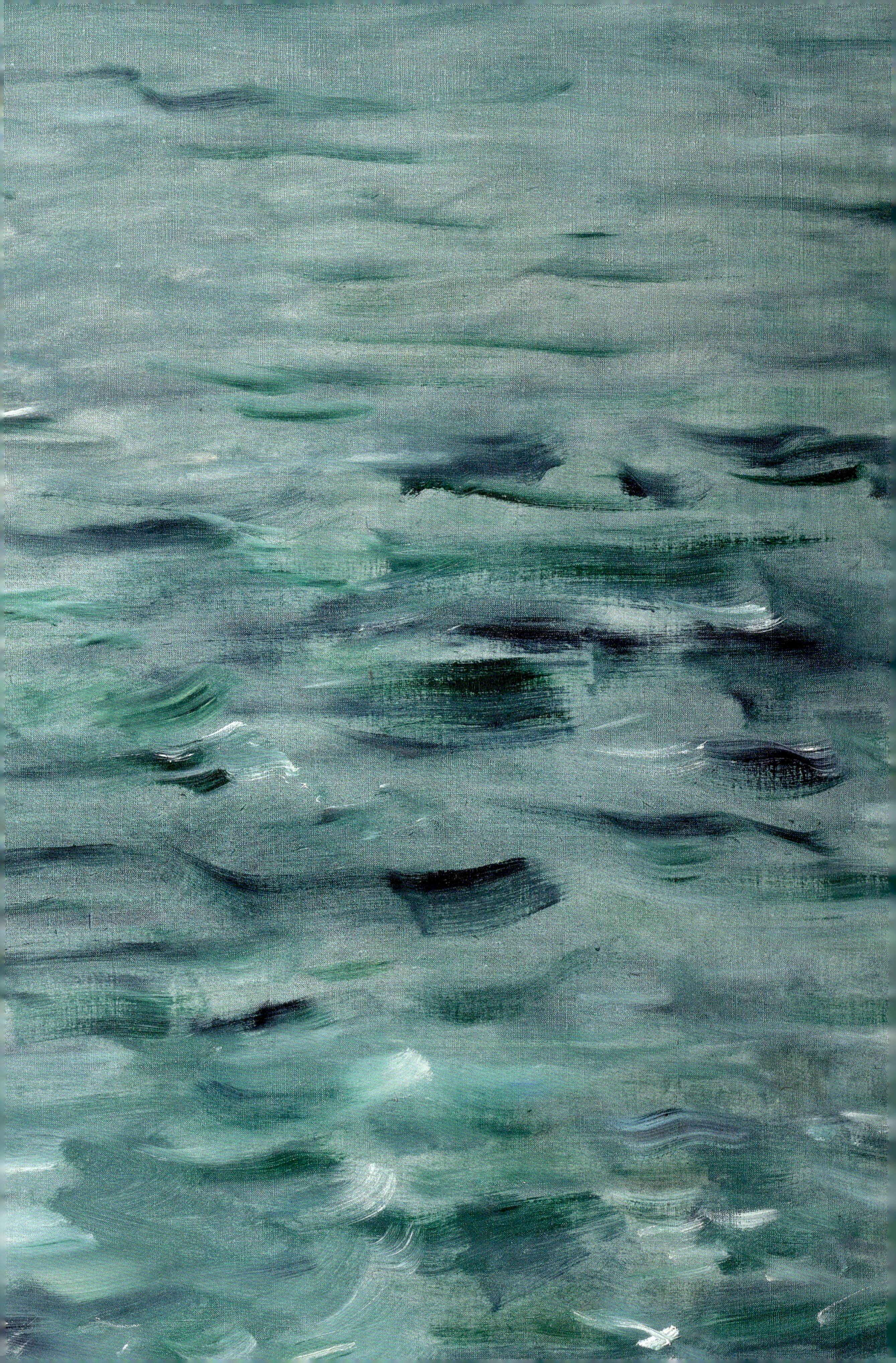

FOREWORD

While the sea holds special significance at the Caisse d'Épargne Normandie—it is based in a region bordered from one end to the other by the English Channel—sport will take on a distinctive role in 2024, as France prepares to host the Olympic Games. A "Premium Partner" of the Paris 2024 Games and official sponsor of the Normandy segment of the Olympic Torch Relay, which will pass through Vernon-Giverny on July 6, the Caisse d'Épargne Normandie is also the historic sponsor of the *Belem*, that jewel of the high seas, which will carry the flame from Greece. With this new exhibition, *Impressionism and the Sea*, the Musée des Impressionnismes Giverny also indulges in the dream of the open sea, evoking life in ports and on beaches, transport, and the maritime industry, as well as untamed nature and a thirst for distant lands. These themes all incite travel and discovery through the works of Claude Monet, Eugène Boudin, Johan Barthold Jongkind, Gustave Courbet, and Paul Gauguin, among others. The museum's dedication to constantly arousing visitors' curiosity, by regularly staging new exhibitions and offering a rich selection of cultural activities, is what defines it.

The Caisse d'Épargne Normandie has been the principal sponsor of this renowned center of impressionism in Normandy for over twelve years, and we are proud to be able to promote culture among a wide audience. A cooperative bank committed to social solidarity and serving both individuals and communities, the Caisse d'Épargne Normandie supports the projects and initiatives that make our region so dynamic, thanks to our shared values: the fostering of close relationships, as well as a commitment to making art and sport accessible to all, and to balancing economic performance with social responsibility.

Over the years, a fruitful cooperation has developed between our two institutions, helping to raise the profile of art and heritage in Giverny, Normandy, and far beyond. Just like the museum's previous exhibitions and publications, *Impressionism and the Sea* is sure to be a resounding success.

Bruno Goré
Chairman of the board of directors of the Caisse d'Épargne Normandie

Édouard Manet, *L'Évasion de Rochefort* (*The Escape of Rochefort*), detail, 1881 (cat. 99).

IMPRESSIONISM AND THE SEA

Editorial direction by Cyrille Sciama

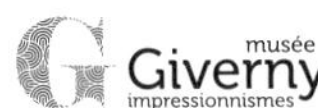

Flammarion

This book is published to accompany the exhibition *L'Impressionnisme et la mer* (*Impressionism and the Sea*), organized by the Musée des Impressionnismes Giverny, from March 29–June 30, 2024.

In 2024, to mark the 150th anniversary of impressionism, the French Ministry of Culture and the Musée d'Orsay have the honor of presenting the exhibition *Paris 1874: Inventer l'impressionnisme* (*Paris 1874: Inventing Impressionism*), held in Paris, with some 180 works on special loan from the Musée d'Orsay on display in more than thirty museums across France.

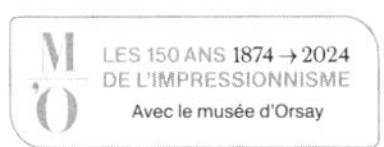

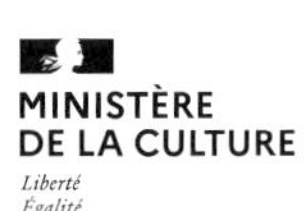

The exhibition *L'Impressionnisme et la mer* (*Impressionism and the Sea*) forms part of the events program organized by the 2024 Normandie Impressionniste festival, held from March 22–September 22, 2024.

The Musée des Impressionnismes Giverny is most grateful for the generosity of the Cercle des Mécènes du Musée des Impressionnismes Giverny, Les Amis du Musée, and the Caisse d'Épargne Normandie.

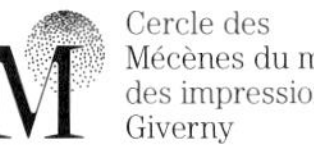

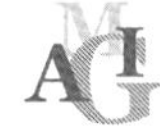

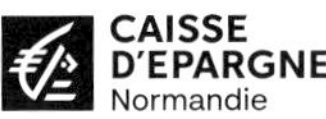

Founding members of the Musée des Impressionnismes Giverny:

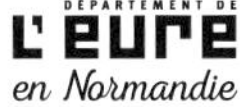

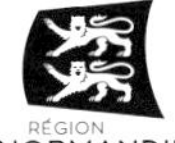

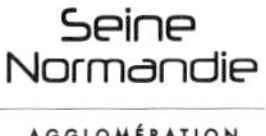

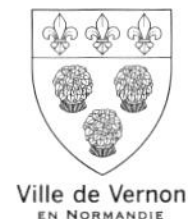

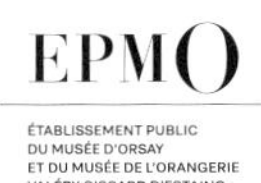

Exhibition curator
Cyrille Sciama
General director and chief curator of the Musée des Impressionnismes Giverny

Musée des Impressionnismes Giverny

President: Sébastien Lecornu
General director: Cyrille Sciama
General secretary: Cécile Stumpf-Meraly
Administration: Vincent Gosselin, Francine Le Massu, Xavier Poc
Curatorial assistance: Marie Delbarre, Valérie Reis, Véronique Roca
Maintenance: Denis Atanné, Didier Guiot, and the maintenance team
Visitor services and security: Olivier Touren and his team
Communication and marketing: Laurine Dallard, Aurore Hoair Fouquet, Romane Pinard, Charlène Potier
Press: Valérie Solvit
Public programs: Élisa Bonnin, Éléonore Coutau-Bégarie, Charlotte Guimier, Laurette Roche, and the education team
Bookstore and boutique: Cassandre Baron, Sandrine Couture, Carole Thuillier
Gardens: Emmanuel Besnard, Nicolas Feray, Aurélien Le Bras

Lenders

France
Château-Musée, Dieppe
FRAC Normandie
Les Franciscaines, Deauville
Musée d'Art et d'Archéologie, Guéret
Musée d'Art et d'Histoire, Saint-Lô
Musée d'Art, d'Histoire et d'Archéologie, Évreux
Musée d'Art Moderne André-Malraux (MuMA), Le Havre
Musée des Beaux-Arts, Angers
Musée des Beaux-Arts, Caen
Musée des Beaux-Arts, La Cohue, Vannes
Musée des Beaux-Arts, Orléans
Musée des Beaux-Arts, Reims
Musée des Beaux-Arts, Rennes
Musée de la Compagnie des Indes – Musée d'Art et d'Histoire de la Ville de Lorient, Lorient
Musée Eugène Boudin, Honfleur
Musée des Jacobins, Morlaix
Musée Lambinet, Versailles
Musée d'Orsay, Paris

Germany
Wallraf-Richartz Museum & Fondation Corboud, Cologne

The Netherlands
The Mesdag Collection, The Hague

Norway
Nasjonalmuseet for Kunst, Arkitektur og Design, Oslo

Spain
Carmen Thyssen Collection, Museo Nacional Thyssen-Bornemisza, Madrid

United States
Memorial Art Gallery, Rochester, NY
National Gallery of Art, Washington, D.C.
Virginia Museum of Fine Arts, Richmond, VA

De Bueil & Ract-Madoux Collection
Nahmad Collection
Hasso Plattner Collection
Private collections through the Galerie de la Présidence, Paris

And the private collectors who wish to remain anonymous.

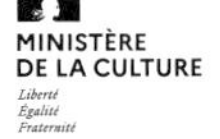
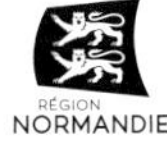
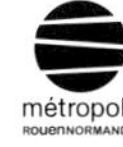
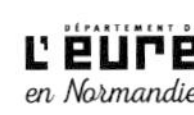
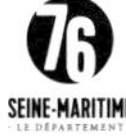
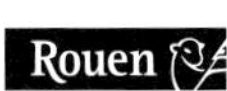
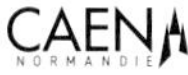
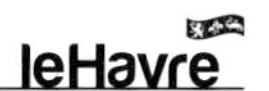
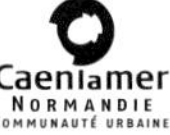
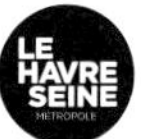

Catalog

Editorial coordination
Annie Dufour, ad.édition

Design and typesetting
Line Martin-Célo

Musée des Impressionnismes Giverny

Picture research and editorial supervision
Marie Delbarre and Valérie Reis

Flammarion

Editorial directors
Kate Mascaro and Julie Rouart
Editor
Helen Adedotun
Administration manager
Delphine Montagne
Translation from the French
Kate Robinson
Copyediting
Lindsay Porter
Proofreading
Rebecca du Plessis
Production:
Corinne Trovarelli

Color separation:
Les Artisans du Regard, Paris

Printed in Belgium by Graphius

Originally published in French
as *L'Impressionnisme et la mer*

English-language edition

editions.flammarion.com
@flammarioninternational

24 25 26 3 2 1
ISBN: 978-2-08-045548-2
Legal deposit: 05/2024

Acknowledgments

We wish to express our warmest thanks to Sébastien Lecornu, president of the Musée des Impressionnismes Giverny and minister for Armed Forces, for the trust he has shown in us and for his support throughout the project.

The exhibition could never have taken place without the unfailing support of the Departmental Council of Eure, in particular Alexandre Rassaërt, Pascal Lehongre, Pierre Stussi, Orlane Jaurégui, Ludivine Ponte, and their teams.
The members of the board of trustees and scientific council of the Musée des Impressionnismes Giverny have also demonstrated their loyalty and faith in the project.

We extend our sincere thanks to the teams of the Musée des Impressionnismes Giverny:
Denis Atanné, Cassandre Baron, Alizée Béatrix, Emmanuel Besnard, Élisa Bonnin, Éléonore Coutau-Bégarie, Sandrine Couture, Laurine Dallard, Marie Delbarre, Hassan El Oundi, Nicolas Feray, Aurore Hoair Fouquet, Vincent Gosselin, Charlotte Guimier, Didier Guiot, Emmanuel Hargous, Frédéric Ksiezarczyk, Aurélien Le Bras, Laurent Lefrançois, Francine Le Massu, Pascal Mérieau, Romane Pinard, Xavier Poc, Charlène Potier, Emmeline Raout, Valérie Reis, Véronique Roca, Laurette Roche, Cécile Stumpf-Meraly, Carole Thuillier, Olivier Touren, and Vincent Turquet.

We would also like to express our appreciation for the generosity of the Cercle des Mécènes (Patrons' Circle) of the Musée des Impressionnismes Giverny, under its president, Alain Missoffe; Les Amis du Musée (Friends of the Museum), under its president, Charles-Élie de La Brosse; as well as that of the museum's principal patron, the Caisse d'Épargne Normandie, under its president, Bruno Goré.

We extend our gratitude to Joachim Pissarro, president of the Normandie Impressionniste 2024 festival, as well as Philippe Platel, director, and Philippe Piguet, general curator of the fifth edition of the festival, for supporting this project.

We are particularly grateful to Annie Dufour for her contribution to the project, and to Line Martin-Célo for her design of the catalog.

Valérie Solvit and her agency provided invaluable assistance.

We would also like to thank all those who helped in the preparation of the exhibition and the catalog: Darren Almond, Marian Aparicio, Catherine Arnold, Marie-Annie Avril, Gérard and Marie-Claude Beaufour, Françoise Berretrot, Nathalie Besson-Amiot, Gilles Blanchard, Beatriz Blanco, Jean-Roch Bouiller, Magali Bourbon, Mai Britt Guleng, Flore Brizé Le Lion, Jean-Gabriel de Bueil, Maxime Carette, Stéphane Cariou, Bridget Chew, Florence Chibret-Plaussu, Françoise Chibret-Plaussu, Estelle Clavel, Caroline Clémensat, Lucille Cocito, Christina Collet Hvolgaard, Pierre Commoy, Sylvain Cordier, Marjolaine David, Sophie De Grande, Renée Dejouany, Marcus Dekiert, Emmanuelle Delapierre, Catherine Delot, Courtney DiMartino, Florence Disson, Clémence Ducroix, Patrick Eoche-Duval, Anne Esnault, Kaywin Feldman, Pascal Foulon, David Gadanho, Alice Gamblin, Émilie Gordenker, Laura Gosse, Camille Gross, Bénédicte Hamard, Nadine Hansen, Annette Haudiquet, Matthias Heitbrink, Grant Holcomb, Nadine Huc, Pierre Ickowicz, Fanny Jacquinet, Kimberly A. Jones, Melanie Krone, Géraldine Lefebvre, Philippe Legouis, Anne-Laure Le Guen, Sophie Levisse-Montfort, Siri Lindberg, Fatima Louli, Paula Luengo, Lisa M. MacDougall, Annie Madet-Vache, Émilie Maisonneuve, Laurène Marin, Odile Michel, Marc Montagne, Marie-Hélène Montout Richard, Mary Morton, Rebecca Myles, David Nahmad, Ezra Nahmad, Esther Navarro, Alexander Nette, Nancy T. Nichols, Brigitte Nicolas, Nancy Norwood, Alex Nyerges, Guillaume Parage, Vincent Pécoil, Paul Perrin, Martine Picat, Michael Philipp, Isolde Pludermacher, Nicolas Pratz, Stanislas Ract-Madoux, Reinhard Rasch, Hermine Ravel, Philippe Remes, Purificacion Ripio, Béatrice Riou, Robert Ritter, Natacha Roehrig, Justin Romeo, Ingrid Roynesdal, Barbara Schaefer, Emmanuelle Siot, Nathalie Sitko, Guillermo Solana, Mary Sullivan, Mélanie Thomas, Giulia Trabaldo Togna, Ambroise Triail-Plaussu, Mathis Triail-Plaussu, Evangelia Tsiantoula, Jean-Pierre Vincens, Olivia Voisin, Ortrud Westheider, Edouard Williamson, Sylvie Winckler, Magali Wunderle, and Daniel Zamani.

AUTHORS

Cyrille Sciama
General director and chief curator of the Musée des Impressionnismes Giverny

Marie Delbarre
Research assistant, Musée des Impressionnismes Giverny

Valérie Reis
Exhibition manager Musée des Impressionnismes Giverny

Editor's note:
Catalog numbers (cat.) refer to works included in the exhibition.
Figure numbers (fig.) refer to works reproduced here for illustrative purposes.

CONTENTS

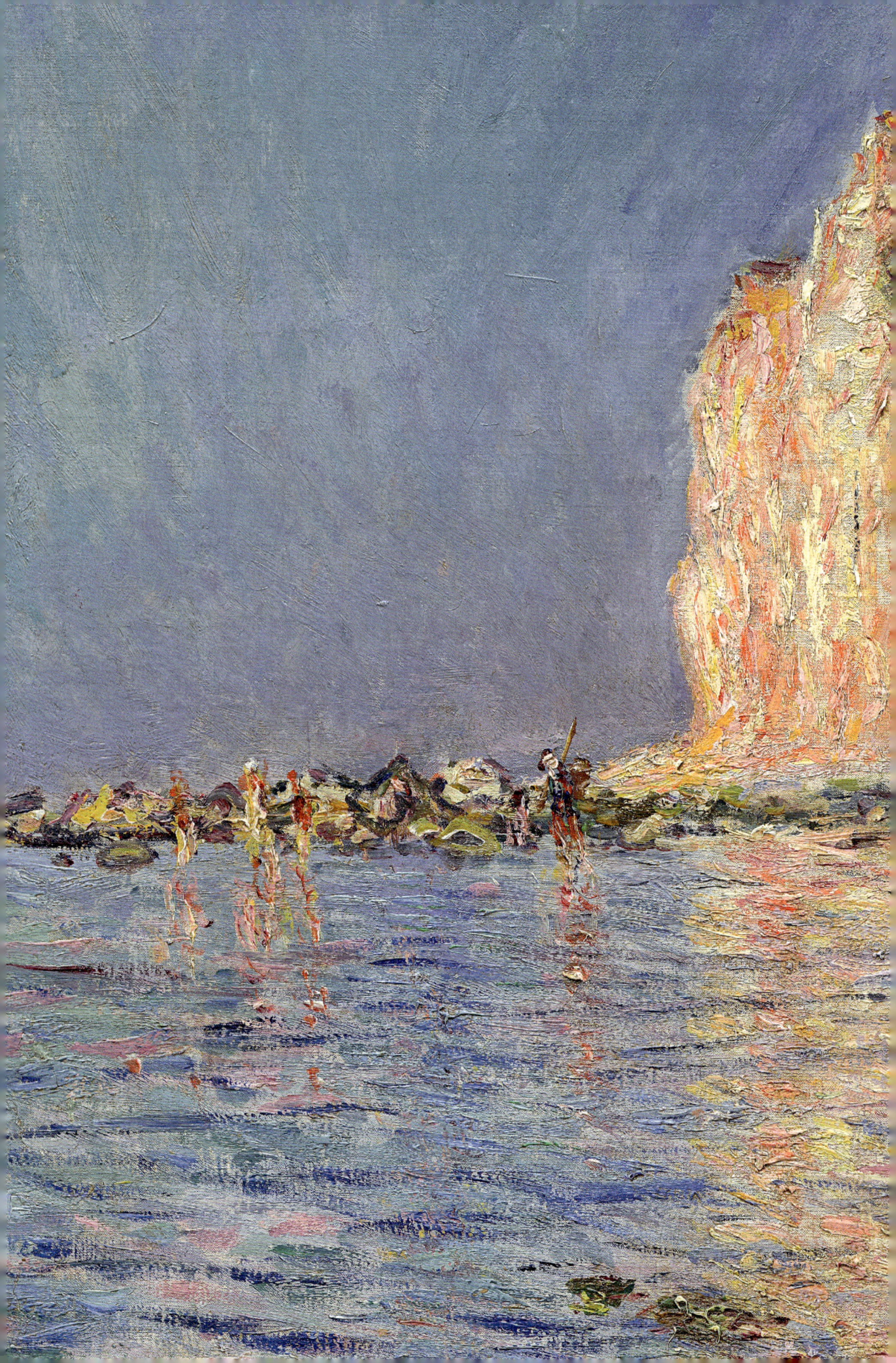

PAINTING THE SEA: IMPRESSIONIST SEASCAPES

By Cyrille Sciama

"I lived in Le Havre as a child. I was raised and have remained faithful to this sea with which I grew up. . . , this sea has always been a wonderful teacher for landscape painters. . . , they have all come to the coast of the English Channel to learn the color of the air and the secrets of the fog."[1]

Claude Monet spoke these words during an interview with a journalist in 1889, at a time when he enjoyed a solid reputation as a painter. Like his friends Édouard Manet, Edgar Degas, and Pierre-Auguste Renoir, Monet never tired of depicting the sea, pebbled beaches, bathers, ships, and changing skies of the Normandy coast. The connection between the impressionist painters and the sea has been addressed in many publications and exhibitions,[2] focusing on such themes as *Un été au bord de l'eau* (*A Summer at the Water's Edge*),[3] *La femme et la mer, 1850–1920* (Women and the sea, 1850–1920),[4] *Impressionists by the Sea*,[5] and *Aux couleurs de la mer* (The colors of the sea).[6] Researchers have highlighted the role of specific locations in developing the individual styles of certain artists: Le Havre for Monet, Guernsey for Renoir, Boulogne-sur-Mer for Manet, and Saint-Valery-sur-Somme for Degas. The artists seem to have each developed a preference for a specific place appropriated by them alone. Yet the impressionists, through their vivid portrayals of the profound social changes taking place along the coasts of France, carried on a tradition of which they were the admiring successors. From Joseph Vernet's spectacular seascapes, lauded by Denis Diderot, to Théodore Gudin's romantic shipwrecks,[7] nautical subjects were incredibly popular. In this context of commercial and critical success, what did the impressionists contribute to marine landscape painting? Did they have a *distinctive* point of view?

Going beyond the pleasing image of the impressionists at work in Deauville or Dieppe, the subject can be explored from new thematic and chronological perspectives. The impressionists were a diverse group, and the ways in which they approached seascapes and the seaside reflect their different dispositions, as well as each artist's personal concerns. Monet and Renoir have little in common when it comes to depictions of the sea. Similarly, Camille Pissarro's vision of Le Havre differed from Monet's. This suggests that there are still a number of themes worth examining that could shed a different light on the attraction the impressionists felt toward the open sea. After all, impressionism emerged by the water's edge. Monet's *Impression, soleil levant* (*Impression, Sunrise*; 1872, Musée Marmottan Monet, Paris) is ultimately a seascape that adheres to a genre previously glorified by Gustave Courbet and Eugène Boudin. Degas, Manet, Gustave Caillebotte, and Johan Barthold Jongkind depicted the coastal landscape with elegance and originality. Researchers have thoroughly studied this vision of the landscape, often focusing on the effects of sunlight, as well as on original points of view, framing devices borrowed from photography, or the lifestyle of summer vacationers during the impressionist period. However, certain other aspects unique to seafaring activity during the impressionist period have been given little consideration: life for dockers and fishermen, the maritime industry and transport, naval warfare, but also storms and a desire to travel to distant lands, among others. The geographic scope remains relatively limited: impressionist artists worked primarily on seascapes in Normandy or on the French Riviera, although it is also important to consider Brittany through the work of Maxime Maufra and Henry Moret, both of whom were strongly influenced by Monet.

1 Claude Monet, quoted by Hugues Le Roux in "L'exposition de Claude Monet," *Gil Blas*, March 3, 1889.
2 Claire Durand-Ruel Snollaerts, *Les Impressionnistes: Loisirs et mondanités* (Rouen: Éditions des Falaises, 2016).
3 Musée des Beaux-Arts, Caen, April 27–September 29, 2013.
4 Musée Eugène Boudin, Honfleur, June 22–September 30, 2013.
5 Royal Academy of Arts, London, July 7–September 30, 2007; The Phillips Collection, Washington, D.C., October 20, 2007–January 13, 2008; Wadsworth Atheneum Museum of Art, Hartford, CT, February 9–May 11, 2008.
6 Musée d'Orsay, Paris, November 6, 1999–January 16, 2000.
7 The exhibition *Tempêtes et naufrages: De Vernet à Courbet* (Storms and shipwrecks: From Vernet to Courbet), Musée de la Vie Romantique, Paris, May 19–September 12, 2021, explored this subject.

Claude Monet, *Marée basse aux Petites Dalles* (*Low Tide at Les Petites Dalles*), detail, 1884 (cat. 45).

GETTING TO THE SEA

In the late eighteenth century, painters began traveling to Normandy, drawn by the light and the region's spectacular natural sites, which were ideal for inspiring artistic production. English painters J.M.W. Turner and Richard Bonington spent time in Honfleur, as did Romantic painters such as Paul Huet and Eugène Isabey—famous for his shipwreck scenes—followed in 1825 by Camille Corot, who would return to Normandy in 1829, after his first stay in Rome. During the Restoration, the Duchess of Berry, accompanied by members of the Parisian nobility, turned Dieppe into the first summer seaside resort. Granville subsequently attracted bathers, before the Duke of Morny, Napoleon III's half-brother, made Deauville fashionable. Artists also catered to prevailing tastes: by painting fashionable places, they found a wealthy clientele willing to purchase their work.

For the impressionists—artists who lived in Paris during the 1870s—traveling to the sea to paint was no easy feat. Often, they began by painting riverbanks, especially those of the Seine, to depict the changing light. With the exception of Monet, who grew up in Le Havre and moved to Paris in 1859, and Manet, who stayed in Boulogne-sur-Mer and Berck in the 1860s, the impressionists discovered Normandy and the sea in the late 1870s. Renoir's first experience was in Wargemont, near Dieppe, in 1879; for Caillebotte, it was in Villers-sur-Mer in 1880; and for Degas, it was in Saint-Valery-sur-Somme in 1896. Later, Brittany was popularized through Paul Gauguin's studies, and the Riviera would cast its charm on Monet and Renoir later in life, in 1884, when they were both over forty.

Getting from Paris to the sea required time and organization. The train was the fastest mode of transport. A rail line between Paris and Rouen opened in 1843 and was extended to Le Havre in 1847; the line to Dieppe opened in 1848, to Cherbourg and to Fécamp in 1858, and to Granville in 1870. The branch line between Lisieux and Trouville opened in 1863. In 1870, the train ride from Paris to Le Havre took about five hours, making it a rather long journey and one subject to delays and construction work, not to mention the frequent obstacles encountered along the track. Trips organized from Saturday evening to Sunday evening enabled passengers, for a reduced fare, to travel at night and spend the day by the sea. From the late 1840s, these *trains de plaisir*, or "excursion trains," were quite popular, especially among travelers of more modest means {fig. 1}.

Once they arrived, vacationers had to find a place to stay. They could rely on guide books to help them in their search, notably the Guide Joanne,

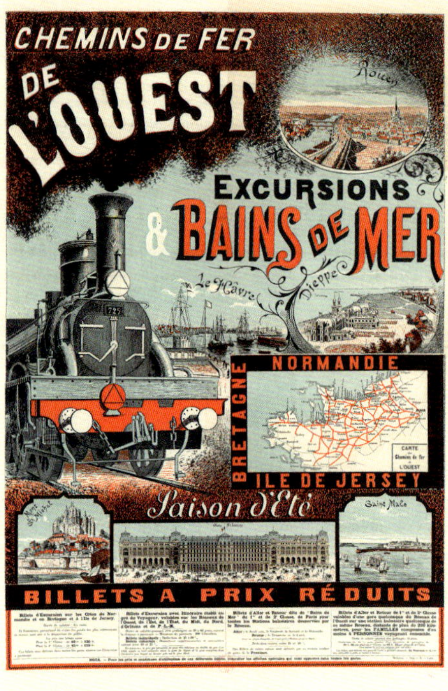

1 {fig.}
Poster for the French Railroad Company Les Chemins de Fer de l'Ouest, 1880.
Lithograph, 3 ft. 9 in. × 2 ft. 8 in. (115 × 81 cm). BNF, Paris.

the most well-known during the Third Republic, which later became Le Guide Bleu.[8] Since hotels in town were expensive for penniless artists, they sometimes sought lodgings further out in the country, as Camille Corot did when he began traveling to Honfleur in the 1830s. Impressionists in search of dramatic themes on the Côte de Grâce congregated at the inn at the Saint-Siméon farm, which became something of an informal artists' colony. The farmhouse made a name for itself thanks to the warm welcome provided by its owner, Mère Toutain, and her daughter. Courbet followed on the heels of Corot, trailed by Jongkind, Boudin, and Monet. On August 6, 1864, Jongkind wrote to Boudin, "In my opinion, Honfleur is an admirable place in which to live and work."[9] For the more well-to-do tourists, a group of luxury hotels was created along the coast, which also drew painters' attention: the Hôtel des Roches Noires in Trouville is one famous example. In the 1880s, Caillebotte—who would paint the urban development taking place along the coast as villages expanded, as in Villers-sur-Mer, for example—rented villas during the summer and participated in regattas, of which he was a great fan {fig. 3}. This was the ideal situation for the most fortunate impressionists—to be both painter and vacationer.

HARBOR SEASCAPES

Before turning their attention to the sea, artists naturally began painting harbors, and these ports became the scene for numerous impressionist depictions. Painters stayed in hotels along the quays, where they observed the ships and the activity of the docks. Corot was able to focus both on the comings and goings in the harbor, as he did in his striking *Vue de Honfleur* (View of Honfleur),[10] and on more specific elements, such as vessels at low tide (*Trouville, bateaux de pêche échoués dans le chenal* [Trouville, fishing boats aground in the channel] {cat. 17}). Jongkind, like Boudin, created a whole series featuring harbors, notably Dordrecht and Antwerp. In 1855, Jongkind painted a rather traditional version of Antwerp's harbor {cat. 15} that is similar in style to the work of Eugène Isabey. The smooth brushwork revisits the codes of seventeenth-century Flemish painting. However, Jongkind's 1868 etching *Le Soleil couchant, port d'Anvers* (*Sunset, Port of Antwerp*) {cat. 14} demonstrates an evolution in his work, foreshadowing the modernity to come in Monet's *Impression, soleil levant*. Here, he is as close as he can get to the water and to the sparkling of the light on its surface. The ships blend gently into the morning landscape. In 1871, Boudin also depicted Antwerp harbor {cat. 16}, using an economy of means reminiscent of Corot's technique. But the following year, he completed a striking illustration of Camaret, in Finistère (western Brittany) {cat. 19}: the interplay between the cloud-filled sky and the rippling surface of the water is rendered dramatically in a muted range of grays and blues. Throughout his entire career, Boudin

8 For more on the subject, see Hélène Morlier, "La Normandie des guides Joanne: L'attrait des stations balnéaires," in *Destination Normandie: Deux siècles de tourisme, XIXe–XXe siècles*, ed. Alice Gandin, exh. cat. (Caen: Musée de Normandie/Milan: 5 Continents Éditions, 2009), 53–59.

9 Georges Jean-Aubry, *Eugène Boudin* (Greenwich, CT: New York Graphic Society, 1968), 33.

10 Circa 1850, Musée des Beaux-Arts, Reims.

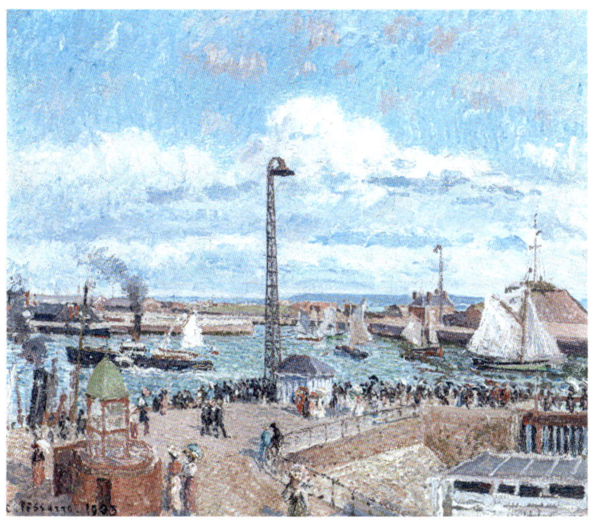

2 {fig.}
Camille Pissarro, *L'Anse des Pilotes et le brise-lames est, Le Havre, après-midi, temps ensoleillé* (*Pilots' Jetty*), 1903. Oil on canvas, 21½ × 26 in. (54.5 × 65.3 cm). MuMA, Le Havre.

displayed a talent for rendering sunsets over water, as seen in *Le Bassin de l'Eure au Havre* (The Eure basin at Le Havre) {cat. 21}.

In the summer of 1903, from the window of the Hôtel Continental, Pissarro painted Le Havre's harbor, focusing on the activity of the quays, cranes, and passersby, in contrast to the movement of the ships {fig. 2, cat. 24}. His fragmented brushwork is perfectly suited to the depiction of the crowds lining the Quai de Southampton, amid the thick smoke of the coasters. After painting a series of twenty-four canvases featuring Le Havre's harbor, he left the maritime city for Paris on September 26 and died on November 13; ports were, therefore, Pissarro's final theme—the ultimate expression of an appreciation for the sea by this artist who was born in Saint Thomas, in the West Indies {cat. 101}.

As a young artist, Paul Signac was drawn to the impressionist movement. Monet was an important model for Signac, who realized the master painter's significance in 1879, during the group's fourth exhibition. In 1882, Signac painted *Port-en-Bessin (étude no. 5, l'avant-port)* (Port-en-Bessin [study no. 5, outer harbor]) {cat. 26} using a technique influenced by Monet and Renoir: his fragmented and vibrant brushwork uses luminous strokes in an attempt to capture the reflection of the sky on the water. Signac had a lifelong fascination with the sea, and in 1929 he began a series featuring the port cities of France, picking up where Vernet had left off two centuries earlier. He wandered the coast until 1931, visiting a hundred or so ports, and produced dramatic scenes, from Barfleur to La Rochelle, and from Bayonne to Menton. Along with Caillebotte and Paul Helleu, Signac was one of the few artists who owned boats, and he took up sailing in the 1890s. As a result, his vision of the sea is a personal one, and he executed some of his harbor scenes from the water. In 1915, he was awarded the title Peintre de la Marine (official painter of the fleet). In 1930, he rented a house in Barfleur, and it is likely that his view of the harbor held in the Musée des Impressionnismes Giverny dates from this period {cat. 25}. Signac's art comes into its own in this large ink wash drawing, in which the movements of the clouds are mirrored in the waves below. The palette of grays reinforces the painting's analogous relationship with black-and-white photography—a resemblance that the artist plays on skillfully.

BOUDIN AND BAUDELAIRE

Eugène Boudin, known for his paintings of the sky and the sea, had a decisive influence on the impressionists—Monet most of all. The two men met in Le Havre in 1858, in the boutique of the paper-maker and framer Gravier where Boudin worked. He encouraged the eighteen-year-old Monet to join him in painting en plein air. Monet would later describe the older artist as being his master, explaining how he was enlightened by him: "Boudin truly initiated me."[11] The two artists saw each other regularly, and painted and drew together; at times, their styles blended, especially

11 *Monet: A Retrospective*, ed. Charles F. Stuckey (New York: Park Lane, 1986), 271.

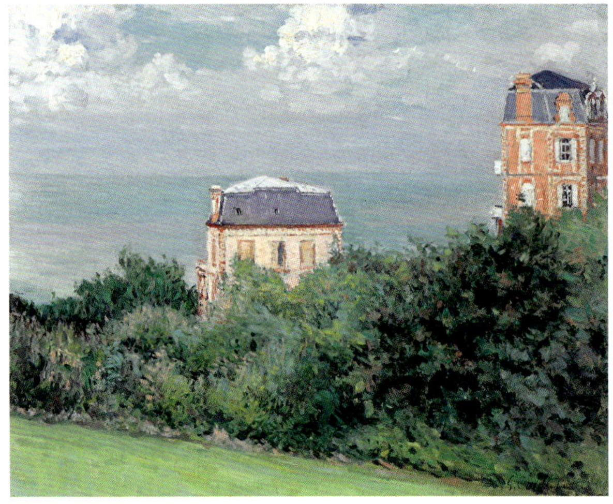

3 {fig.}
Gustave Caillebotte, *Villas à Villers-sur-Mer* (Villas at Villers-sur-Mer), 1880.
Oil on canvas, 25½ × 32 in. (64.8 × 81.3 cm). Private collection.

when they used pastel to depict the countryside around Honfleur, the sunsets, the skies, and the sea. The two men shared an ongoing, respectful, and admiring exchange. Recent reconsideration of their relationship has revealed that both artists mutually influenced each other's work throughout their respective careers.[12] The two friends grew apart over time, and at the end of his life, Boudin appeared somewhat bitter, insisting that Monet give him a painting in memory of the time they had spent together in their youth.[13] In Le Havre, in 1862, Monet met Jongkind, who, according to Monet, "completed the teachings that I had already received from Boudin. From that time on he was my real master, and it was to him that I owed the final education of my eye."[14]

The water, sky, and reflections that shaped the works of Boudin and Jongkind were also of crucial importance for the impressionists. It was at this time that Honfleur began attracting a more bourgeois, Parisian clientele in search of sea air and artistic inspiration. As a result, Boudin met Charles Baudelaire by chance—an encounter that would help to forge the painter's reputation in Paris. Boudin moved to the capital in 1861, hoping to find new clients for his work. The relationship between Boudin and Baudelaire was most active in 1859, when the poet made several trips to Honfleur. On his return to Paris, he wrote an article commending Boudin, for which the painter was grateful. "So far I have met only Baudelaire, who wrote quite well of me in a review he was editing at the time, and which has recently ceased publication."[15] The two men were not really friends, and they did not grow close after Baudelaire's stay in Honfleur. Nevertheless, Baudelaire praised Boudin's work, which he discovered during this period:

> These studies, so swiftly and accurately sketched, after what, in terms of force and color, are the most inconstant, the most fleeting of the things, after waves and clouds, always have written in their margins the date, the hour and the wind.... At the end, all these clouds, with their fantastic, luminous shapes, these chaotic shadows, these green and pink immensities suspended and added one on top of the other, these yawning ovens, these firmaments made from black or violet satin, crumpled, rolled or torn, these horizons in mourning or streaming with molten metal, all these depths, all these splendors, went to my head like an intoxicating drink or the eloquence of opium.[16]

For the poet, Boudin's art enabled a perfect synesthesia between the senses of sight, smell, and taste: he was intoxicated not on wine but on art, as he would recommend some time later, in his 1864 sonnet "Enivrez-vous!" ("Get Drunk"). In his review of the Salon, Baudelaire extolled Boudin's "meteorological beauties." Within his visionary approach, the poet included Boudin in his pantheon of painters of modern life, no doubt due to his own fondness for the sea, which he had declaimed in his collection *Les Fleurs du mal* (*The Flowers of Evil*) in 1857:

12 *Monet/Boudin*, ed. Juan Ángel López Manzanares, exh. cat. (Madrid: Museo Nacional Thyssen-Bornemisza, 2018).

13 Boudin to Monet, July 28, 1892, in Jean-Aubry, *Eugène Boudin*, 116–118.

14 *Monet: A Retrospective*, ed. Charles F. Stuckey, 217.

15 Boudin to Louis Boudin, February 2, 1861, in Jean-Aubry, *Eugène Boudin*, 30.

16 Charles Baudelaire, *Curiosités esthéthiques*, cited in Anne-Marie Bergeret-Gourbin, *Eugène Boudin: Paintings and Drawings. Catalogue Raisonné, Musée Eugène Boudin, Honfleur* (Paris: Somogy Éditions d'Art, 1996), 76.

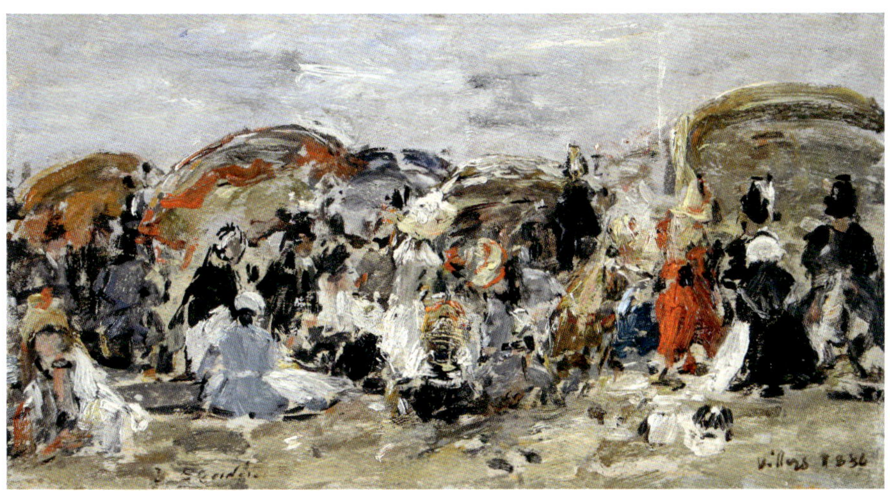

4 {cat.}
Eugène Boudin, *Crinolines sur la plage de Villers* (Crinolines on the beach at Villers), 1886. Oil on panel, 5½ × 10½ in. (14 × 26 cm). Private collection.

5 {fig.} – *The Casino and Beach at Trouville*, c. 1900.

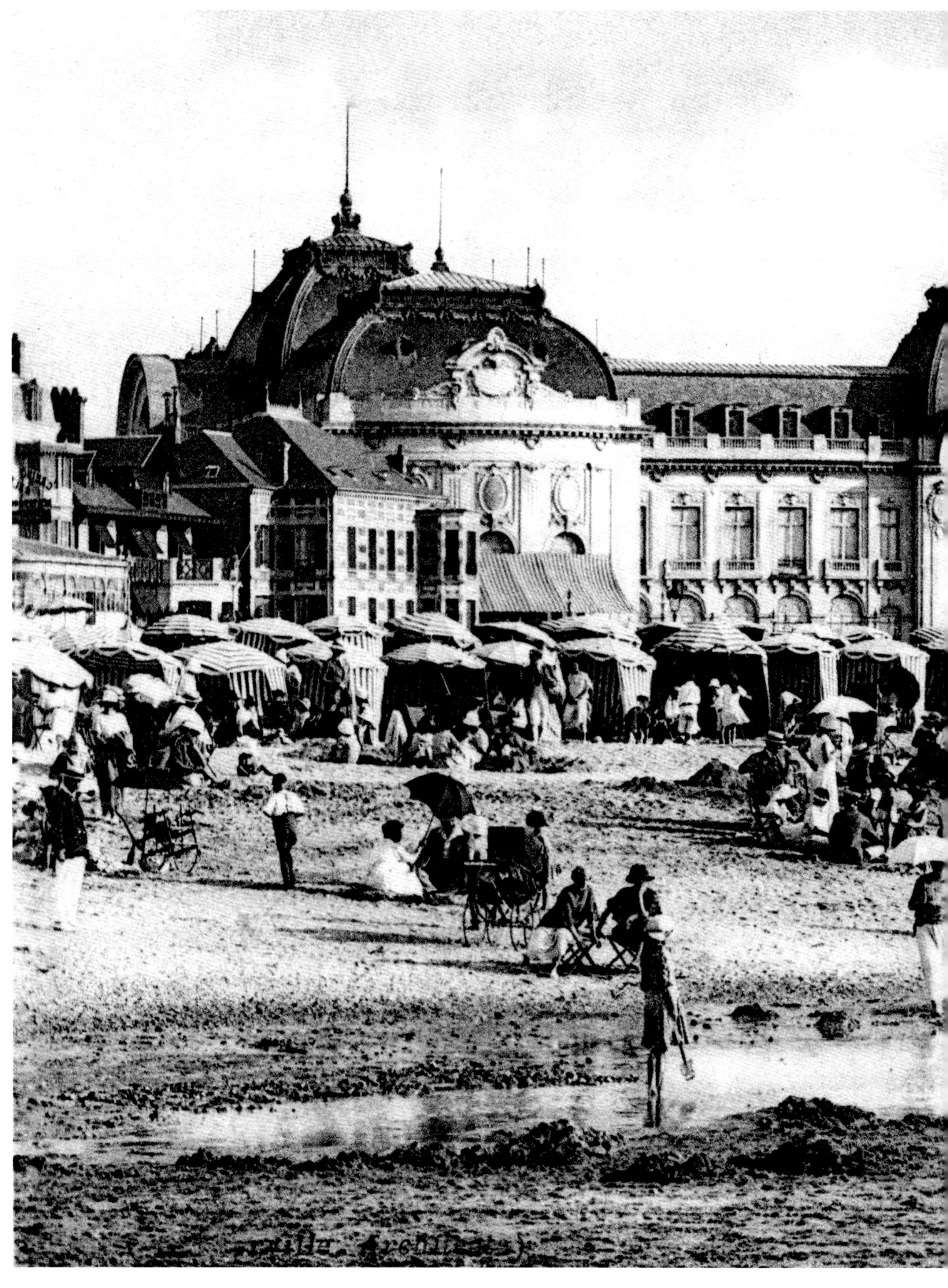

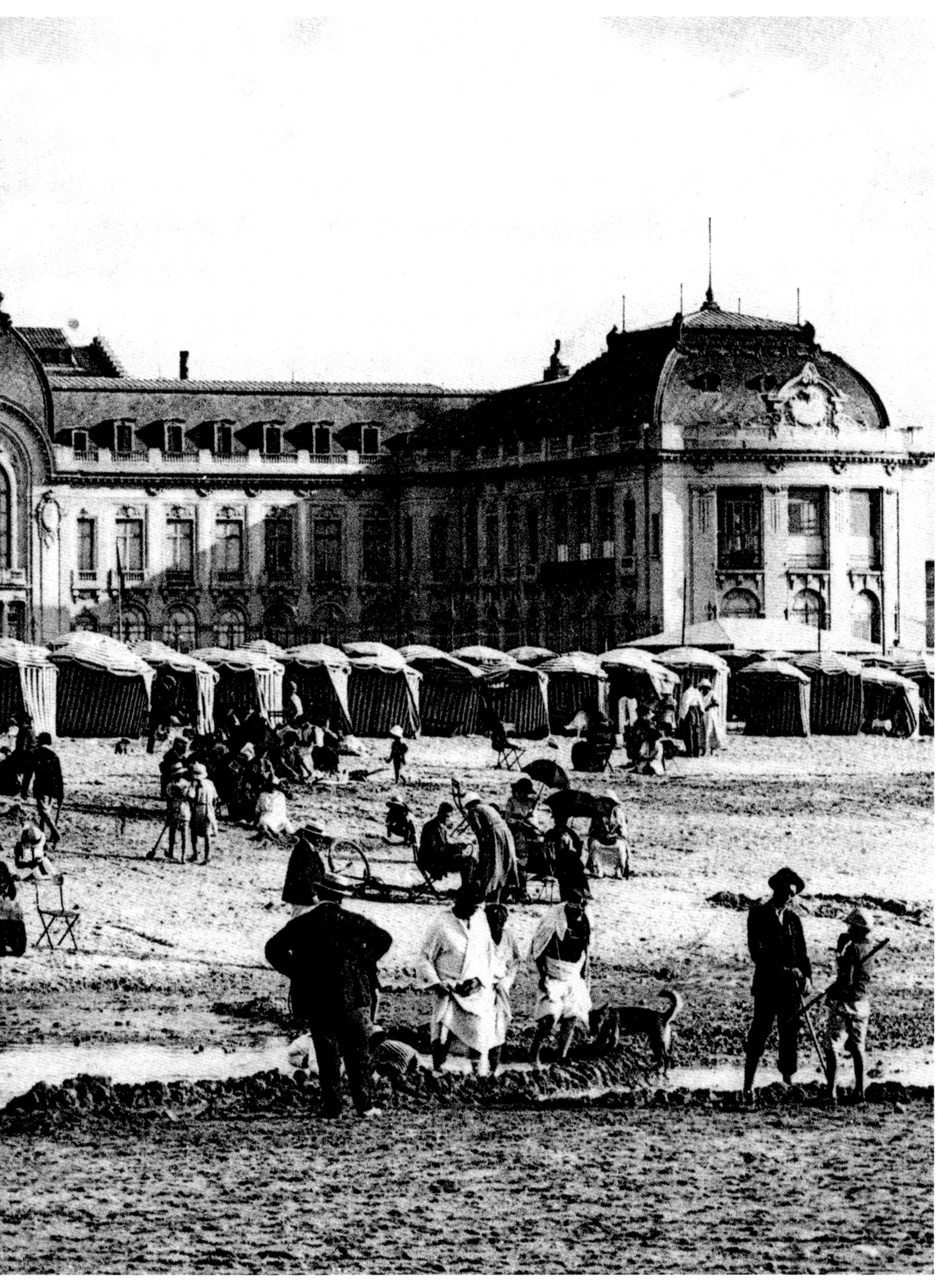

Man and the Sea

Free man, the sea is to thee ever dear!
The sea is thy mirror, thou regardest thy soul
In its mighteous waves that unendingly roll,
And thy spirit is yet not a chasm less drear.

Thou delight'st to plunge deep in thine image down;
Thou tak'st it with eyes and with arms in embrace,
And at times thine own inward voice would'st efface
With the sound of its savage ungovernable moan.

You are both of you, sombre, secretive and deep:
Oh mortal, thy depths are foraye unexplored,
Oh sea—no one knoweth thy dazzling hoard,
You both are so jealous your secrets to keep!

And endless ages have wandered by,
Yet still without pity or mercy you fight,
So mighty in plunder and death your delight:
Oh wrestlers, so constant in enmity![17]

In 1859, Monet, who was living in Paris at the time, wrote the following to Boudin: "I would add that there is a total lack of marine painters, and it is up to you to set off on the road that will lead you far" (June 3, 1859).[18] Monet was right. Boudin was aware that his art was original and capable of attracting a large clientele. In a letter to his friend Ferdinand Martin, a merchant from Le Havre, he explained, "They love my little ladies on the beach, and some people say that there's a thread of gold to exploit there. I am working on a regatta scene for the next exhibition" (February 12, 1863).[19] Two years later, on March 26, 1865, Boudin wrote to his mother, "We experienced another significant loss with the passing of Morny. I had hoped to catch the attention of this serious art enthusiast someday. This year, I had even prepared a small painting of his concert in Deauville—it would surely have flattered him. I was putting the finishing touches on it when we received the news. Deauville will surely miss him."[20] Boudin's perseverance eventually paid off: he was recognized as the foremost painter of seascapes in the late nineteenth century. The first of his paintings acquired, somewhat belatedly, by the French state was *Coucher de soleil à marée basse* (Sunset at low tide) {cat. 46}, and, during the twentieth century, Boudin's beach scenes became the most sought after, especially by American collectors, with Paul Mellon at the top of the list. The art critic Duranty, echoing Baudelaire, showed foresight when he wrote, "Nearly twenty years ago, if not more, Mr. Boudin ... began painting the harbors, the fishermen, the endlessly changing skies of the English Channel, the Parisians bathing in the sea. From then on, the modern sea—with its fishermen, boats, harbors, Parisians on jetties or beside bathing cabins—suddenly interested painters who had previously known only shipwrecks, storms, collisions, fires, in short, a dramatic and melodramatic sea."[21] In this way, Boudin can be said to have invented the modern seascape.

THE SEA VIEWED FROM THE SHORE

It is strange that so few painters were sailors. Caillebotte, Gauguin, and Helleu may have been, but neither Renoir, Monet, nor Pissarro possessed sailboats. When artists did own a boat, it was used for navigating the Seine, like Monet's studio-boat, inspired by Daubigny and his *Botin*. In fact, Monet, who grew up in Le Havre, rarely made reference to being at sea: he was a landsman who observed it from the shore. When he stayed

17 Charles Baudelaire, "Man and the Sea," *Baudelaire: The Flowers of Evil*, trans. Cyril Scott (London: Elkin Mathews, 1909).
18 Jean-Aubry, *Eugène Boudin*, 35.
19 Ibid., 50.
20 Durand-Ruel Snollaerts, *Les Impressionnistes*, 65.
21 Edmond Duranty, "Réflexions d'un bourgeois sur le Salon de peinture," *La Gazette des Beaux-Arts*, June (1877), 566–567.

in Belle-Île-en-Mer from September 12 to November 25, 1886, he painted craggy rocks, storms, rain, and light on the wild coast of Brittany. But he did not linger over picturesque aspects: there are no scenes of the harbor in Palais or Sauzon, or of fishermen. Furthermore, he painted the Breton island in the fall, when the weather takes a turn for the worse and the wind blows in, whipping up dramatic waves on the coast {cat. 68}. These spectacular sights attracted Monet, who was always ready for a challenge. "I know that to paint the sea really well, you need to look at it every hour of every day in the same place so that you can understand its way in that particular spot; and that is why I am working on the same motifs over and over again, four or six times even," he wrote to his companion, Alice Hoschedé, on October 30, 1886.[22] While staying on Belle-Île-en-Mer, Monet had the idea of painting in series, a practice he later developed in the 1890s, with *Peupliers* (*Poplars*) and *Cathédrales de Rouen* (*Rouen Cathedrals*). In 1887, he presented his suite of thirty-nine canvases painted on the Breton island at Georges Petit's gallery, where they met with great success. For Parisian collectors, the series had an exotic charm that showed Brittany in another light. The sea, by nature ever-changing, was a natural theme for this generation of artists who were intent on capturing ephemerality.

The impressionists rarely depicted sailors: portraits were not their priority. Monet is a notable exception; he painted *Poly*,[23] a sailor from Belle-Île-en-Mer who would help him to carry his canvases across the island's rocky slopes. And when the weather was too inclement—which enraged the artist—he painted the rain from his window.[24] Unlike the Concarneau School—whose ranks included artists such as Fernand Legout Gérard and Henri Barnoin, who painted fisherman returning home from sea—the first impressionist group was not interested in painting portraits of people who lived along the coast. Even Renoir, a portraitist, preferred to illustrate his seaside landscapes with female figures on the beach, either bathing or walking, rather than with sailors or dockers. In late summer of 1883, he spent five weeks on Guernsey.[25] He marveled at the island's relaxed manners and the bathers who were not afraid to swim in the nude, as he wrote to his dealer, Paul Durand-Ruel: "Here people bathe among the rocks, which serve as cabins, since there's nothing else; nothing is more attractive than this mixture of women and men crowded on these rocks. One would believe oneself in a landscape by Watteau rather than in the real world . . . and just as in Athens the women are not at all afraid of the proximity of men on the nearby rocks. Nothing is more amusing, when one is strolling through these rocks, than to surprise young girls getting ready to bathe; even though they are English, they are not particularly shocked."[26] This relaxed behavior led to a keen sense of lightness in Renoir's style, with brushstrokes that would enhance the ethereal effect of the landscapes. His technique became more atmospheric and his themes changed. This self-defined "painter of figures"

22 Daniel Wildenstein, *Claude Monet: Biographie et catalogue raisonné*, vol. II (Lausanne/Paris: Bibliothèque des Arts, 1979).
23 Musée Marmottan Monet, Paris.
24 *Pluie à Belle-Île*, 1886, Musée des Jacobins, Morlaix.
25 For more about this visit, see Cyrille Sciama, *Renoir in Guernsey, 1883* (Giverny: Musée des Impressionnismes Giverny, 2023), 21.
26 Renoir to Durand-Ruel, September 27, 1883, in John House, *Renoir, 1841–1919* (St. Peter Port, Guernsey: Guernsey Museum & Art Gallery, 1988), 15.

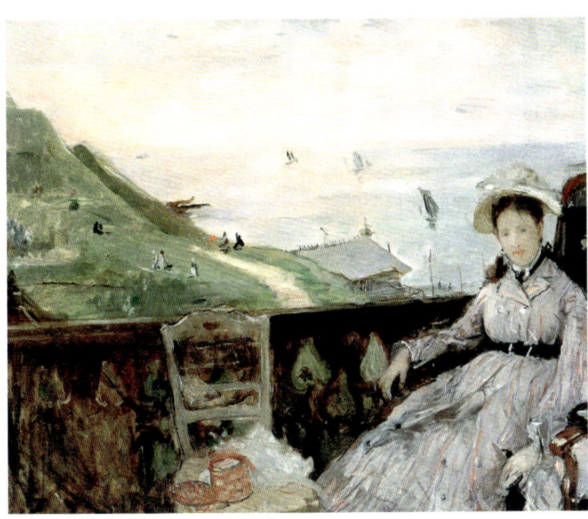

6 {fig.} – Berthe Morisot, *Sur la terrasse à Fécamp* (*On the Terrace*), 1874. Oil on canvas, 25½ × 28½ in. (65.5 × 73 cm). Tokyo Fuji Art Museum, Tokyo.

began to paint nudes en plein air, using the pretext of the Guernsey seaside. The ambivalence inherent in beach scenes enabled Renoir to make portraits of summer vacationers and to paint seascapes. Berthe Morisot also makes use of this ambiguity in *Sur la terrasse à Fécamp* (*On the Terrace*) {fig. 6}:[27] the ocean, bordered by a large hill, serves as a backdrop for a portrait of a woman. One of the rare canvases from this period that appears to have been painted from the water rather than the shore is Manet's *L'Évasion de Rochefort* (*The Escape of Rochefort*) {cat. 99}. The vast foreground depicts the sea's quivering green surface bearing a small vessel; Rochefort is depicted on the right, fleeing the penal colony in Nouméa, New Caledonia, to board the *Peace, Comfort, Ease*,[28] an English ship that is visible in the distance. Here, the ocean is portrayed as a source of freedom.

ON THE BEACH

Over time, several images came to epitomize nineteenth-century beach resorts, and Boudin was the undisputed master of the genre. He was renowned for his "crinolines" and his portraits of the resort elite at Deauville or Trouville {cat. 4}, and yet he also took a keen interest in local coastal life, such as the washerwomen on the beach and the nearby fish market {cat. 22}. Born in Honfleur, the artist remained close to the locals and was a hardworking and prolific draftsman who constantly traveled up and down the shores of Normandy. He enjoyed painting views from the beach, portraying the locals or fishermen at work, and although he conveyed the charm of Normandy's vacation destinations in numerous works, he also selected motifs from everyday life. For example, *Normandes étendant du linge sur la plage* (Norman women drying laundry on the beach; 1865) {cat. 50} highlights the domestic tasks that fell to women while their husbands were at sea. *Lavandière près de Trouville* (*Washerwoman near Trouville*; c. 1872–1876) {cat. 49} depicts a subject from everyday life, while also forming a seascape in which the water blends into the sky, with the ships in the background. In this way, Boudin blurs his themes and blurs boundaries. Nevertheless, Boudin became the painter par excellence of the social life that flourished on Normandy's coast. His beach scenes—splendid images of a lost world, where crinolines compete with straw boaters—have come to exemplify a casual-chic lifestyle typical of French seaside resorts. Despite a certain reluctance to paint scenes like this, which he felt were too commercial, Boudin worked particularly hard to create this image of the Norman coast. And the young Monet drew inspiration from him, as he worked on several paintings in Trouville: *L'Hôtel des Roches Noires. Trouville* (*The Hôtel des Roches Noires at Trouville*) {fig. 8}[29] and *Camille sur la plage* (*Camille on the Beach*)[30] were both influenced by Boudin's work.

Adolphe-Félix Cals, who remains a relatively unknown painter, depicted scenes painted from life with great precision. In the 1860s, he moved to Honfleur, where he painted the Saint-Siméon farm, as well as

27 1874, Tokyo Fuji Art Museum, Tokyo.
28 Henri Rochefort (1831–1913), a fierce opponent of the Second Empire, was sentenced to prison in 1871 for his involvement with the Paris Commune. He was deported to the penal colony in Nouméa in December 1873. On March 19, 1874, he managed to escape by swimming his way to a whaling ship with five other accomplices.
29 Musée d'Orsay, Paris.
30 Musée Marmottan Monet, Paris.

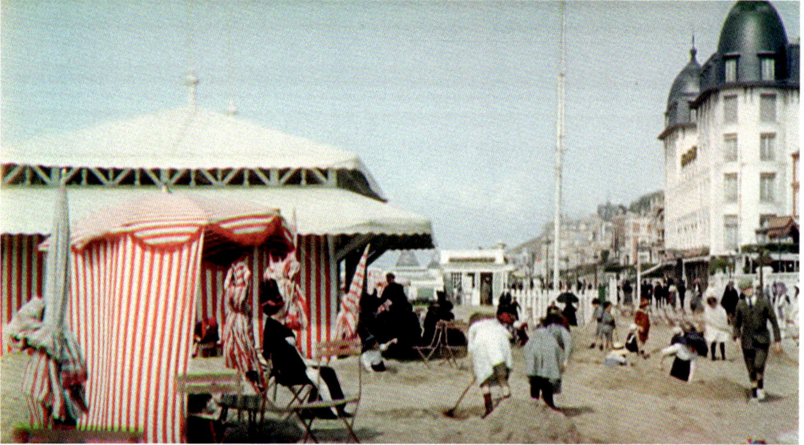

7 {cat.} – Société des Établissements Gaumont, *Deauville-Trouville: The Beach and Seafront*, 1912.
Chronochrome film, 6 min. 30 sec.

the coast, with great freedom of expression. His *Pêcheur* (Fisherman) {cat. 43} has the charm of an in situ sketch: walking along the strand, holding his rod across his back, a man appears miniscule next to the cliffs. To the left, the sea stretches to the horizon, where a steamboat chugs along. Painted in 1874, this canvas shares similarities with works carried out by Monet and Boudin during the same period. That very year, Cals presented two paintings at the first impressionist exhibition held on Boulevard des Capucines: *Le Bon Père Pêcheur à Honfleur* (Old fisherman in Honfleur; no. 37) and *Le Vieux pêcheur* (Old fisherman; no. 38),[31] and it is likely that no. 37 is the aforementioned *Pêcheur*. At Monet's invitation, Cals exhibited with the impressionists in 1874, 1876, and 1877. He had ties to the Barbizon School in addition to being a friend of Jongkind; as such, he formed a bridge between two generations of plein air painters.

Both Degas and Manet painted original scenes of summer vacationers on the beach, depicted variously as tourists lying on the ground, deep in thought (as in Degas's *Scène de plage* [*Beach Scene*]);[32] as abstract gray and black silhouettes (as in Manet's *Sur la plage* [*On the Beach*]);[33] or as figures that are placed as decorative elements (as in Manet's *Sur la plage de Boulogne* [*On the Beach, Boulogne-sur-Mer*]).[34]

When it comes to Gauguin's work, the beaches of Normandy do not immediately spring to mind. However, Gauguin, too, turned his attention to the genre and produced paintings with great emotional force. *Baigneuses à Dieppe* (Bathers at Dieppe) {fig. 9}[35] depicts four women in black bathing suits against a background of green. Behind them, a mustachioed man is also bathing. In the distance, three ships serve to remind the viewer that Dieppe is a port city. Gauguin revisits the theme in *La Plage de Dieppe* (The beach at Dieppe),[36] which combines depictions of sailboats, fishermen, and bathers. In both paintings, the highly fragmented brushwork reveals the influence of Gauguin's close friend Pissarro.

UNTAMED NATURE

Following Théodore Gudin's success at the official Salons held in the 1830s, members of the French art scene began painting storms. Joseph Vernet had already explored this artistic vein in the 1770s; it was revitalized by the Sturm und Drang movement, followed by developments in German and French Romanticism. Gudin, who was appointed painter for the French navy in 1830, was one of the first to paint Belle-Île-en-Mer.[37] The impressionists, therefore, did not invent the genre; they took a realist approach to it. Dramatic landscapes no longer conveyed personal sentiments, the plight of travelers, or the torments of the viewer, but rather the raging elements and the beauty of untamed nature. In 1859, Courbet began traveling regularly to the Normandy coast. He met Monet, and they painted spectacular seascapes together. Courbet often depicted beaches in Normandy or near Montpellier {cat. 30} that were being subjected to a battering from the elements. Of the thirty-nine canvases Monet painted of Belle-Île-en-Mer, five are scenes of the island during a storm. Some sites were particularly suited to dramatic subjects: the rocky shores that appeared at low tide and the cliffs plunging into the lashing sea fascinated the impressionists. Quick to recognize the emotional potential of these scenes that Vernet had popularized in the eighteenth century, certain of Boudin's fellow artists produced views of Brittany and Normandy featuring long stretches of beach. In a small panel, Édouard Dantan conveys the peculiar atmosphere of a beach at low tide in Villerville, a village near Trouville, where the painter

31 *Le Vieux pêcheur* (Old fisherman) is held at the Musée Eugène Boudin in Honfleur (1873, oil on canvas, 3 ft. 9¾ in. × 2 ft. 11 in. [116.5 × 89 cm], inv. 2018.5.1).

32 1869–1870, National Gallery, London.

33 1873, Musée d'Orsay, Paris.

34 1868, Virginia Museum of Fine Arts, Richmond.

35 1885, The National Museum of Western Art, Tokyo.

36 1885, Ny Carlsberg Glyptotek, Copenhagen.

37 *Tempête sur les côtes de Belle-Île* (Storm on the coast of Belle-Île; 1851), Musée des Beaux-Arts, Quimper.

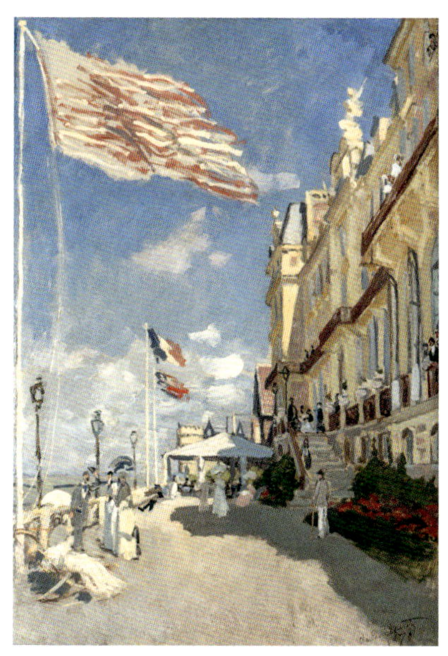

8 {fig.} – Claude Monet, *Hôtel des Roches Noires. Trouville* (*The Hôtel des Roches Noires at Trouville*), 1870. Oil on canvas, 32 × 23 in. (81× 58 cm). Musée d'Orsay, Paris.

owned a villa. This view of a punt—a small boat authorized to travel up the Seine estuary—seen from higher ground was painted in the style of a Japanese woodblock print. Shades of ocher, blue, and gray accentuate the landscape's autumnal character, and the sailor appears to blend into the boat itself {cat. 42}.

In 1895, Armand Guillaumin, like Monet, stayed on Belle-Île-en-Mer. He painted a striking view of Port Goulphar in which a huge rock formation occupies most of the canvas {cat. 71}. A portrait of stone being battered by the ocean, this work captivates viewers with its balance of ochers and greens against the blue of the Breton sea, whipped into a frenzy by the wind. *Rocher à la pointe de la Baumette* (Rock at Pointe de la Baumette) {cat. 62}, painted in Agay, on the French Riviera, also illustrates Guillaumin's taste for dramatic views that are reminiscent of Monet's *Les Rochers à Pourville, marée basse* (*The Rocks at Pourville, Low Tide*) {cat. 47}. The subject was in vogue, creating a flourishing market of enthusiastic buyers for these kinds of paintings.

In 1897, toward the end of his life, Alfred Sisley traveled to Scotland, where he worked on new motifs, including two rather dramatic views of rock formations that were unlike his usual preferred themes of landscapes in Moret-sur-Loing. His sudden death cut short these new explorations in his art, which would have surely ushered in other forms of impressionism in the early twentieth century.

FLIGHT

Sea Breeze

The flesh is sad, alas! and all the books are read.
Flight, only flight! I feel that birds are wild to tread
The floor of unknown foam, and to attain the skies!
Nought, neither ancient gardens mirrored in the eyes,
Shall hold this heart that bathes in waters its delight,
O nights! nor yet my waking lamp, whose lonely light
Shadows the vacant paper, whiteness profits best,
Nor the young wife who rocks her baby on her breast.
I will depart! O steamer, swaying rope and spar,
Lift anchor for exotic lands that lie afar!

A weariness, outworn by cruel hopes, still clings
To the last farewell handkerchief's last beckonings!
And are not these, the masts inviting storms, not these
That an awakening wind bends over wrecking seas,
Lost, not a sail, a sail, a flowering isle, ere long?
But, O my heart, hear thou, hear thou, the sailors' song![38]

In this famous poem published in French in 1865 and republished in 1887 (*Poésies*), Stéphane Mallarmé describes the intoxicating nature of the sea. In this self-portrait, the poet—a friend of Gauguin and Renoir—reveals the particularities of his erratic and depressed personality using maritime metaphors.

A desire for travel infused the late nineteenth century. Rather than traveling beyond the borders of France for a change of scenery, certain painters ventured into *terra incognita*: Brittany. Recent exhibitions have celebrated artists who were inspired by impressionism in Brittany.[39] At first relegated to Breton schools of painting, they have gradually been given the place they deserve, among the most important. The painters of the period from 1880 to 1900 who split from the Pont-Aven School chose the impressionist style inherited from Monet and Renoir, both in terms of their subject matter and expression. Artists close to Monet had gone to Brittany in the wake of the latter's travels to the region. In 1869, Berthe

38 Stéphane Mallarmé, "Sea Breeze," trans. Arthur Symons, reprinted in Scott Horton, "Mallarmé's 'Sea Breeze,'" *Harper's Magazine*, April 4, 2008.

39 *La Modernité en Bretagne 1: De Claude Monet à Lucien Simon. 1870–1920*, eds. Jacqueline Duroc, Estelle Guille des Buttes-Fresneau et al., exh. cat. (Pont-Aven: Musée de Pont-Aven/ Milan: Silvana Editoriale, 2017); *Henry Moret (1856–1913): De Pont-Aven à l'impressionnisme en Bretagne*, eds. Guillaume Ambroise and Florence Rionnet, exh. cat. (Quimper: Musée des Beaux-Arts/ Lyon: Libel, 2021).

Morisot stayed in Lorient. In 1886, the year Monet stayed on Belle-Île-en-Mer, Renoir traveled to Saint-Briac and in 1892, he was in Pont-Aven. Guillaumin very likely visited Belle-Île-en-Mer in 1895, as did Henri Matisse, in 1896. The latter met John Peter Russell during his stay: the Australian painter himself had met Monet on the Breton island in 1886. Captivated by the area, Russell had a house built at Port Goulphar and lived there year-round until 1908. The Breton island became a hotspot for painters. The generation born in the 1850s and 1860s turned to Gauguin for inspiration around 1886 to 1890, before taking up impressionism again toward the 1900s. This later school—which existed at the same time as Monet was conducting his explorations of water—was strongly influenced by impressionist precepts, while adapting them to Breton subjects. Ferdinand Loyen du Puigaudeau, Henry Moret, and Maxime Maufra, for example, developed a form of impressionism based on a local sensibility unique to Brittany. All three met Gauguin around 1890 and were profoundly influenced by his artistic experimentations.

Maufra—a friend of Gauguin with ties to Émile Bernard and the leading symbolists—focused his talent on celebrating the south coast of Brittany. He captured dramatic views from Quiberon to Concarneau, and his fascination with Japanese art comes across in many of his works. The "avant-garde artist," as Gauguin referred to him, maintained a lifelong search for new experiences, perspectives, and encounters. While on a trip to England, the amiable and inquisitive young man abandoned the business studies chosen for him by his parents after discovering the light in the works of J.M.W. Turner, which were a revelation. He painted wholeheartedly, first depicting Nantes, his native city, before going on to draw and paint the Breton coast. He stayed regularly in Quiberon, then settled permanently in Kerhostin, on the Quiberon peninsula, in 1910. Maufra's skill earned him fame, and in 1916 he was awarded the title Peintre de la Marine—official recognition of his talent for seascapes. Throughout his life, he remained loyal to Gauguin, who left for Tahiti in 1894, then in 1901 moved to the Marquise Islands, where he died. Painted ten years earlier, far from Dieppe, *Te Vaa* ("dugout canoe" in Tahitian) {cat. 103} illustrates Gauguin's esthetic voyage and his break with civilization: "to take flight, to flee," as Mallarmé intones, was for Gauguin the only solution, and his final canvas, *D'où venons-nous ? Qui sommes-nous ? Où allons-nous ?* (*Where Do We Come From? Who Are We? Where Are We Going?*),[40] is its tragic illustration. After turning away from European civilization, and facing hostility from colonialists and the Church, Gauguin created his own artistic world, in his "Maison du jouir" (pleasure house), where the sea—a lagoon—remained one of his favorite motifs. Through his explorations of this enigmatic subject, which continued to play a fundamental role in his artistic creation, he paved the way for modernity in the twentieth century.

40 1897–1898, Museum of Fine Arts, Boston.

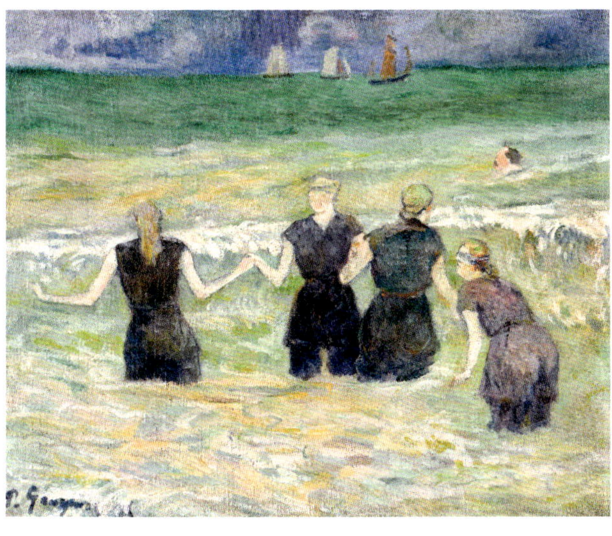

9 {fig.} – Paul Gauguin, *Baigneuses à Dieppe* (Bathers at Dieppe), 1885. Oil on canvas, 15 × 18 in. (38.1 × 46.2 cm). National Museum of Western Art, Tokyo.

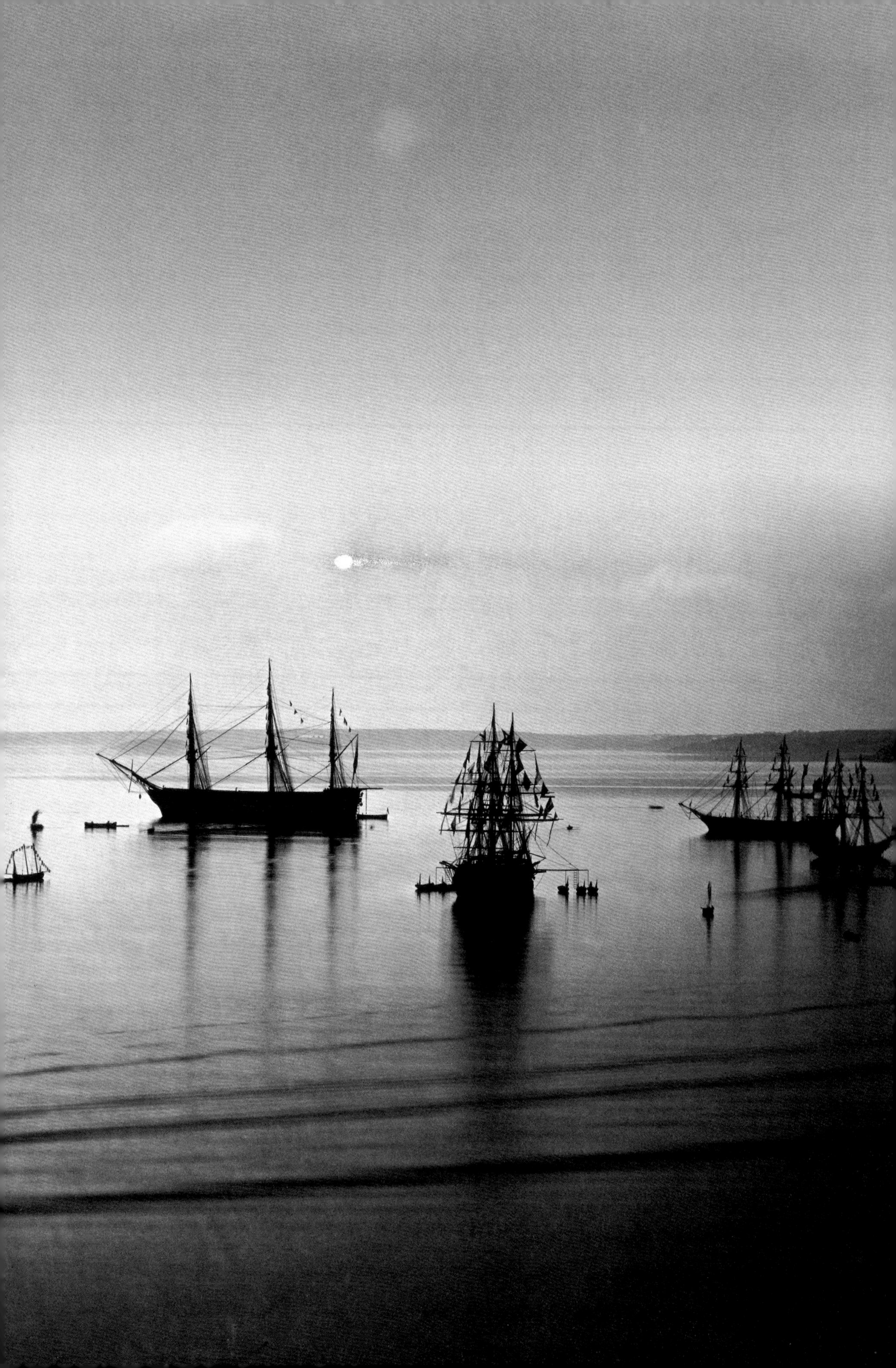

“These great, beautiful vessels, imperceptibly swaying (rocking) on the tranquil waters, these sturdy ships, with their idle, homesick air, do they not ask us, in a silent tongue: When do we sail for happiness?”

—Charles Baudelaire, *Rockets*, XI
In “Intimate Papers from the Unpublished Works of Baudelaire,” trans. Joseph T. Shipley, in *Baudelaire: His Prose and Poetry*, ed. T. R. Smith (New York: Boni and Liveright, Inc., 1919)

10 {fig.} – Gustave Le Gray, *Flotte française en rade de Cherbourg* (*The French Fleet, Cherbourg*), detail, 1858. Monochrome on paper. BNF, Paris.

HARBORS

From Johan Barthold Jongkind's traditional images to Paul Signac's modern vision, artists were particularly drawn to harbors throughout the eighteenth century. They followed a path glorified by Joseph Vernet in the 1770s, in his series of fifteen paintings of French harbors entitled *Vues des ports de France* (*The Ports of France*).

The impressionists renewed the genre, setting up their easels on the quays to portray the activity of dockers and sailors. Camille Corot was one of the first members of the Barbizon School to take an interest in painting the harbors of Normandy. *Trouville, bateaux de pêche échoués dans le chenal* (Trouville, fishing boats aground in the channel) {cat. 17} offers a picturesque view of ships in the harbor; the oil sketch shares similarities with Eugène Boudin's *Barques de pêche et voiliers* (Fishing boats and sailboats) {cat. 23}. In 1855, Jongkind depicted a view of Antwerp harbor that was still somewhat traditional in style, *Le Port d'Anvers* (Port of Antwerp) {cat. 15}: the lines are clearly visible and the work retains a picturesque structure, but the artist's particular attention to the sky is apparent. In 1868, Jongkind produced an etched version {cat. 14} with a low, centrally placed sun that would inspire Claude Monet's *Impression, soleil levant* (*Impression, Sunrise*; 1872): his famous view of Le Havre at dawn. In 1871, Boudin also painted Antwerp harbor, in muted, impressionistic tones {cat. 16}. The theme of ports inspired artists from Pierre-Auguste Renoir to Signac, who rendered them in shades of gray {cat. 26} and produced a more graphic and decorative composition in *Barfleur* {cat. 25}. One of the last series of canvases that Camille Pissarro painted, dating from 1903, features views of the harbor in Le Havre {fig. 2 and cat. 24}.

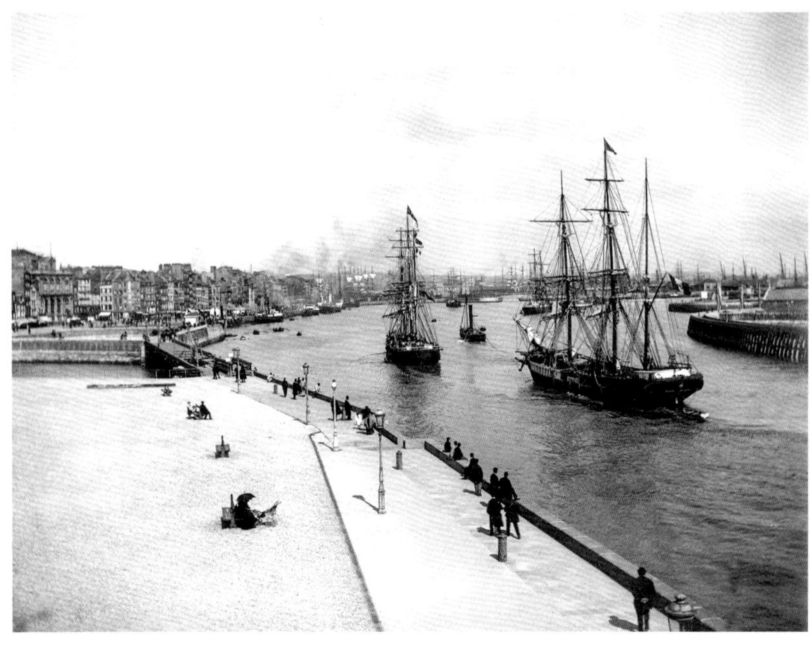

11 {fig.} – *View of Le Havre's Port*, c. 1880.

12 {cat.} – Eugène Boudin, *Deauville, le bassin* (Deauville, the basin), 1884.
Oil on panel, 18½ × 15 in. (46.5 × 38 cm). Musée des Impressionnismes, Giverny.

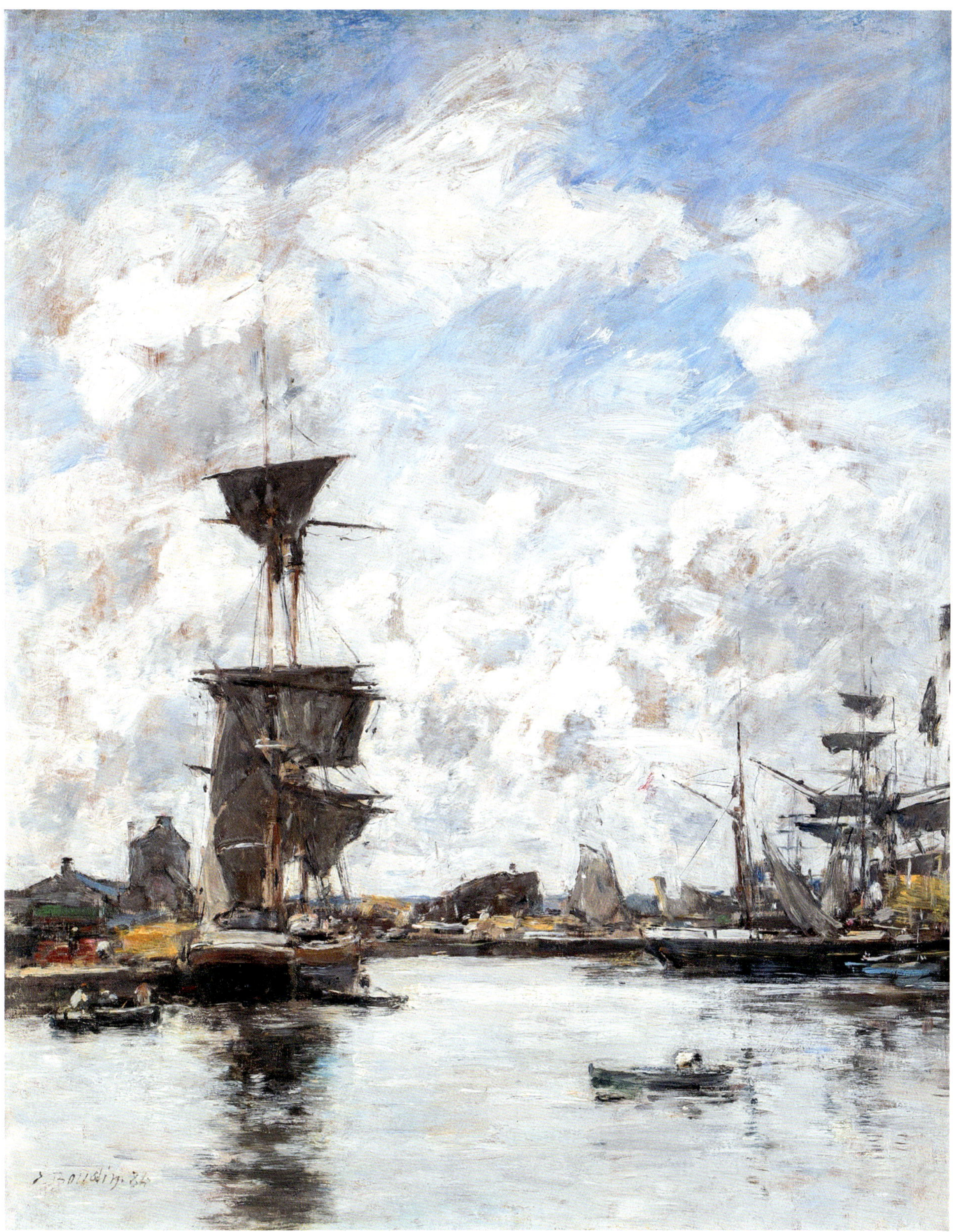

13 {cat.} – Eugène Boudin, *Deauville, le bassin* (Deauville, the basin), 1887.
Oil on panel, 10½ × 8 in. (27 × 21 cm). Private collection.

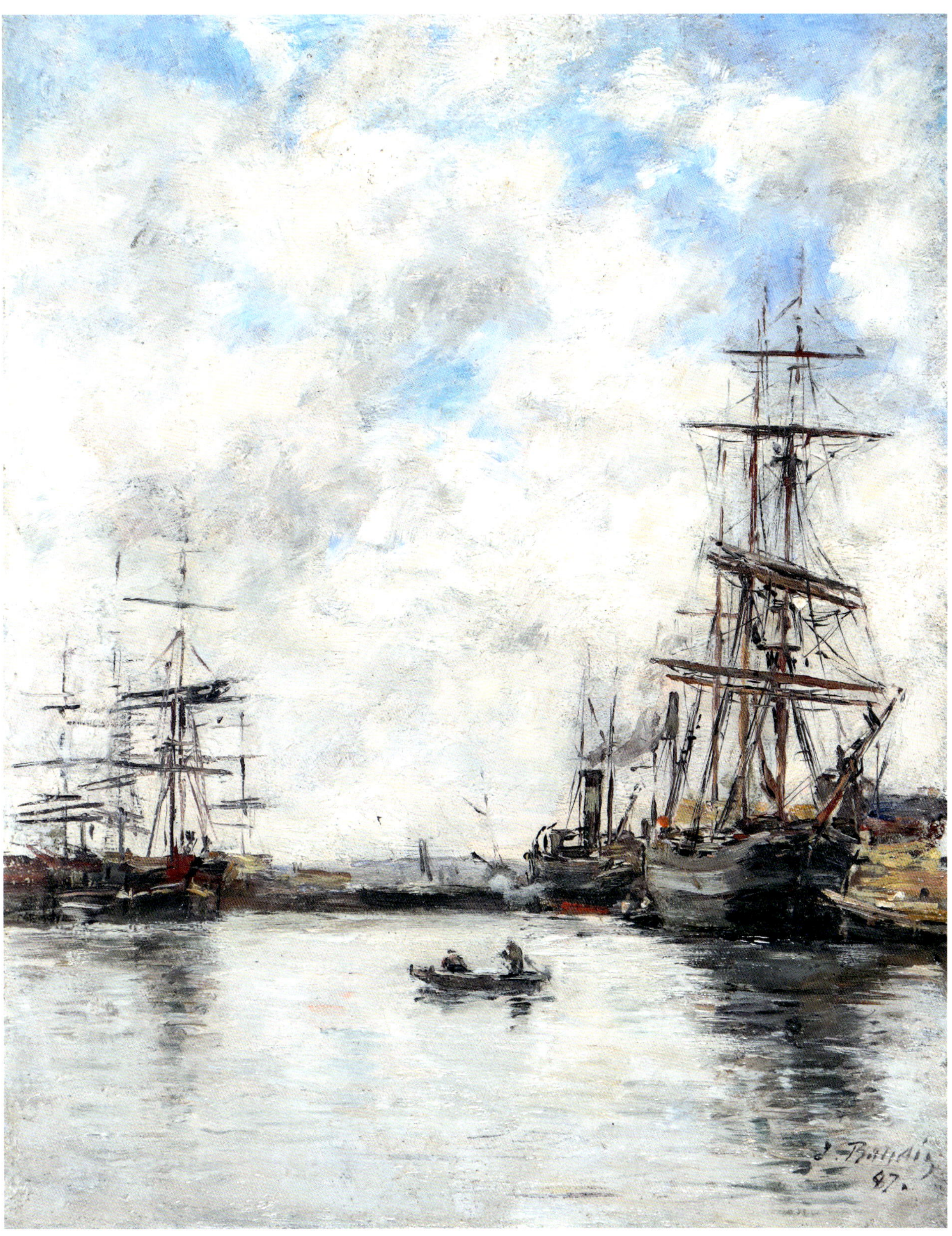

14 {cat.} – Johan Barthold Jongkind, *Le Soleil couchant, port d'Anvers* (*Sunset, Port of Antwerp*), 1868. Etching, 14½ × 22 in. (37 × 56 cm). Musée des Impressionnismes, Giverny.

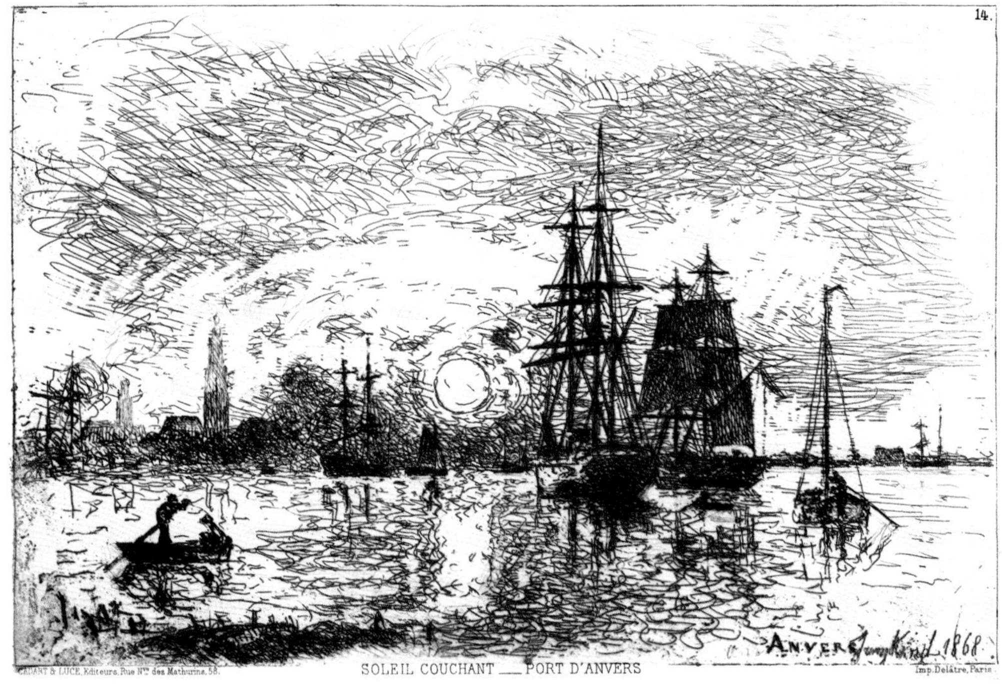

15 {cat.} – Johan Barthold Jongkind, *Le Port d'Anvers* (Port of Antwerp), 1855. Oil on canvas, 2 ft. 8 in. × 3 ft. 6 in. (82 × 107 cm). Musée d'Orsay, Paris, on long-term loan to the Musée des Beaux-Arts, Rennes, MNR 499.

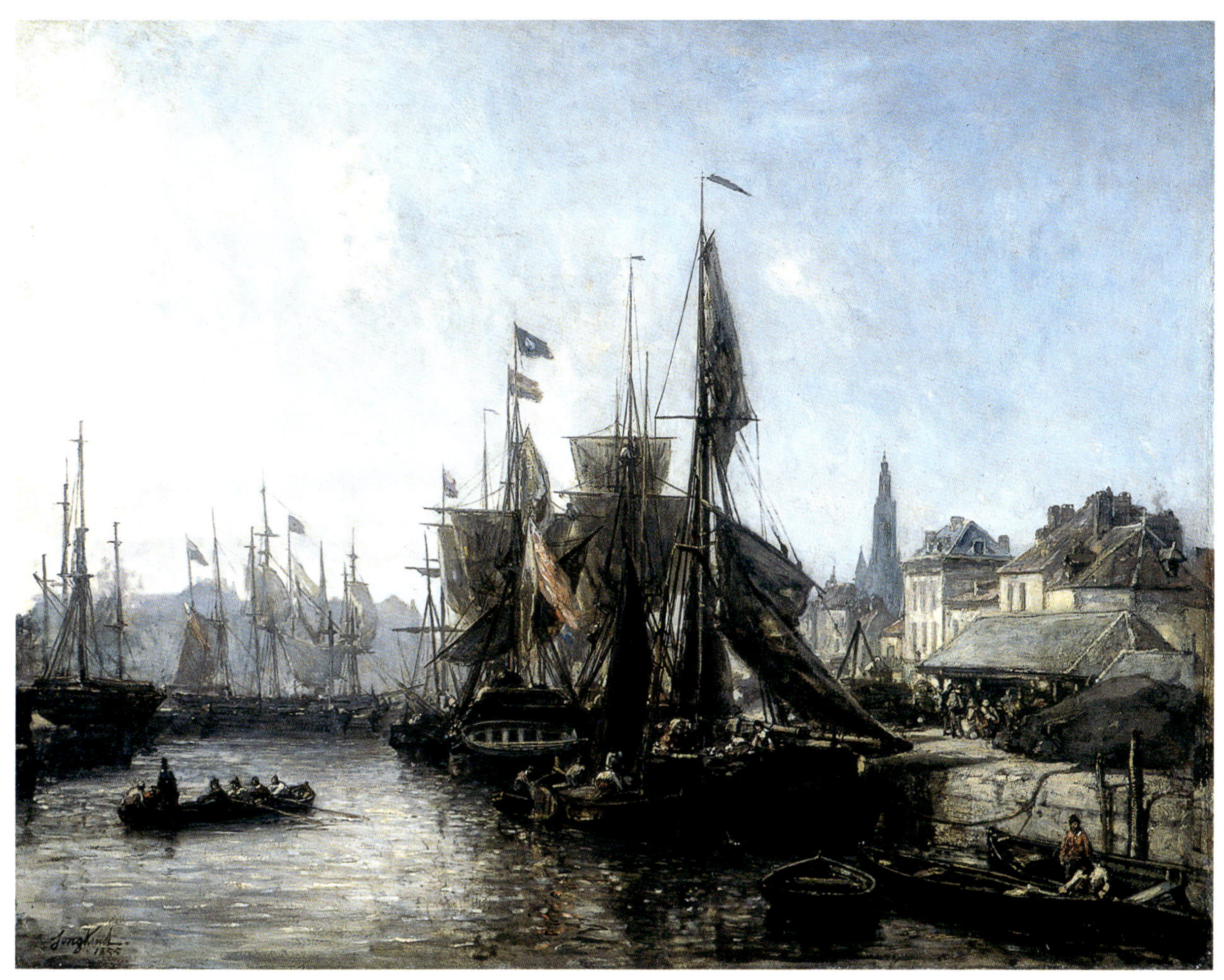

Trained as a draftsman and watercolorist in The Hague, Jongkind met French painter Eugène Isabey in 1845, and the latter artist invited him to study in his studio in Paris. Jongkind quickly earned recognition within French artistic circles and was admitted to the Salon in 1848, where he received several prizes. Although he did not make his paintings outdoors, preferring to work in the studio using his watercolors, Jongkind succeeded in conveying the freshness of his initial observations in his finished canvases. This was to have a profound influence on the impressionists, including the young Claude Monet, whom he met in 1862, several years after completing this painting.

16 {cat.} – Eugène Boudin, *Port d'Anvers* (Port of Antwerp), 1871. Oil on wood, 12½ × 18 in. (31.5 × 46.5 cm). Musée d'Orsay, Paris.

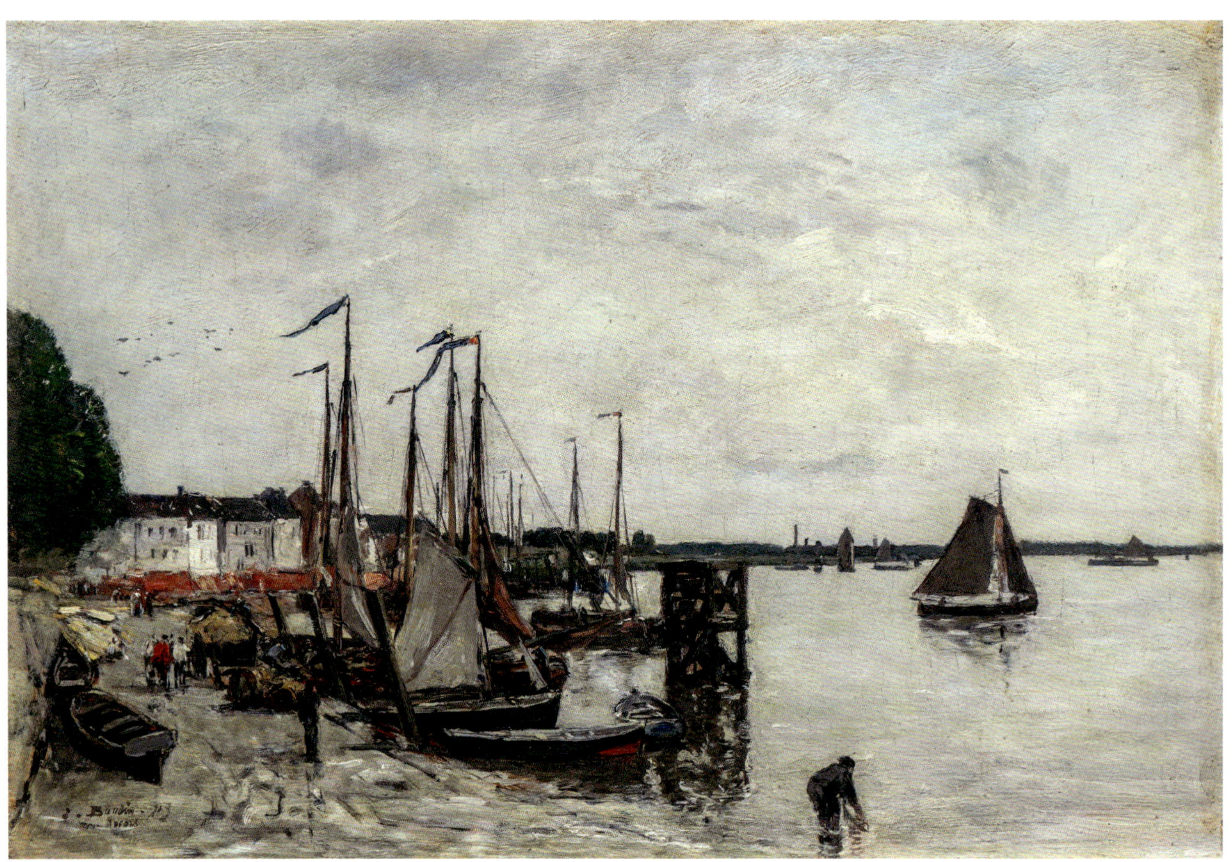

17 {cat.} – Camille Corot, *Trouville, bateaux de pêche échoués dans le chenal* (Trouville, fishing boats aground in the channel), 1875. Oil on paper mounted on canvas, 8 × 9 in. (21 × 23.5 cm). Musée d'Orsay, Paris.

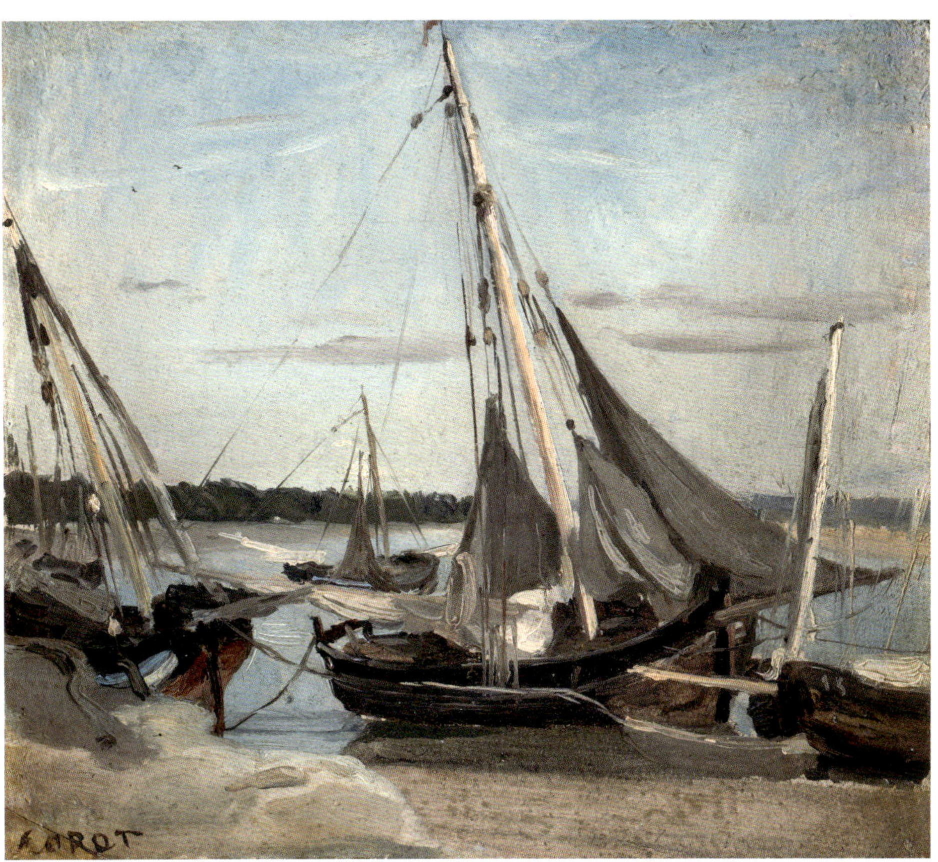

18 {fig.} – Gustave Le Gray, *Vapeur* (*The Tugboat*), 1856. Albumen silver print, 11 × 16 in. (33 × 41.3 cm). Musée d'Orsay, Paris.

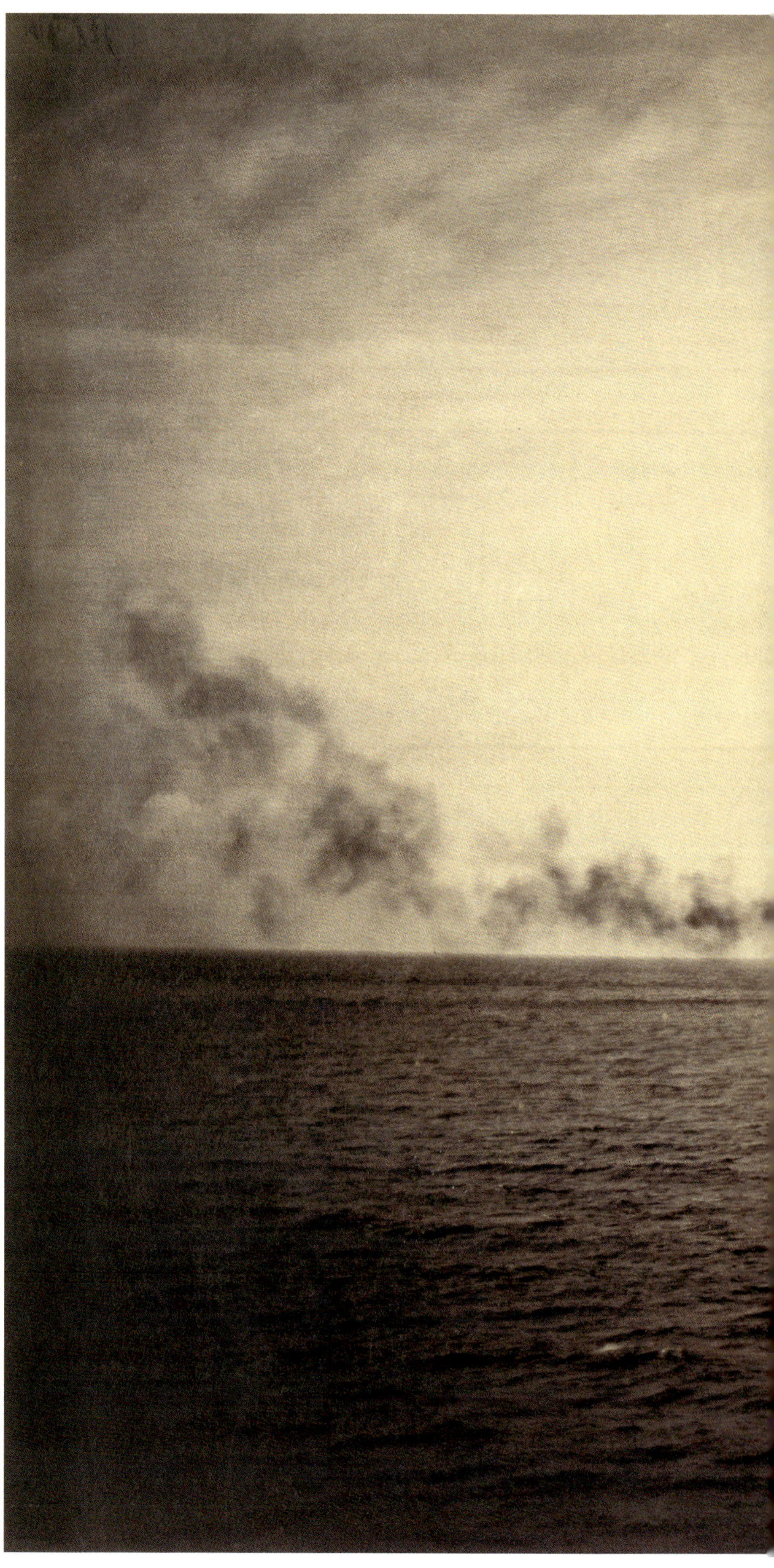

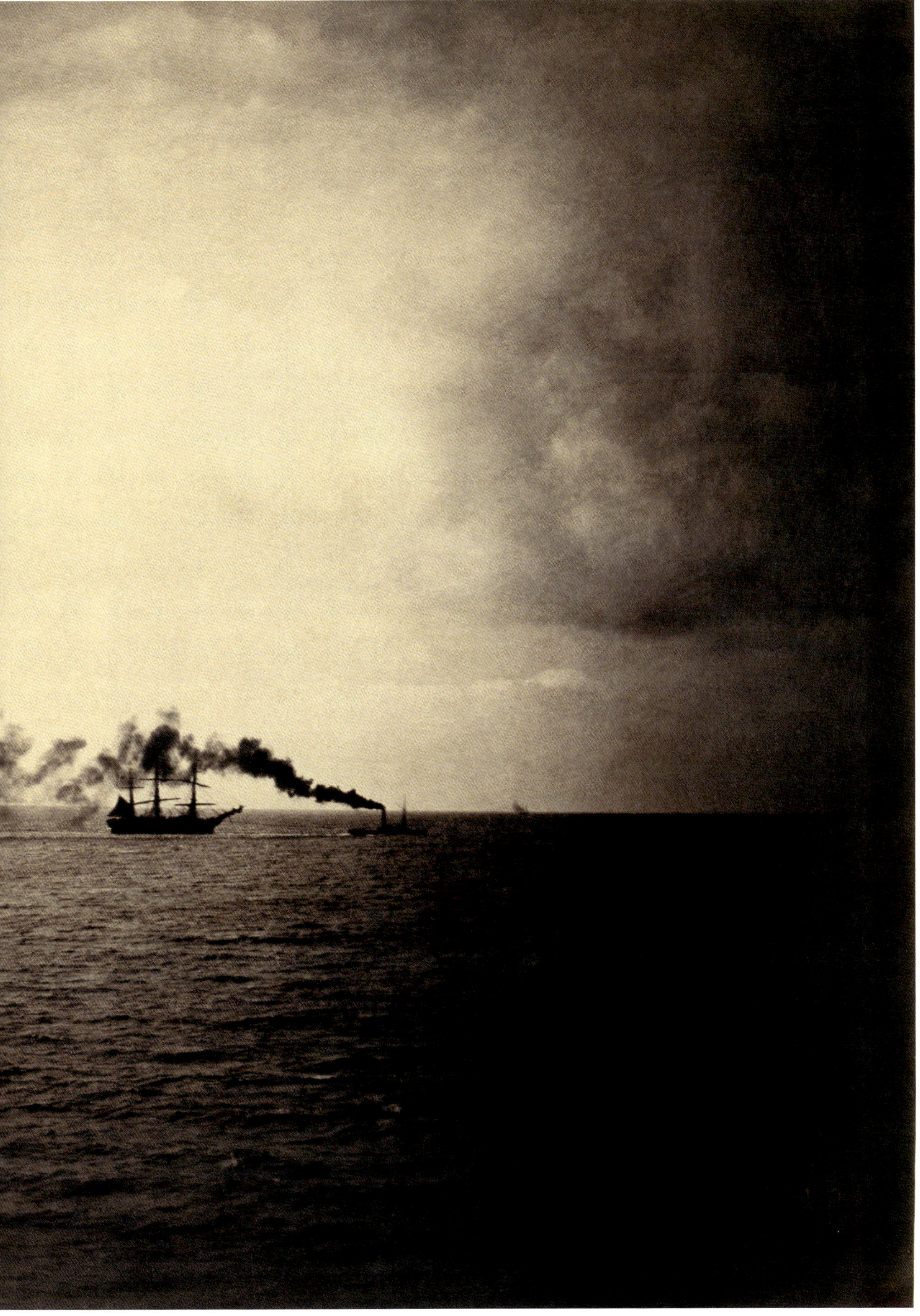

19 (cat.) – Eugène Boudin, *Port de Camaret* (Port of Camaret), 1872. Oil on canvas, 22 × 35½ in. (55.5 × 89.5 cm). Musée d'Orsay, Paris, on long-term loan to the Musée des Beaux-Arts, Angers.

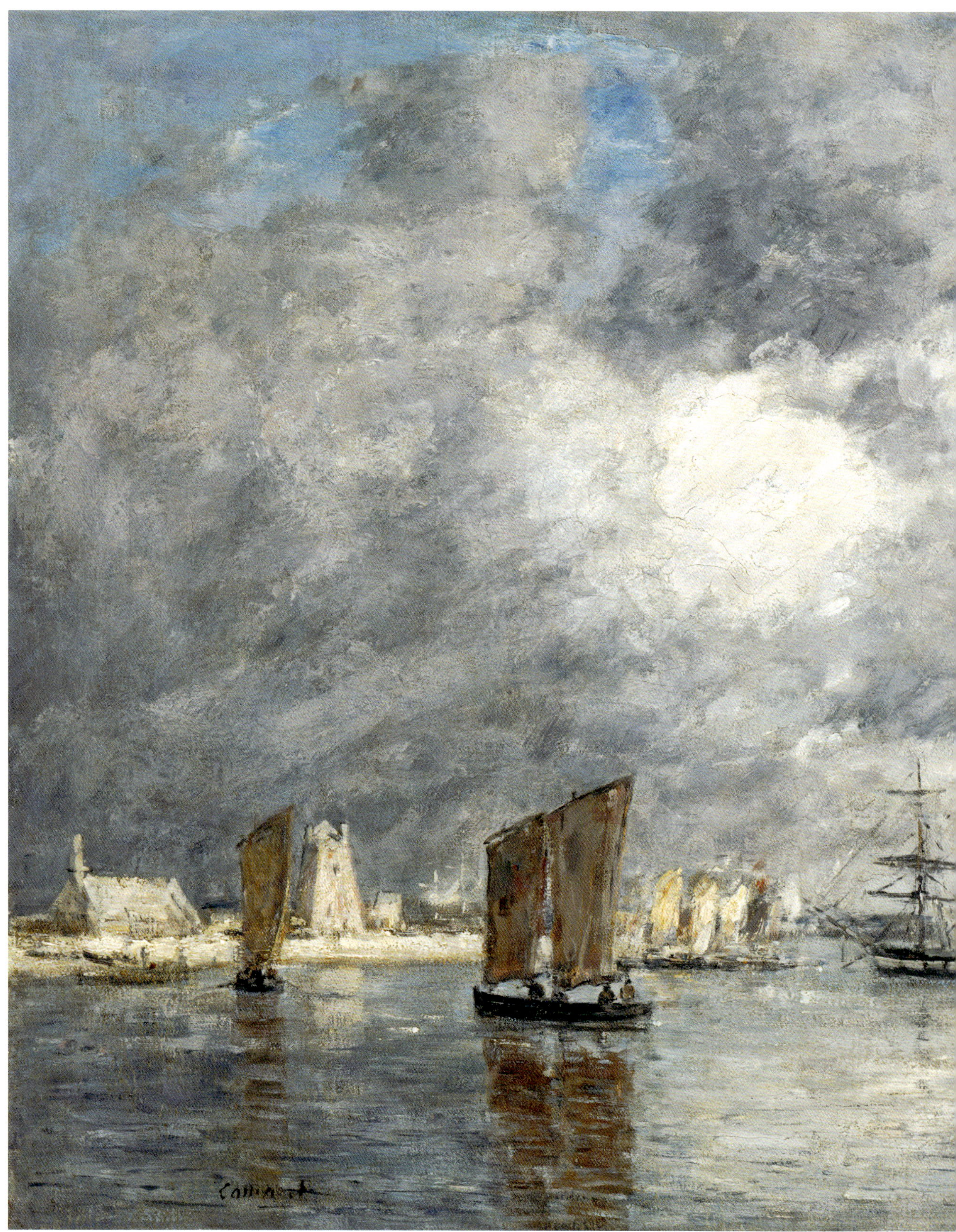

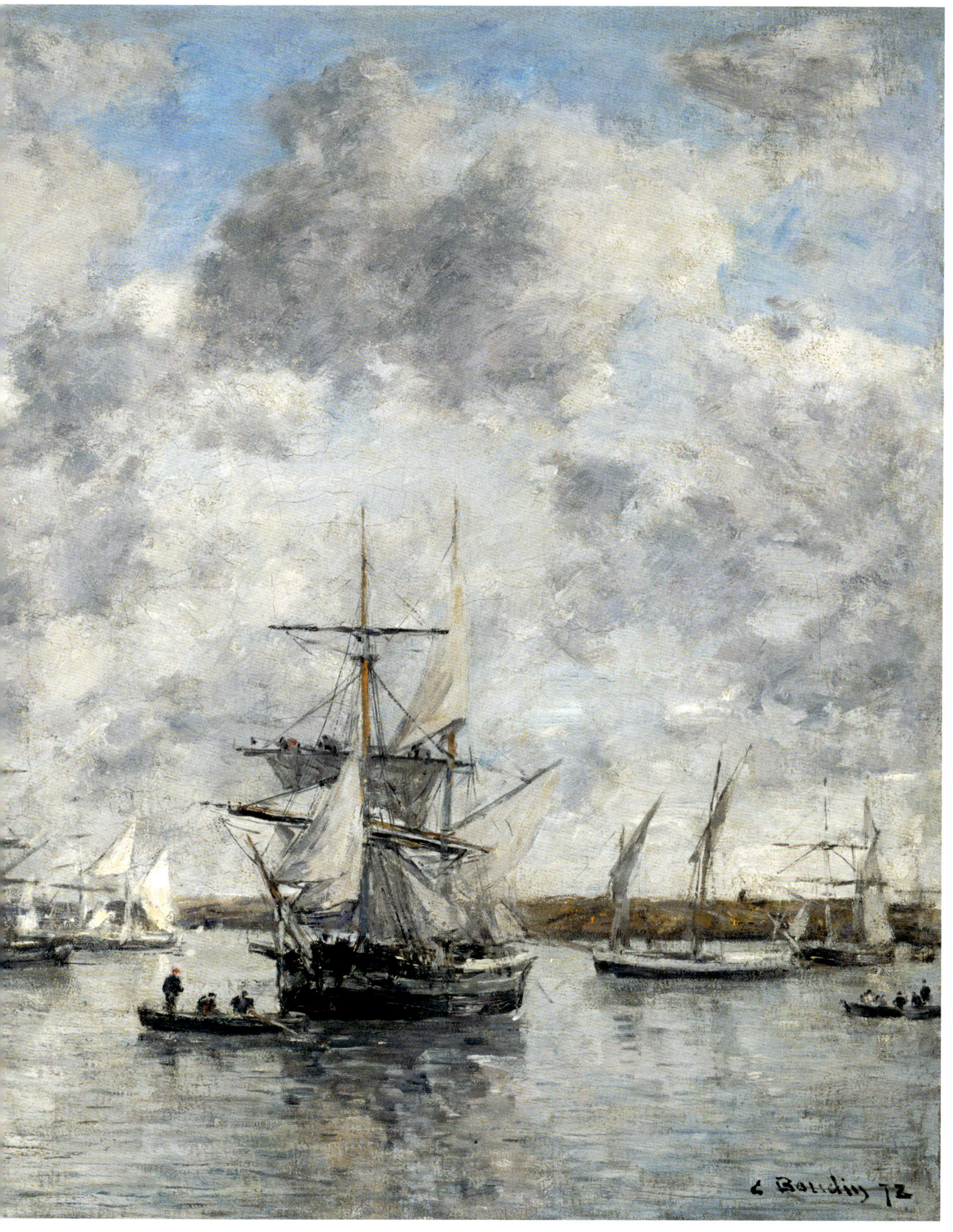

20 {fig.} – Paul Lancrenon, *Vue sur le bassin de radoub, le chantier naval et l'hôtel de ville d'Honfleur* (View of the drydock, shipyard, and town hall in Honfleur), July 21, 1900. Médiathèque du Patrimoine et de la Photographie, Charenton-le-Pont.

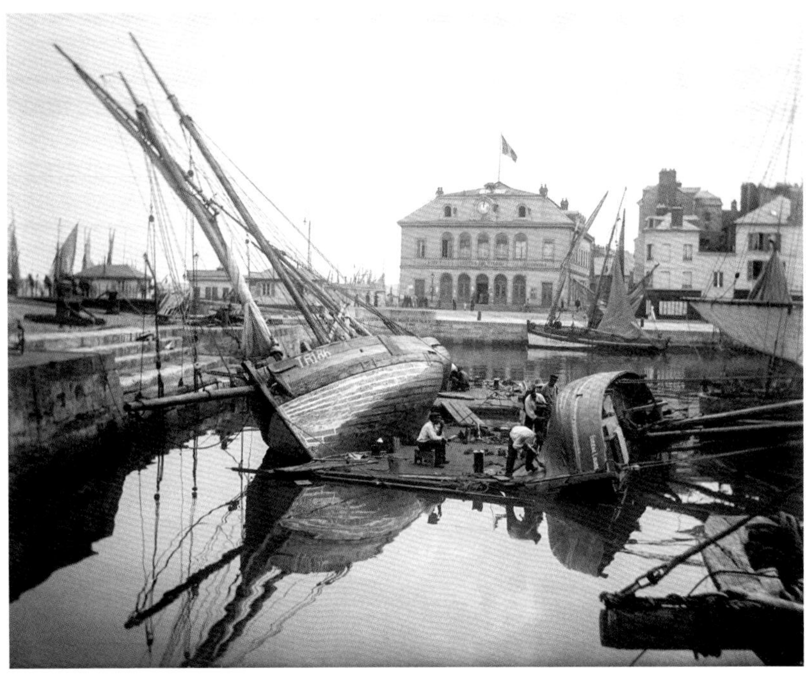

21 {cat.} – Eugène Boudin, *Le Bassin de l'Eure au Havre* (The Eure basin at Le Havre), 1885.
Oil on canvas, 25½ × 35½ in. (65 × 90 cm). Musée d'Art, d'Histoire et d'Archéologie, Évreux.

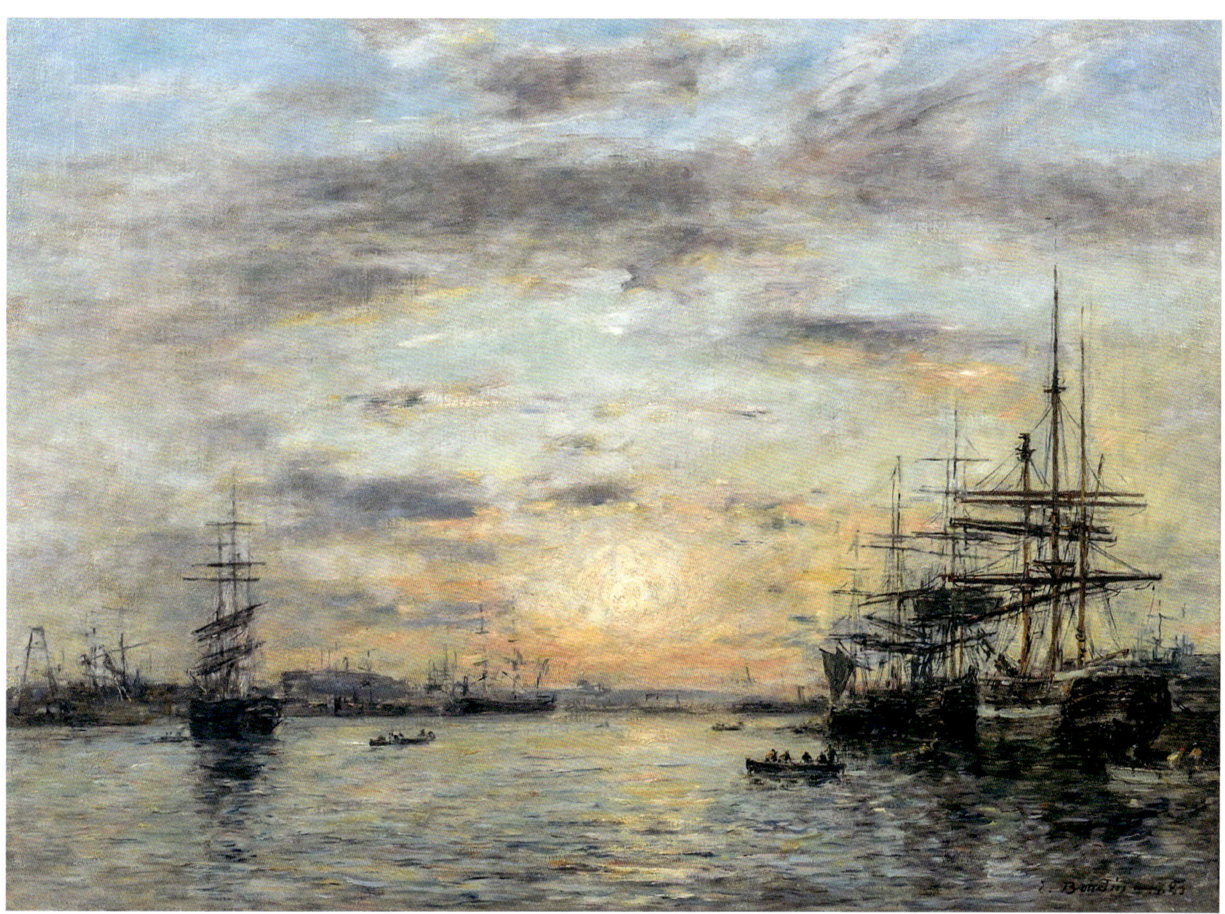

22 {cat.} – Eugène Boudin, *La Poissonnerie de Trouville* (The fish market in Trouville), 1875.
Oil on wood, 9½ × 14 in. (24 × 36 cm). Musée des Impressionnismes, Giverny.

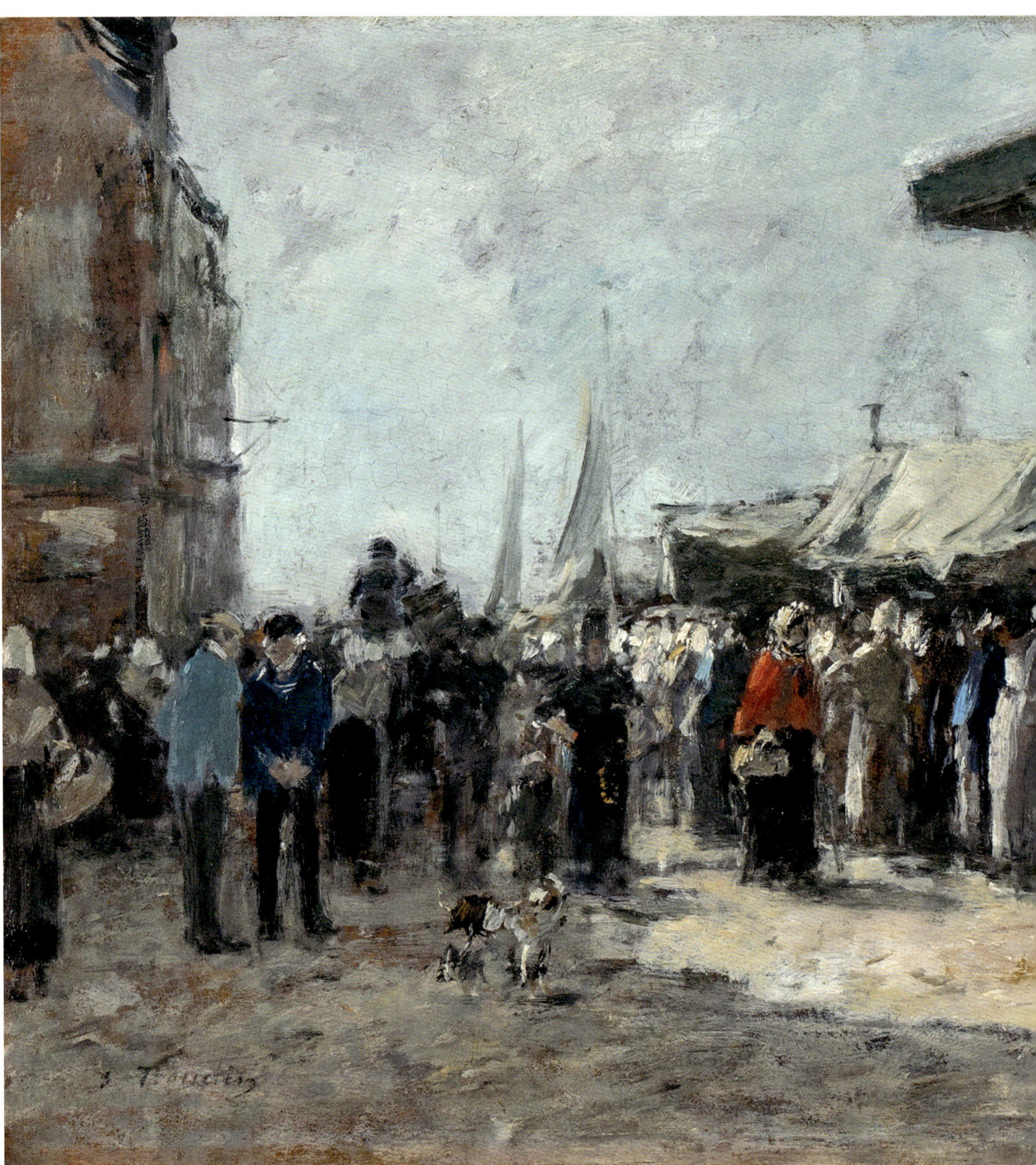

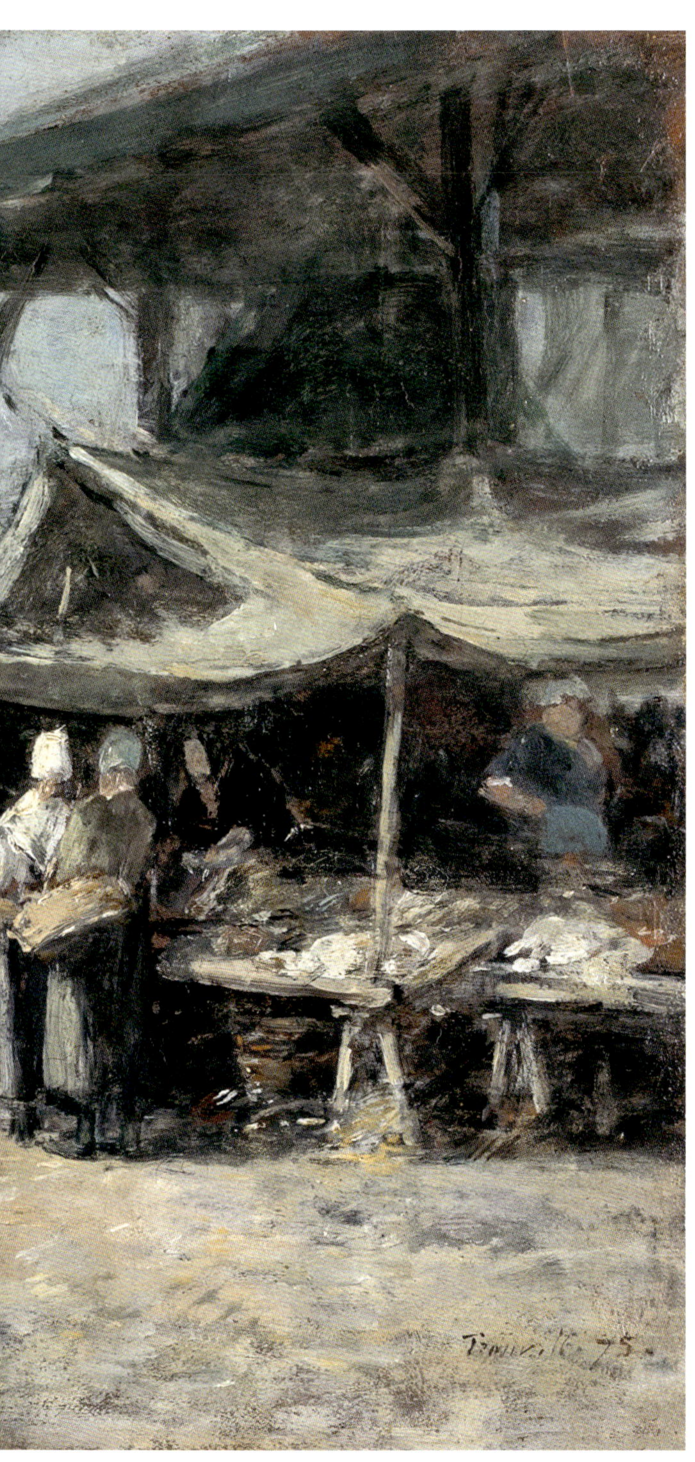

23 {cat.} – Eugène Boudin, *Barques de pêche et voiliers* (Fishing boats and sailboats), 1853–1859.
Oil on board, 8½ × 12½ in. (22 × 32.4 cm). MuMA, Le Havre.

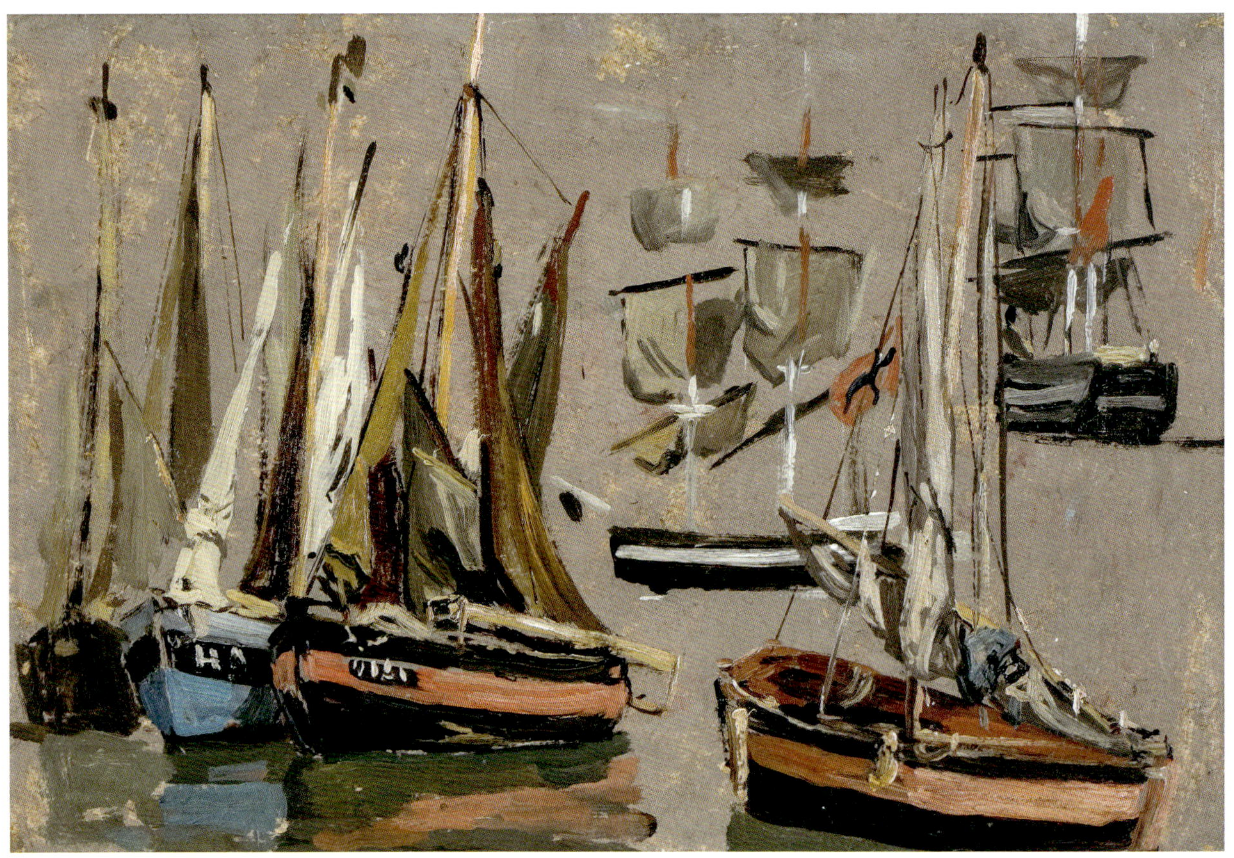

24 {cat.} – Camille Pissarro, *L'Anse des pilotes. Le Havre, matin, soleil, marée montante* (*The Outer Harbour of Le Havre, Morning, Sun, Rising Tide*), 1903. Oil on canvas, 21½ × 25½ in. (54.5 × 65 cm). MuMA, Le Havre.

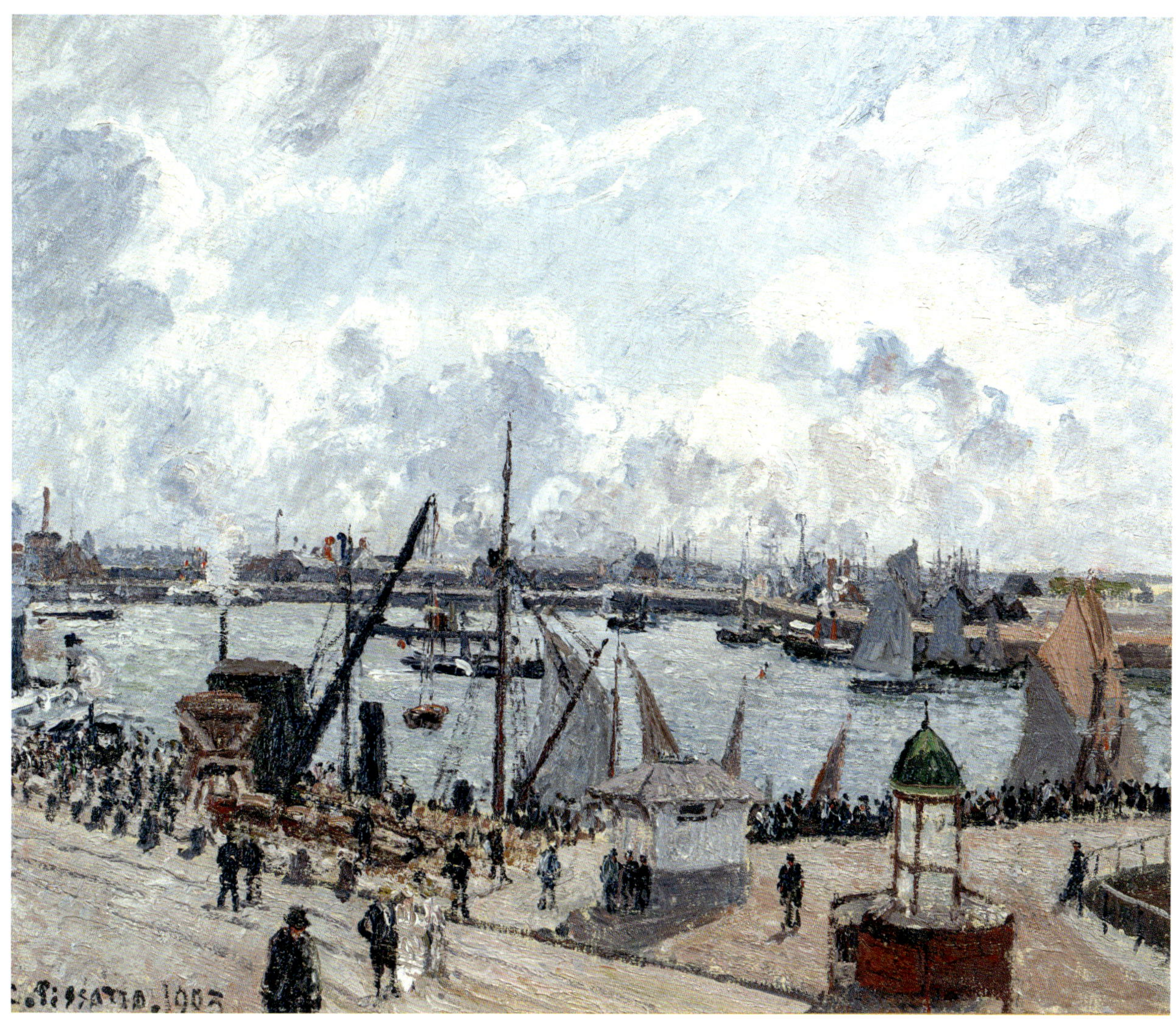

Between July and September 1903, Pissarro carried out a series of twenty paintings of the port of Le Havre—the port at which he had arrived, as a boy, from the Danish West Indies (now the United States Virgin Islands), where he was born. This painting was commissioned by a collector from Le Havre. The artist set up his easel in a hotel room to protect his eyes from the dust, but also to take advantage of a wider view. The cropped framing is reminiscent of Japanese woodblock prints and photography, which fascinated Pissarro. This painting was one of his final works.

25 {cat.} – Paul Signac, *Barfleur* (preparatory sketch for the eponymous painting), 1931.
India ink wash on paper, 2 ft. 4½ in. × 3 ft. (73 × 92 cm). Musée des Impressionnismes, Giverny.

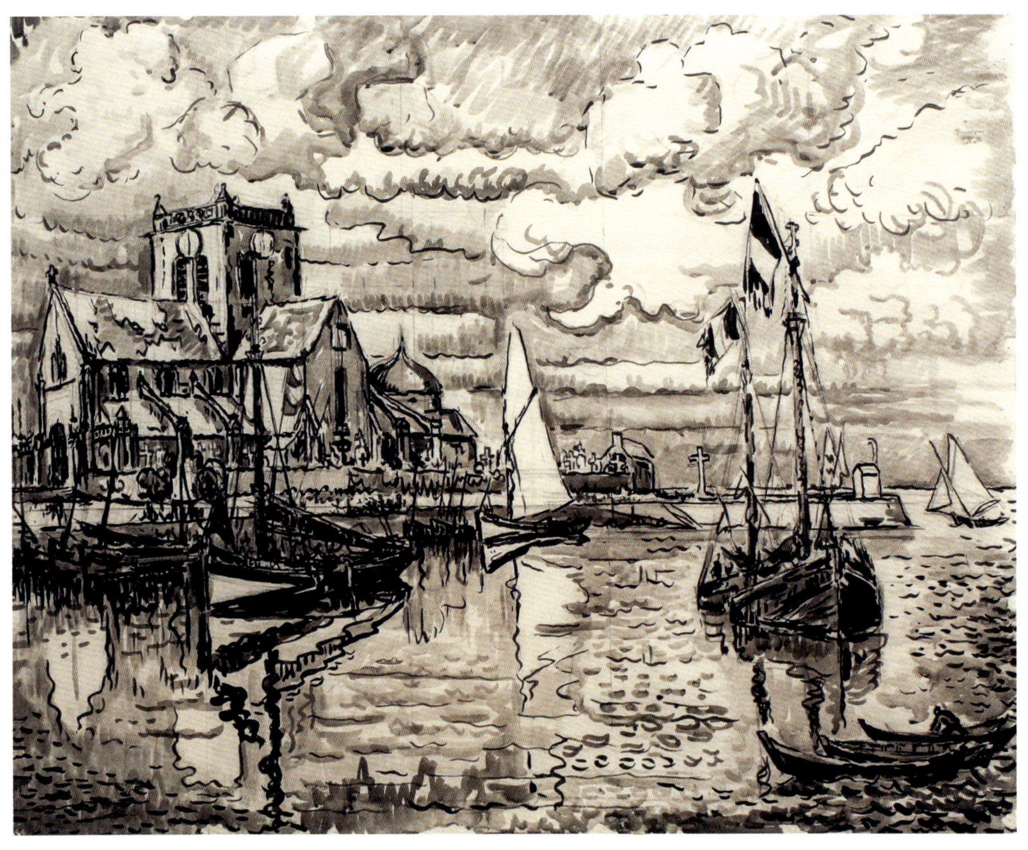

26 {cat.} – Paul Signac, *Port-en-Bessin (étude no. 5, l'avant-port)* (Port-en-Bessin [study no. 5, outer harbor]), summer 1882. Oil on canvas, 12½ × 21½ in. (32 × 55.5 cm). Musée des Impressionnismes, Giverny.

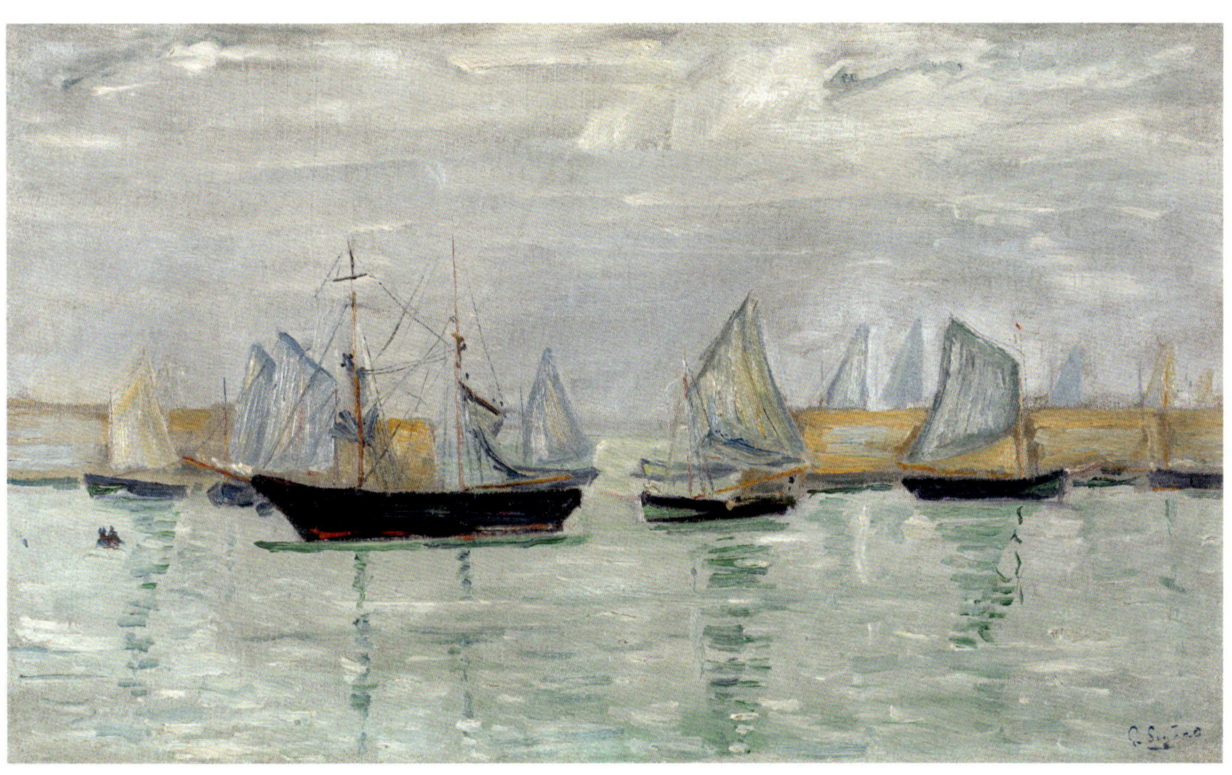

In his youth, Signac took an interest in painting, and was particularly drawn to the impressionist works that he admired in Parisian galleries. In 1880, he visited Monet's first solo exhibition and decided to follow in the footsteps of the master painter. In 1882, the seventeen-year-old Signac spent his first summer painting in Port-en-Bessin, on the coast of Normandy. His working method was similar to Monet's: he strove to portray every aspect of the docks, port, and especially the seashore, which allowed him to explore the effects of light on the surface of the water. Here, the young painter focuses on the outer port of Port-en-Bessin, which was built between 1845 and 1864 to adapt existing structures to the needs of modern ships.

27 {cat.} – Pierre-Auguste Renoir, *Petit port* (Small port), 1919.
Oil on canvas, 18 × 22 in. (46 × 56 cm). Musée d'Orsay, Paris, MNR 840.

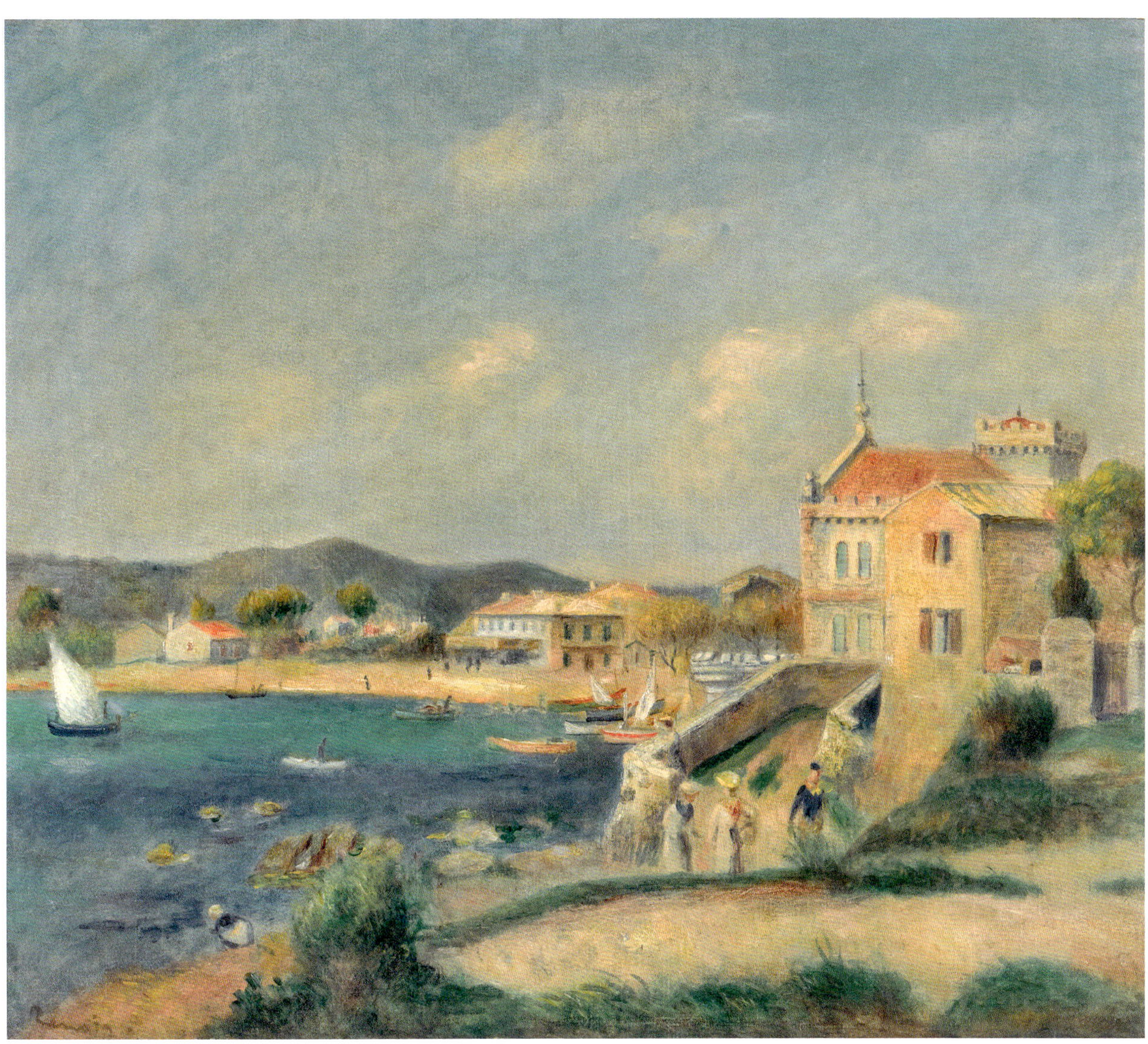

LIGHT

From the early nineteenth century onward, many artists were attracted to Normandy, with its singularly beautiful landscapes that were enhanced by exceptional light. Painters were fascinated by the reflections created by the sea against the jagged coastline, from Dieppe to Deauville. Gustave Courbet was among the first to depict the coastal effects of light, first near Montpellier, then in his Normandy waterscapes from the 1860s, which resulted in his famous series *Vagues* (*Waves*). At the same time, his friend Charles-François Daubigny painted a view of Villerville as a dramatic sunset panorama {cat. 35}. Eugène Boudin, described as "the king of the skies" by Charles Baudelaire, best portrayed the way in which air and water fuse in Normandy, blending colors to convey the soft green, gray, and ocher of the sea near Trouville. His highly original works inspired other artists, such as Dieppe native Théodore de Broutelles {cat. 36} and Maxime Maufra, who took a similar approach in Brittany {cat. 38}: the artists, drawn to the effects of light produced by the moon, were prolific, and in their paintings reflections of the celestial body converse with the frothing waves. Today, this same attraction is palpable in the work of photographer Darren Almond, who plays with the effects of moonlight on the sea in a striking view of the British coast, as seen in *Fullmoon@ Dunluce* {cat. 40}.

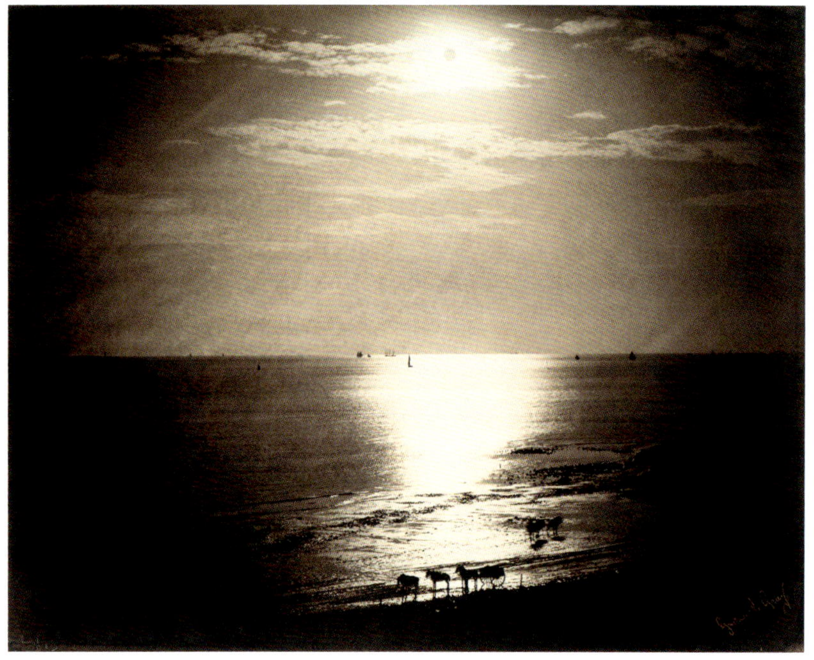

28 {fig.} – Gustave Le Gray, *Le Soleil au Zénith, Normandie* (*The Sun at Its Zenith—Ocean*), 1856.
Albumen print from a collodion-on-glass negative, 16 × 11 in. (40.7 × 27.5 cm). Victoria and Albert Museum, London.

29 {cat.} – Eugène Boudin, *Rivage normand* (Normandy coastline), c. 1858–1869.
Pastel on gray paper, 4 × 7 in. (10 × 18 cm). Private collection.

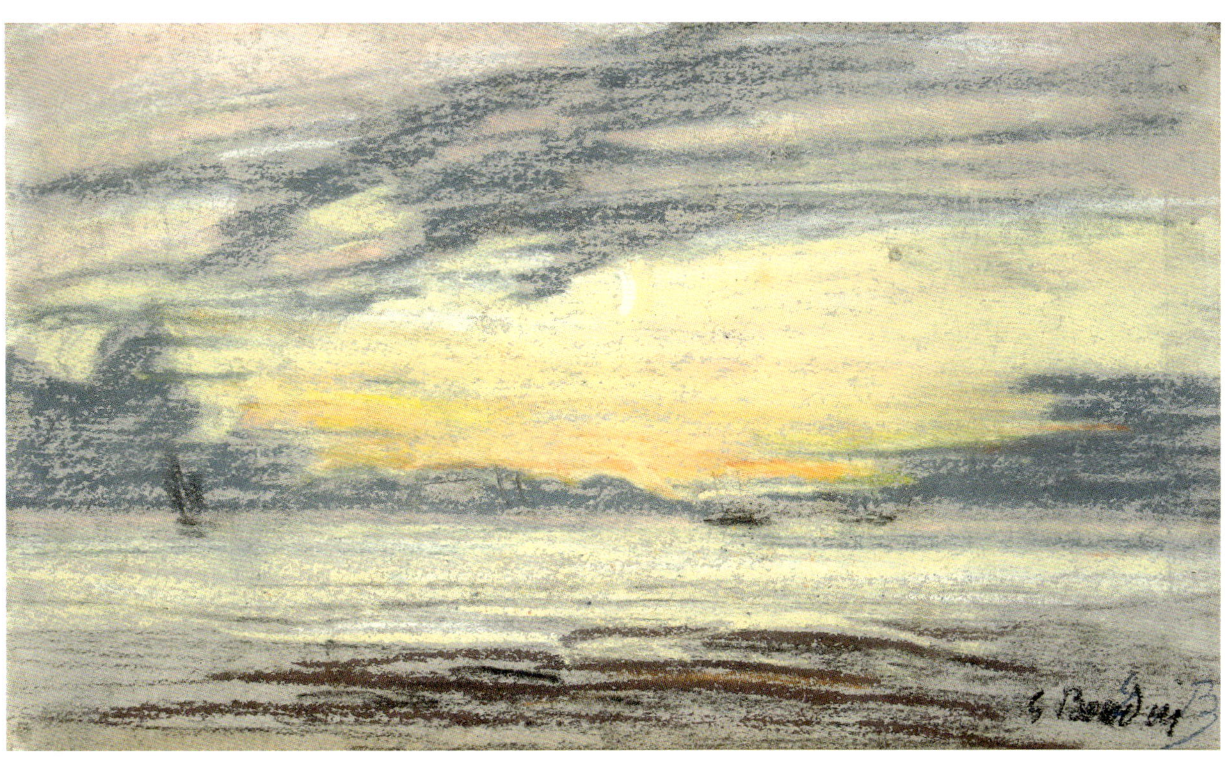

30 {cat.} – Gustave Courbet, *Les Bords de la mer à Palavas* (*The Seashore at Palavas*), c. 1854.
Oil on canvas, 23½ × 29 in. (60 × 73.5 cm). Olivier Senn Collection, gift of Hélène Senn Foulds, MuMA, Le Havre.

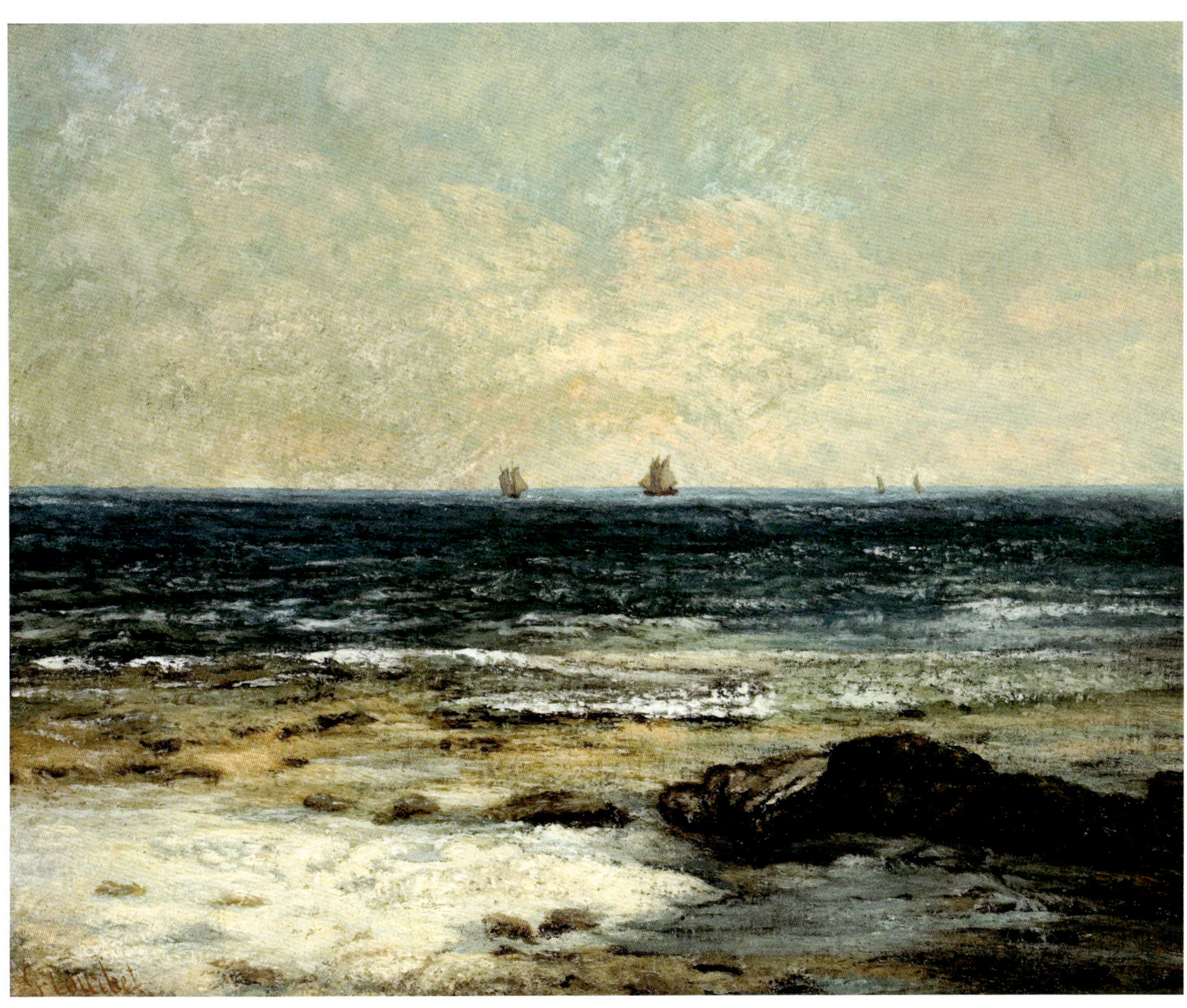

Courbet often painted the sea, which he first got to know when he visited Le Havre in 1841. Here, he depicts a beach near Montpellier that he knew well. The view is skillfully composed: the horizon line is placed high on the canvas, plunging the viewer into a marine landscape full of contrasts. In the foreground, the colors of the sand are rendered subtly, while the background conveys more intensity: the waves froth and four ships sail by in the distance. In 1865, Courbet painted Norman beaches with James Abbott McNeill Whistler in Trouville, before carrying out his famous series of *Vagues* (*Waves*) in 1869.

31 {cat.} – Eugène Boudin, *Soleil couchant sur l'estuaire de la Seine vers Honfleur* (Sunset over the Seine estuary near Honfleur), n.d. Pastel on paper, 5½ × 8½ in. (14.5 × 21.8 cm). Musée des Impressionnismes, Giverny.

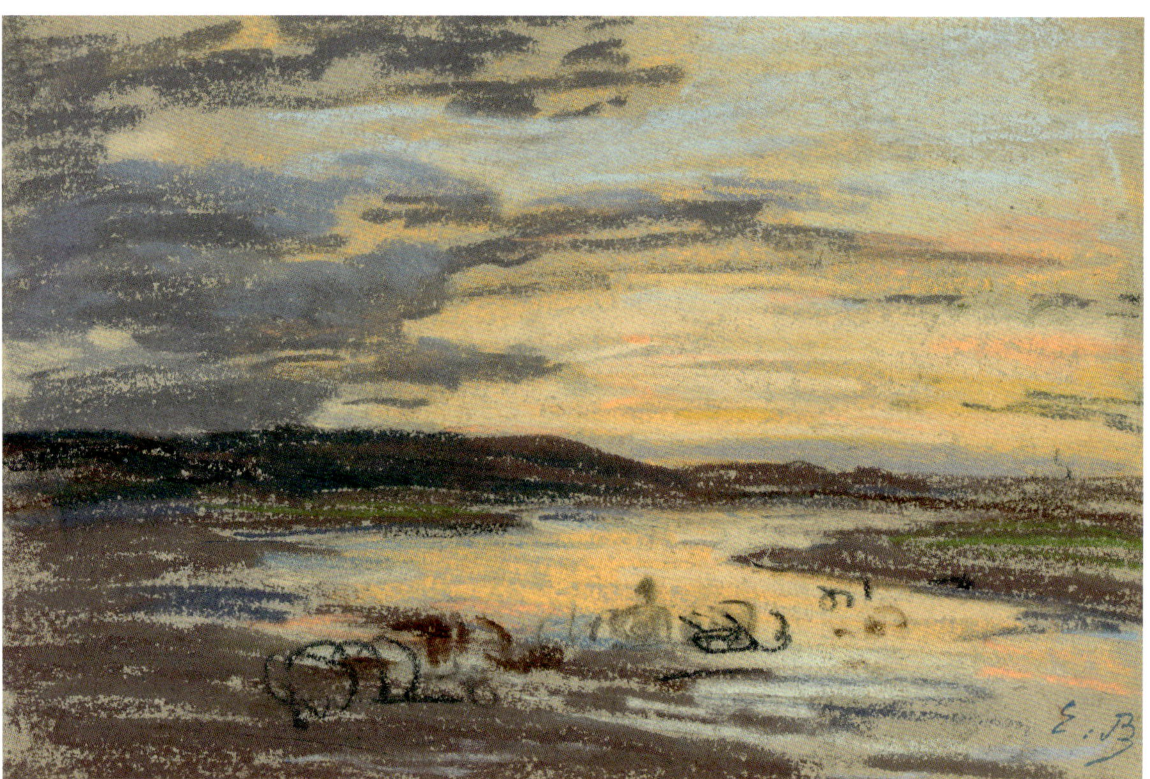

32 {cat.} – Eugène Boudin, *Ciel* (Sky), c. 1855–1860.
Pastel on paper, 3½ × 6½ in. (9.5 × 16.5 cm). Private collection.

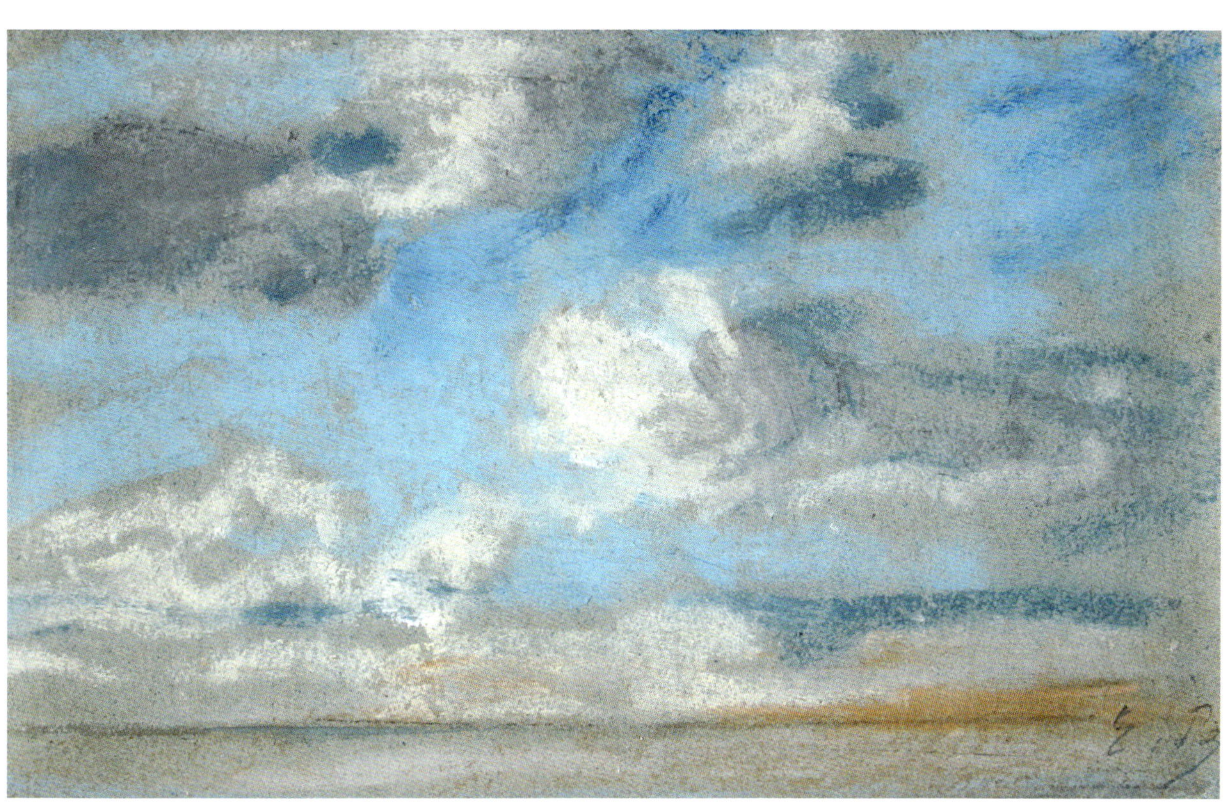

"I want to be on the battlefield already! Chasing boats … following clouds, paintbrush in hand."
Eugène Boudin to Ferdinand Martin, June 16, 1882

33 {fig.} – Gustave Le Gray, *Le Brick au clair de lune* (*Brig on the Water*), c. 1856.
Albumen silver print from a collodion-on-glass negative, 12½ × 16 in. (32.2 × 41.5 cm). Musée d'Orsay, Paris.

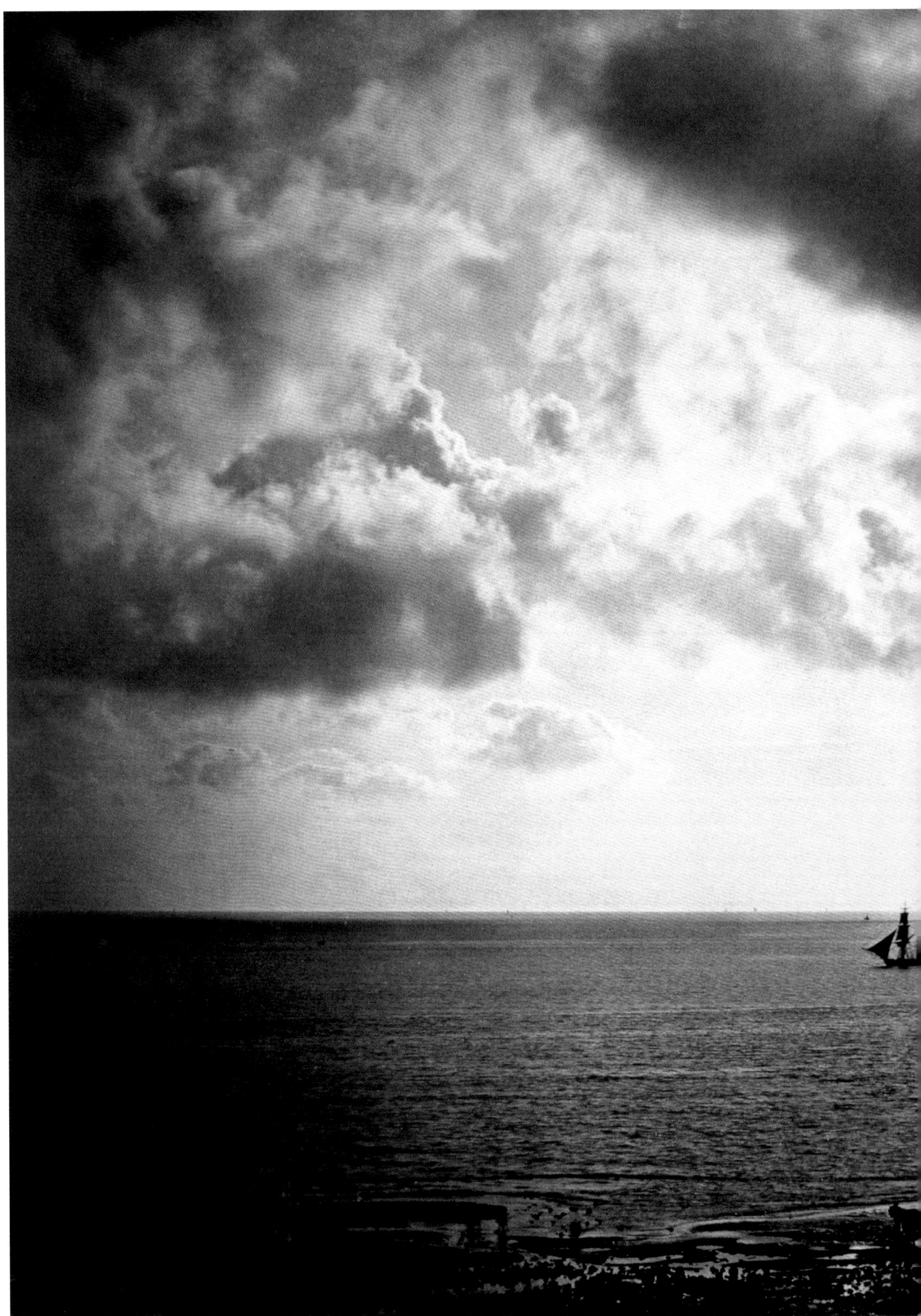

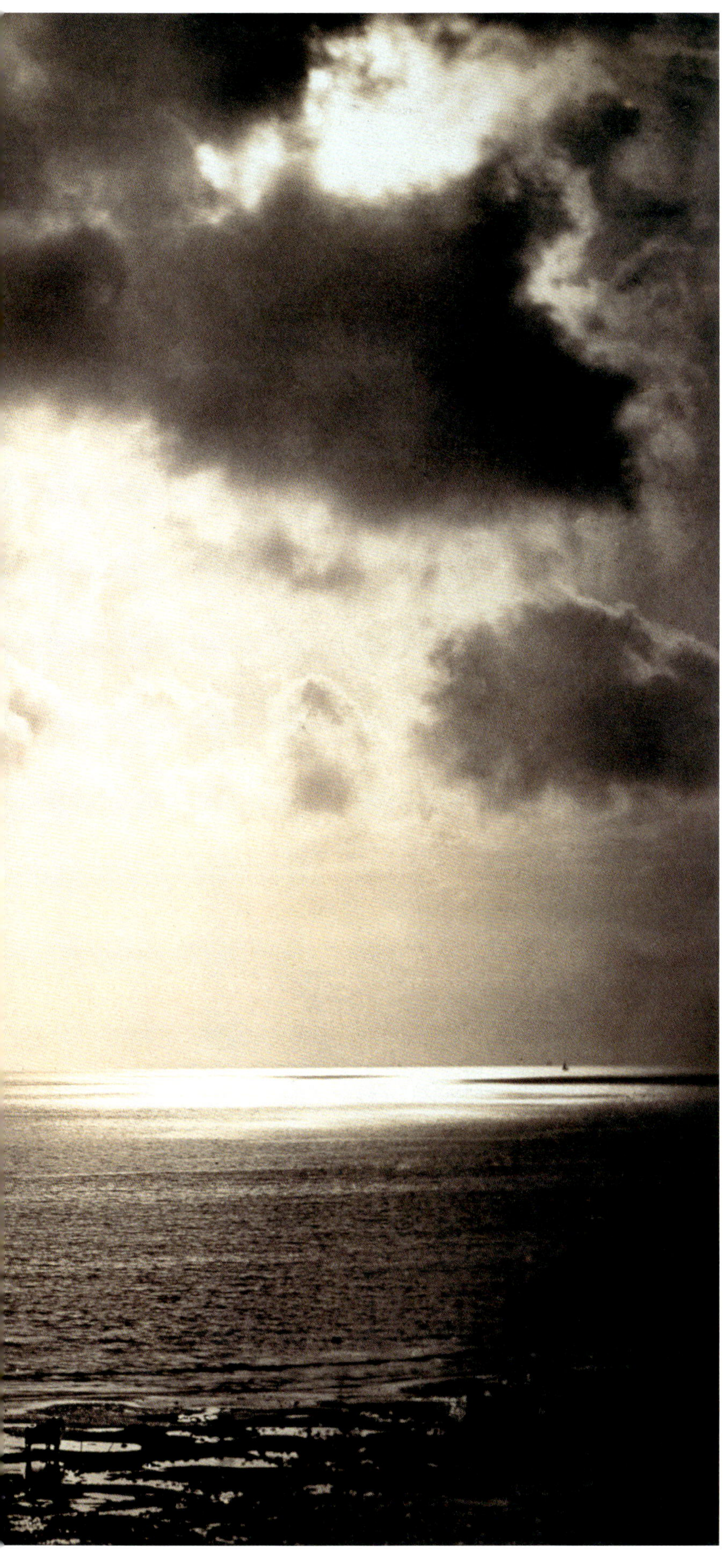

34 {cat.} – Eugène Boudin, *La Plage de Bénerville, coucher de soleil* (The beach at Bénerville, sunset), also known as *Les Vaches noires* (The Vaches Noires rocks), 1894. Pastel on paper, 10 × 15½ in. (26 × 40 cm). Musée des Impressionnismes, Giverny.

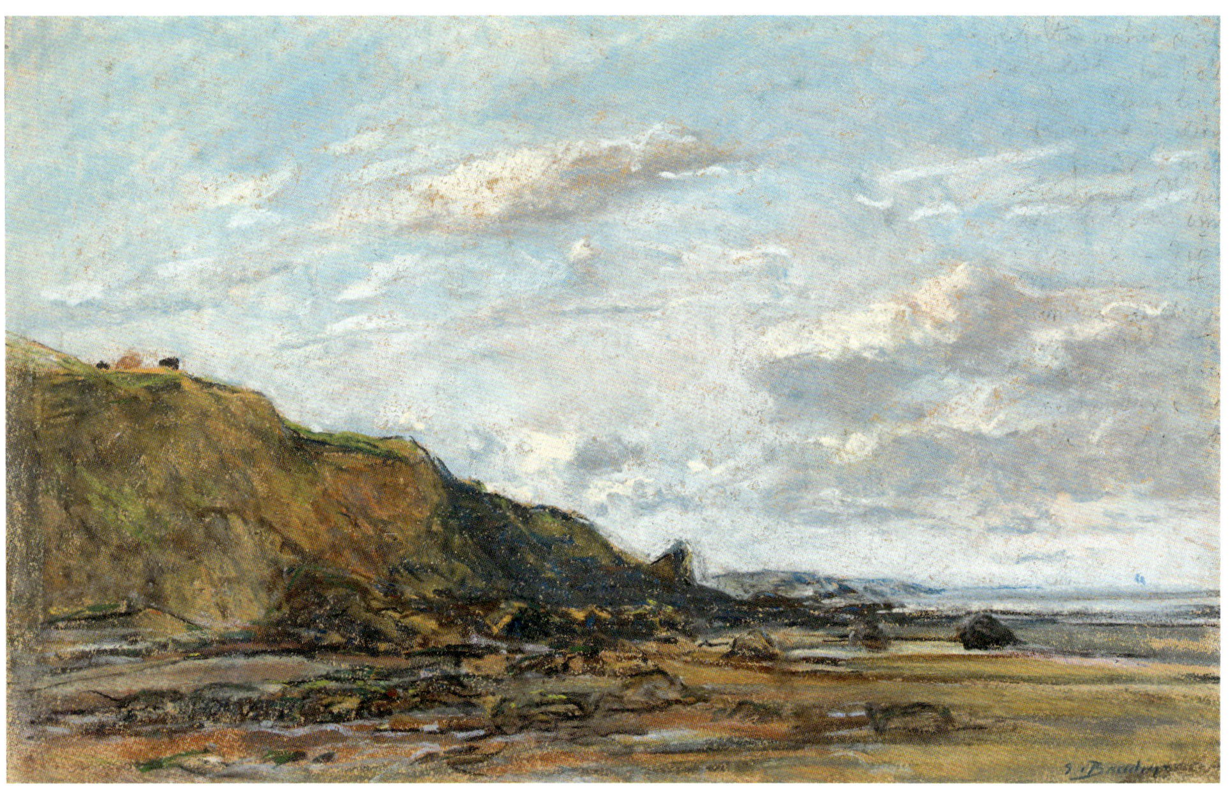

35 {cat.} – Charles-François Daubigny, *Coucher de soleil près de Villerville* (*Sunset near Villerville*), c. 1876. Oil on canvas, 2 ft. 11 in. × 4 ft. 3 in. (89 × 130 cm). The Mesdag Collection, The Hague.

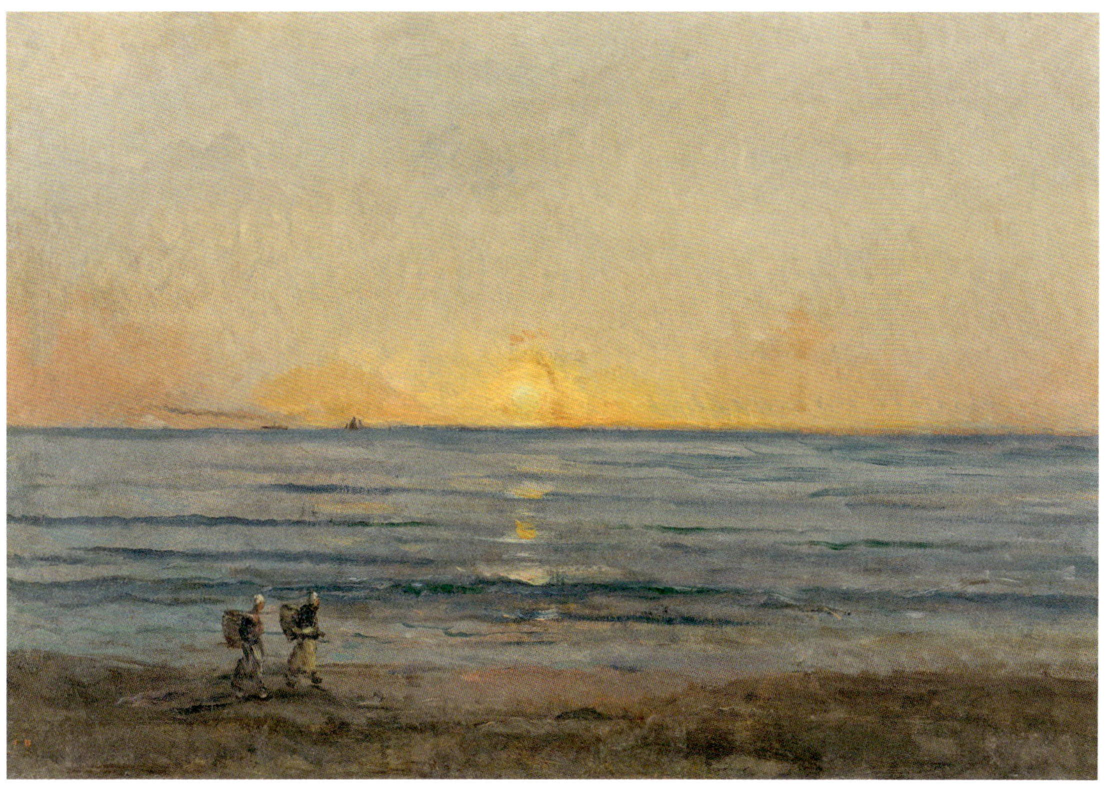

36 (cat.) – Théodore de Broutelles, *Paysage côtier* (Coastal landscape), c. 1900. Pastel on board, 13 × 8½ in. (33 × 22 cm). Musée des Impressionnismes, Giverny.

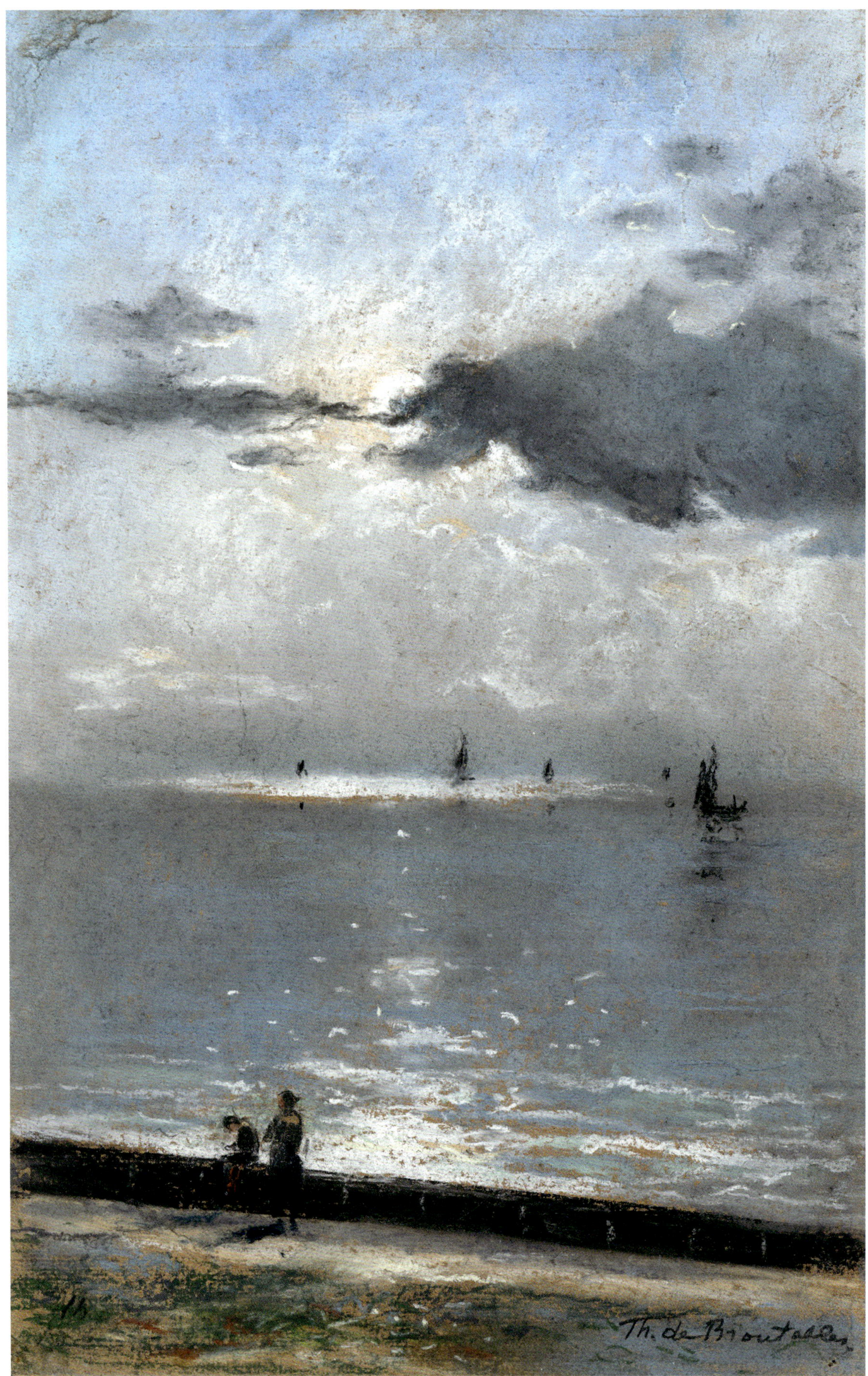

37 {cat.} – Octave de Champeaux, *Clair de lune en mer* (Moonlit sea), 1897.
Oil on canvas, 2 ft. 3½ in. × 3 ft. 3 in. (70 × 100 cm). Musée d'Orsay, Paris.

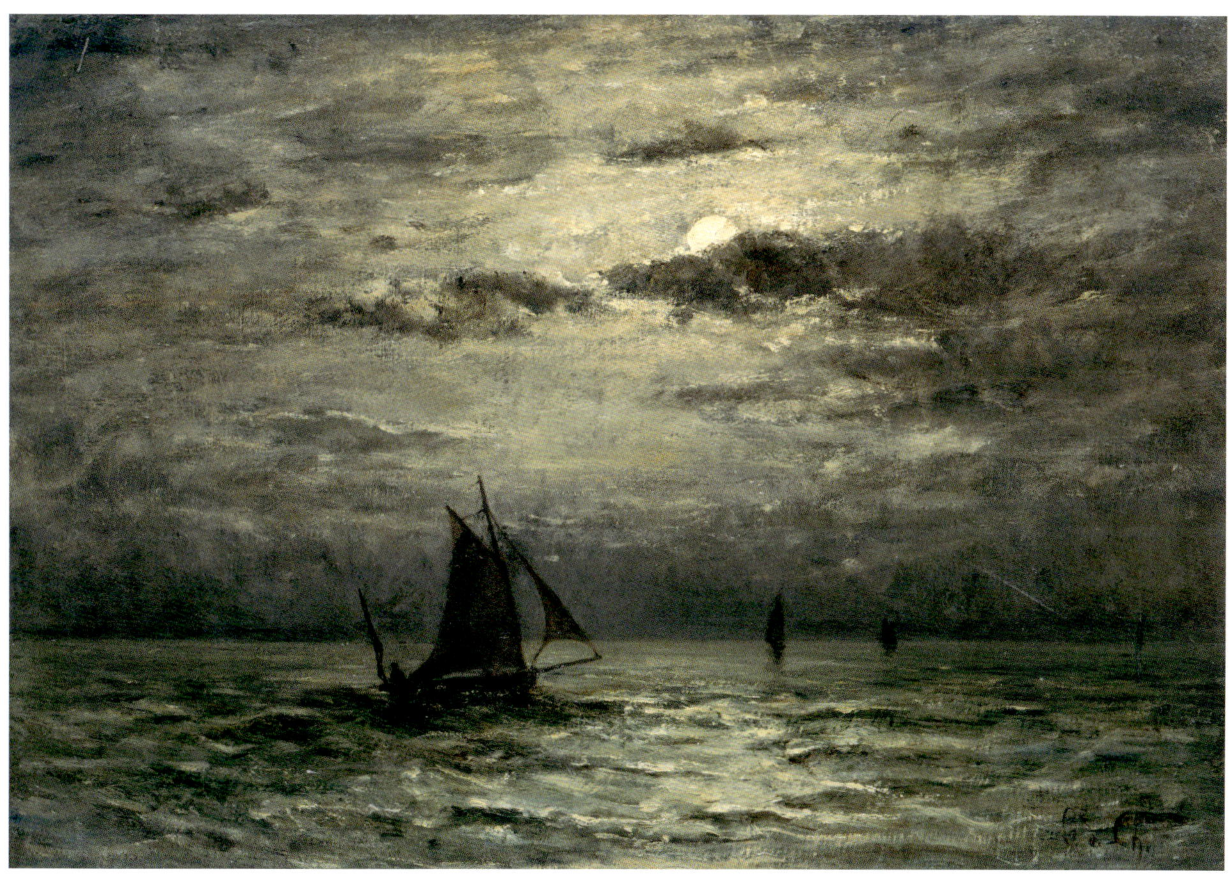

38 {cat.} – Maxime Maufra, *Effet de lune* (Moonlight), 1899.
Oil on canvas, 18½ × 21½ in. (46.6 × 55.4 cm). Musée des Beaux-Arts, Reims.

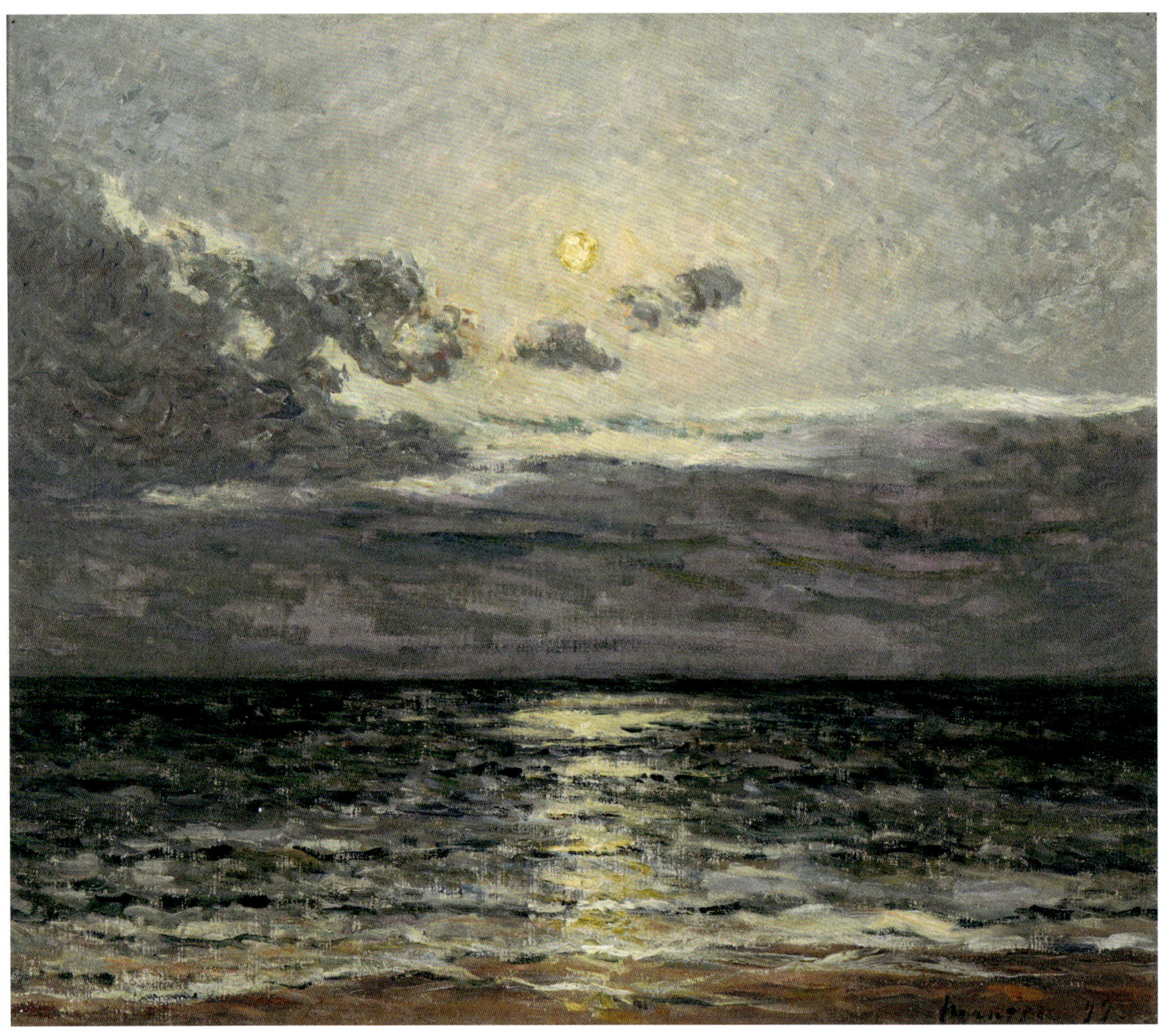

39 {cat.} – Jacques-Émile Blanche, *La Plage de Dieppe* (The beach at Dieppe), n.d.
Oil on canvas, 19½ × 23½ in. (50 × 60 cm). Château-Musée, Dieppe.

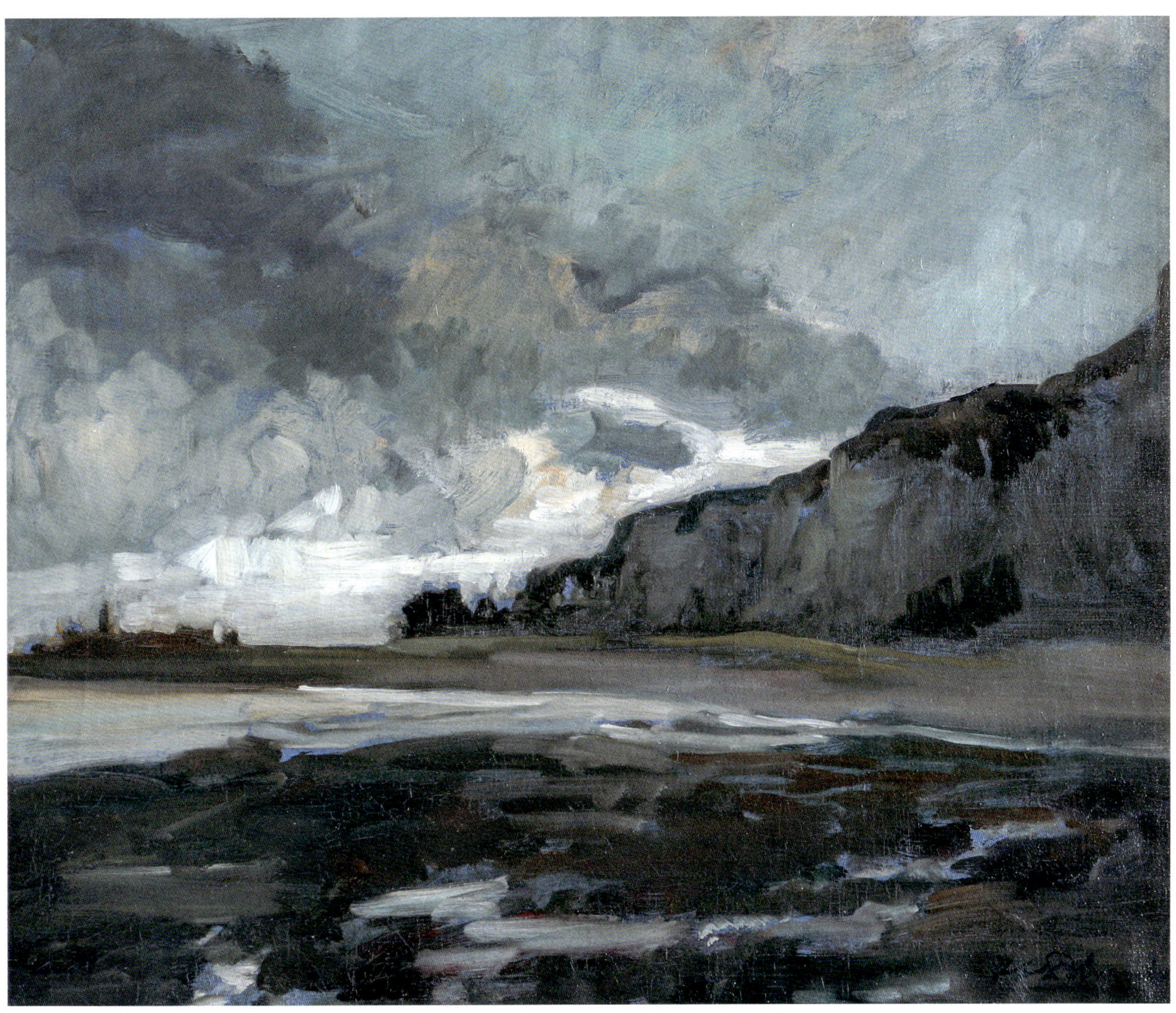

40 {cat.} – Darren Almond, *Fullmoon@Dunluce*, 2007.
C-print mounted on aluminum, 4 ft. 2 in. × 4 ft. 1½ in. (128 × 126 cm). FRAC Normandie Collection.

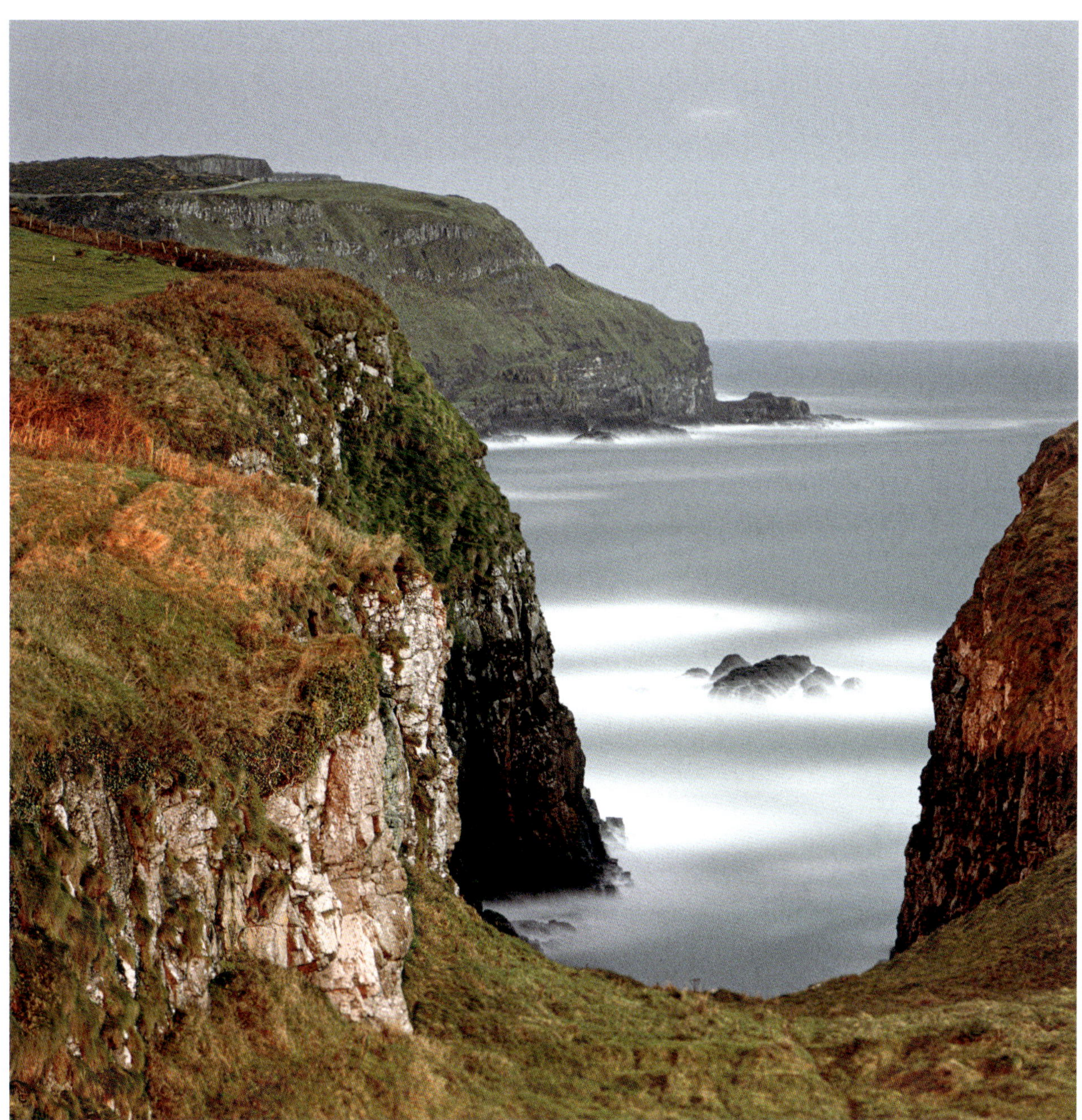

Initiated in 2001, the photographic series *Fullmoon* transforms nighttime landscapes into images of surreal beauty. In this series, the artist photographs mostly remote areas on nights when the moon is full. Using an exposure time of fifteen minutes, he achieves a particular luminosity that gives his landscapes a strange atmosphere in which water takes on a vaporous quality. Darren Almond's explorations and reflections are reminiscent of the impressionists' attempts to render the effects of light.

LOW TIDE

It is striking to note just how much effort the impressionists devoted to conveying the effects of the tide in their work. Low tide became a commonly treated subject. Cals, Monet, Dantan, Boudin, among others, all used a pictorial technique that enhanced the effects of light on ocher ground and strove to impart emotion. While Dantan created a powerful image of a fisherman in a punt in Villerville {cat. 42}, Cals painted the portrait of a sailor walking among the pebbles at low tide {cat. 43}. Both works portray the deserted beach with a certain ghostly atmosphere. Boudin turned his attention to locals working on the beach, such as kelp harvesters and washerwomen. His views create sweeping perspectives that capture the immensity of Normandy's beaches in Deauville and Trouville. On the other hand, Monet succeeds in conveying the subtleties of light in three works reproduced here {cats. 45, 47, 48}: whether depicting the Sainte-Adresse shore in Le Havre in shades of gray, or dramatic boulders in a storm, the painter plays on the dialogue between fragmented brushwork and the effects of the light on the water, through which other rocky elements are just barely visible. In this regard, *Marée basse aux Petites Dalles* (*Low Tide at Les Petites Dalles*) {cat. 45} presents a dramatic view of Dieppe at low tide, with the sun reflecting on the water.

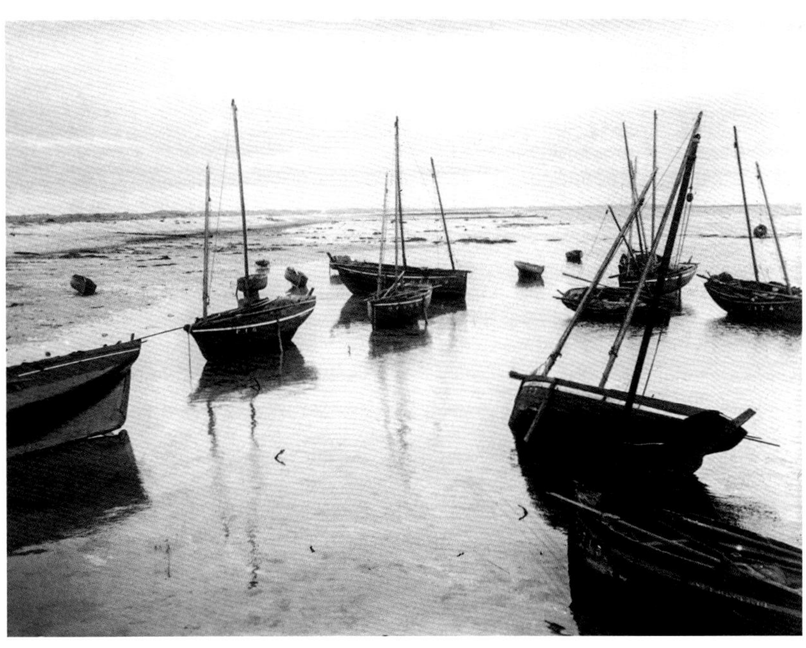

41 {fig.} – Touring Club de France, *Boats in the Port of Penmarc'h at Low Tide*, n.d.
Médiathèque du Patrimoine et de la Photographie, Charenton-le-Pont.

42 {cat.} – Édouard Dantan, *Plate à Villerville, marée basse* (*Boat at Villerville, Low Tide*), October 1881. Oil on wood, 15½ × 7½ in. (40 × 19.5 cm). Musée des Impressionnismes, Giverny.

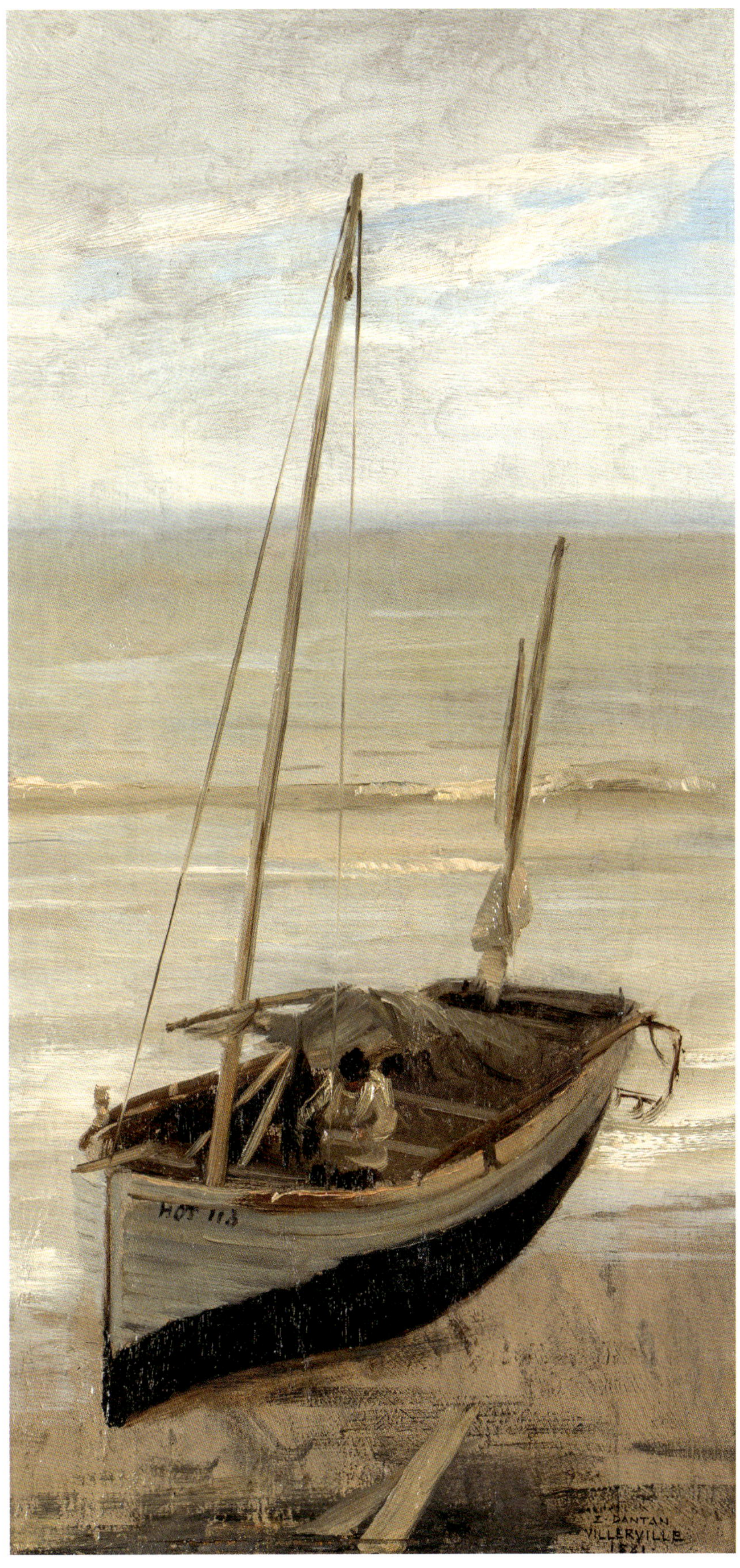

43 {cat.} – Adolphe-Félix Cals, *Pêcheur* (Fisherman), 1874. Oil on canvas, 10 × 12 in. (26 × 31 cm). Musée d'Orsay, Paris, on long-term loan to the Musée Eugène Boudin, Honfleur, MNR 627.

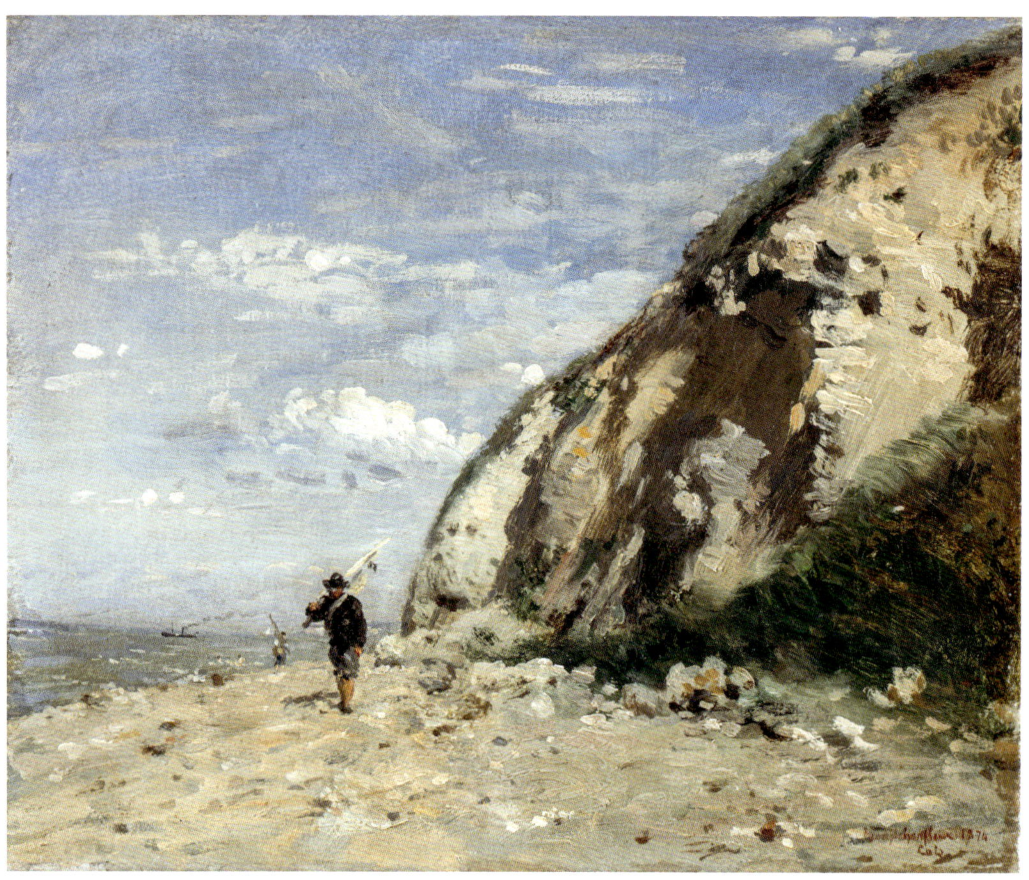

44 {cat.} – Eugène Boudin, *La Plage de Deauville* (The beach at Deauville), 1893.
Oil on canvas, 20 × 29½ in. (50.5 × 74.5 cm). Musée des Beaux-Arts, Caen.

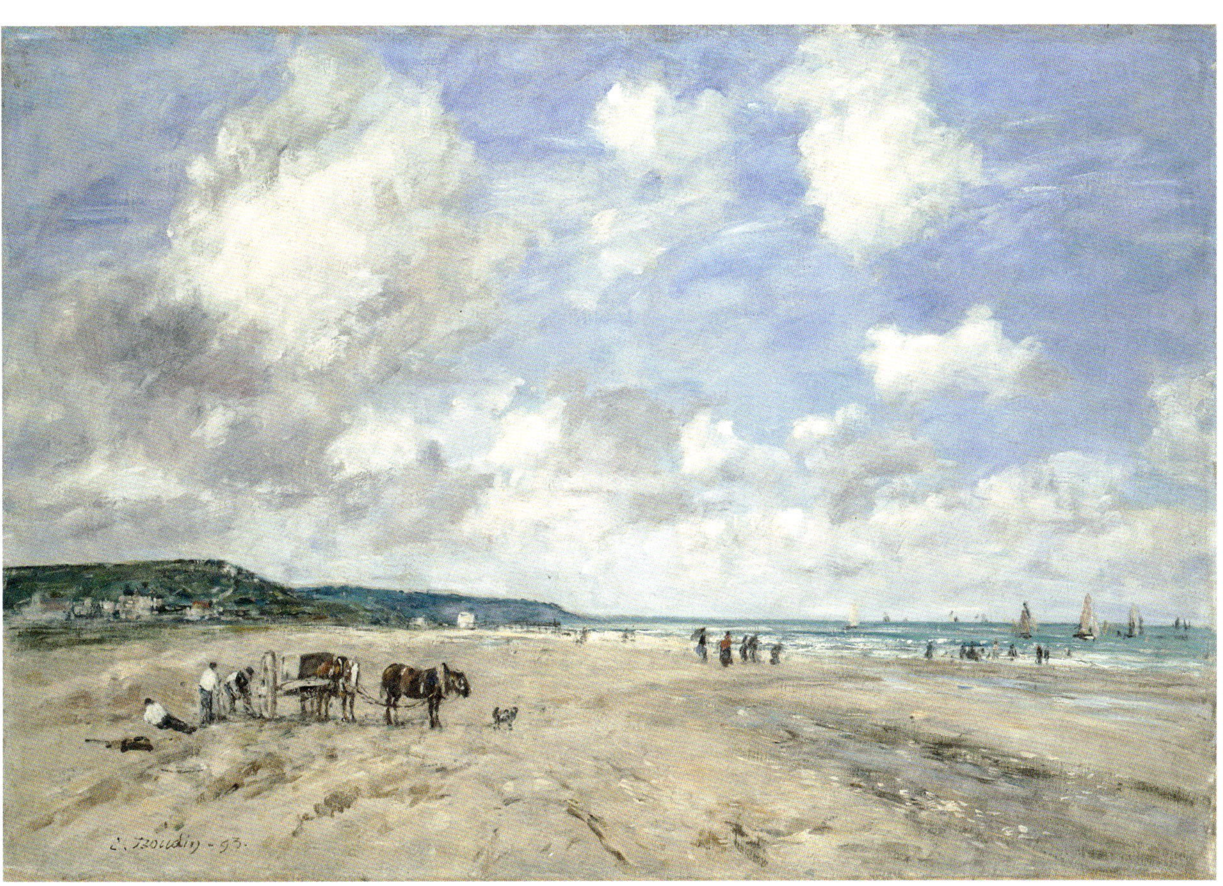

45 {cat.} – Claude Monet, *Marée basse aux Petites Dalles* (*Low Tide at Les Petites Dalles*), 1884.
Oil on canvas, 23½ × 28½ in. (60 × 73 cm). Hasso Plattner Collection.

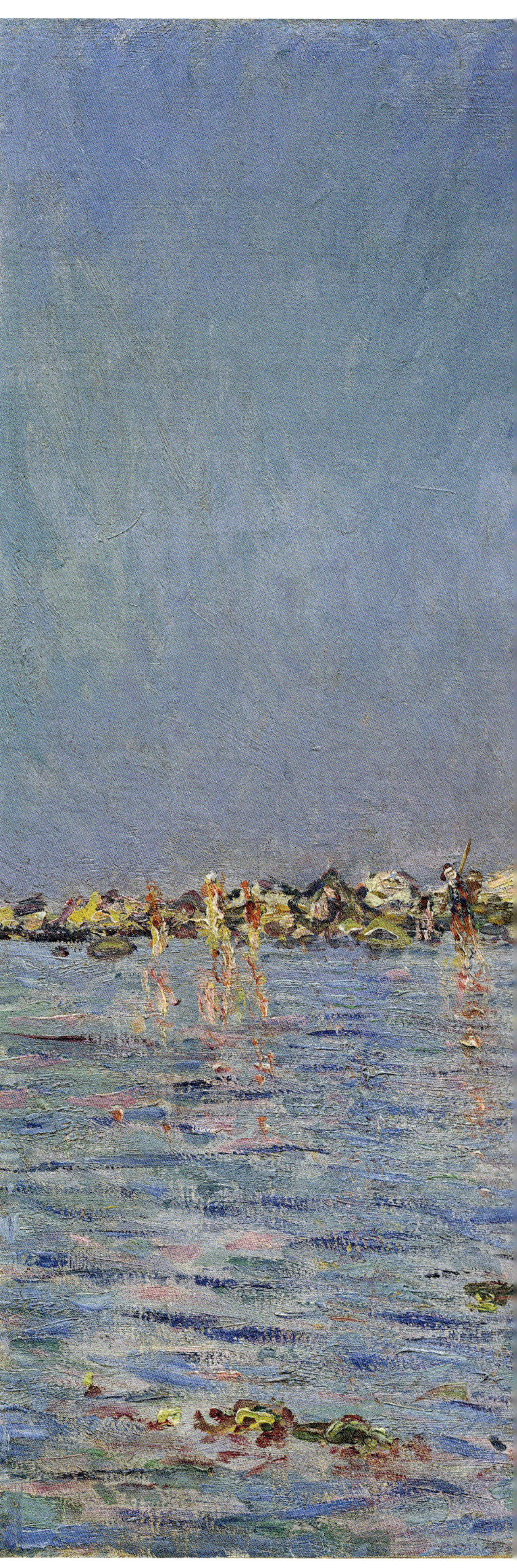

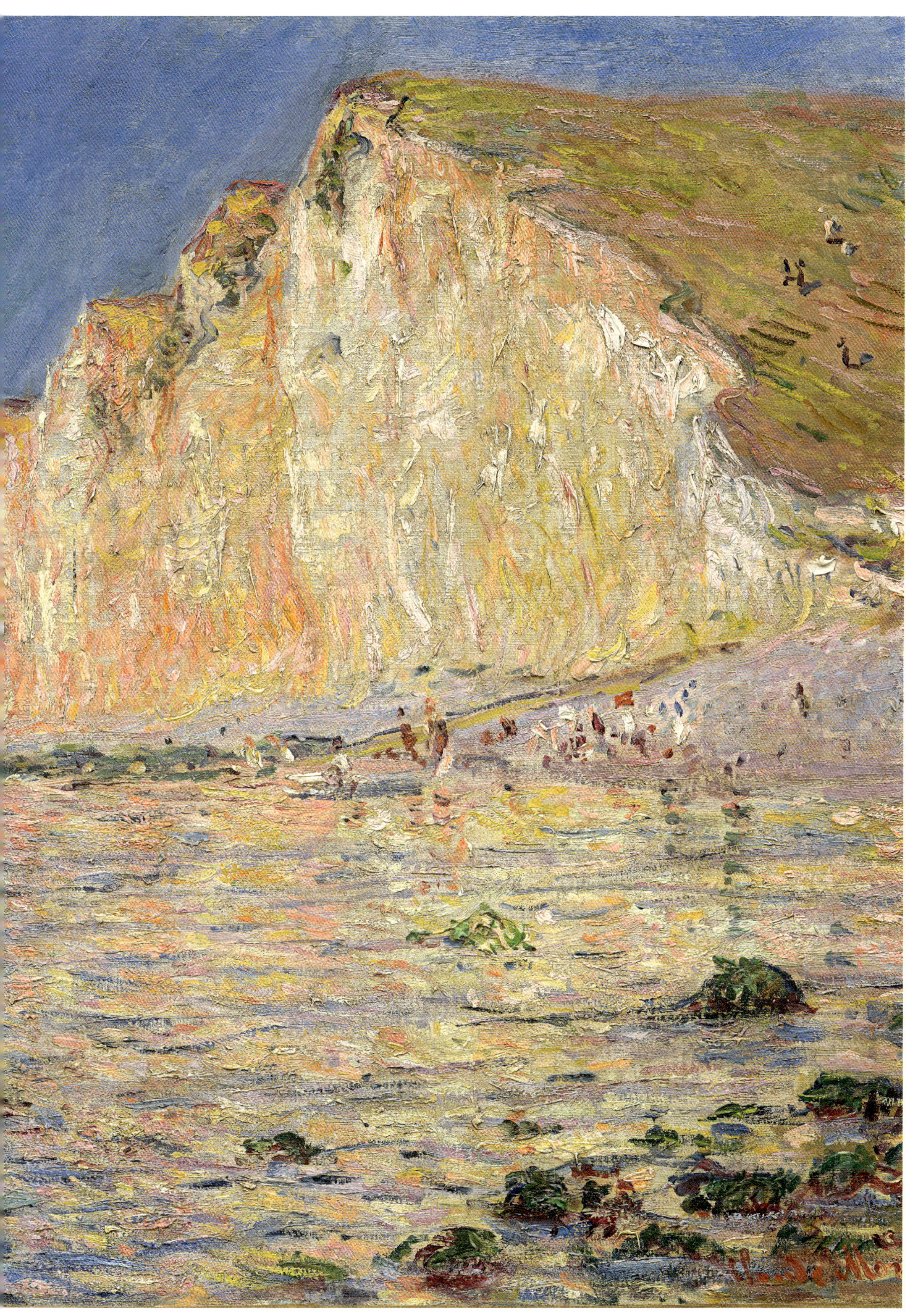

46 {cat.} – Eugène Boudin, *Coucher de soleil à marée basse* (Sunset at low tide), 1884. Oil on canvas, 3 ft. 10 in. × 5 ft. 3 in. (117 × 161 cm). Musée d'Art et d'Histoire, Saint-Lô.

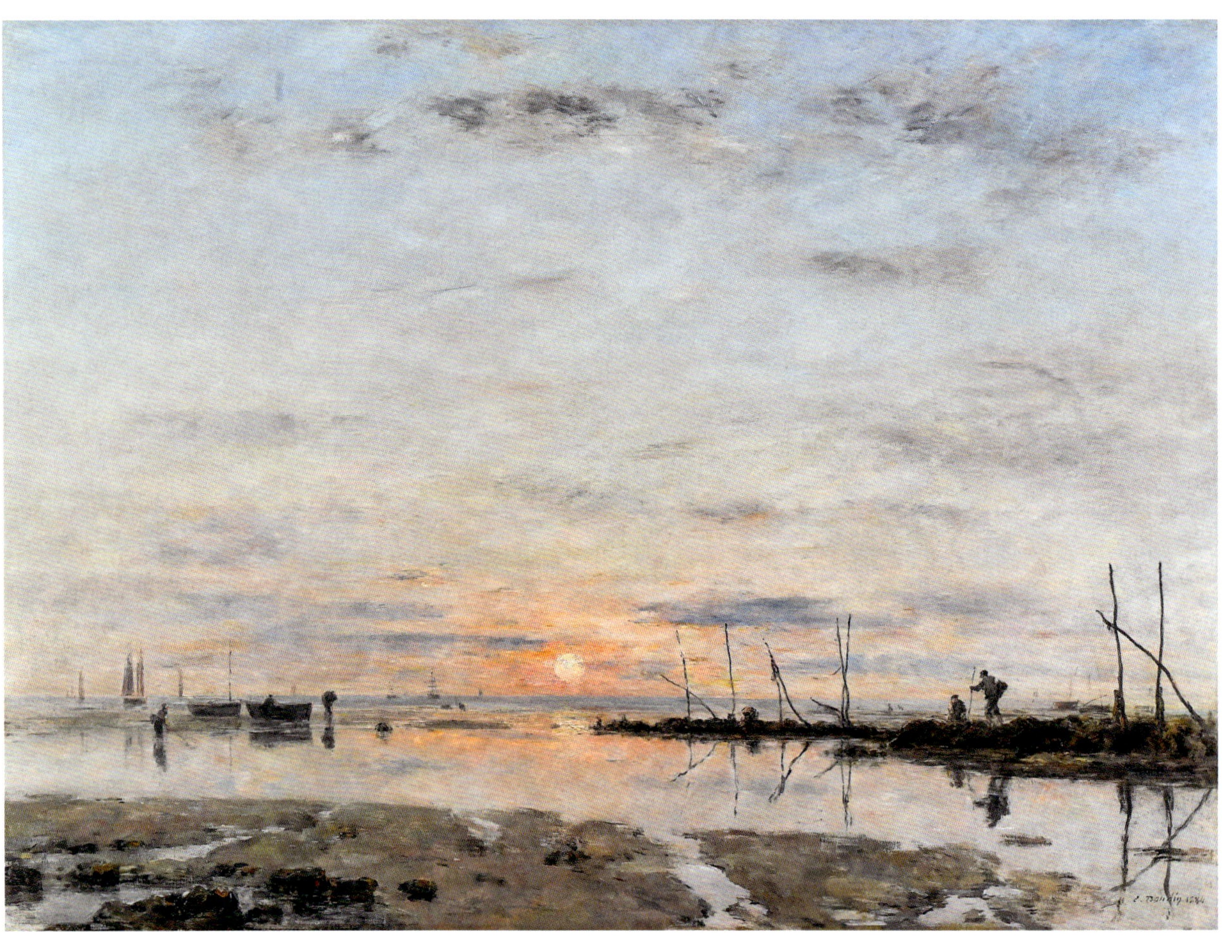

47 {cat.} – Claude Monet, *Les Rochers à Pourville, marée basse* (*The Rocks at Pourville, Low Tide*), 1882. Oil on canvas, 25½ × 31 in. (64.3 × 78.7 cm). Memorial Art Gallery, Rochester, NY.

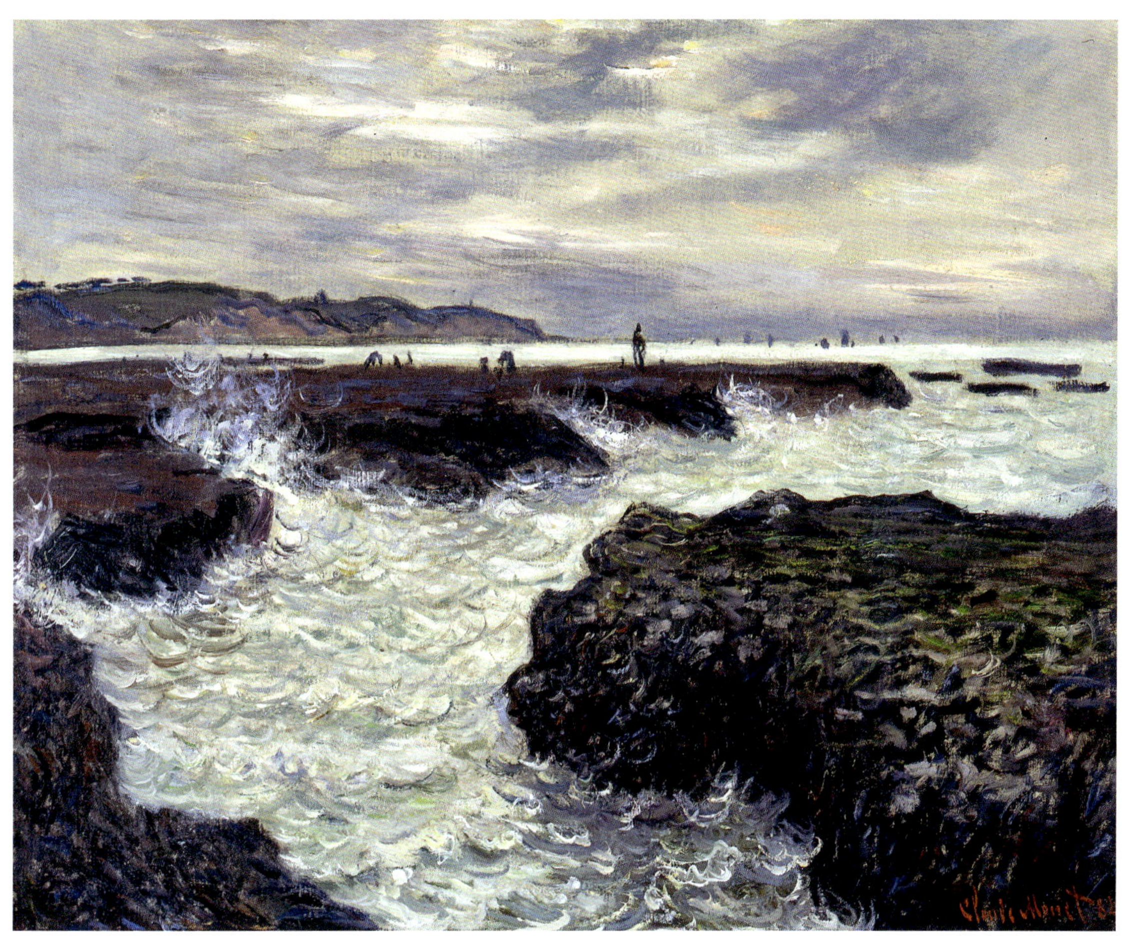

"The painter [Monet] waited before his subject, stalked the sun and shadows, gathered up the ray of sun that fell or the cloud that passed in a few brushstrokes, and, scornful of all that is false or conventional, swiftly placed them on his canvas."

Guy de Maupassant, "La vie d'un paysagiste" (The life of a landscape painter), *Gil Blas*, September 28, 1886

48 (cat.) – Claude Monet, *Sainte-Adresse*, 1867. Oil on canvas, 22½ × 31½ in. (57 × 80 cm). National Gallery of Art, Washington, D.C.

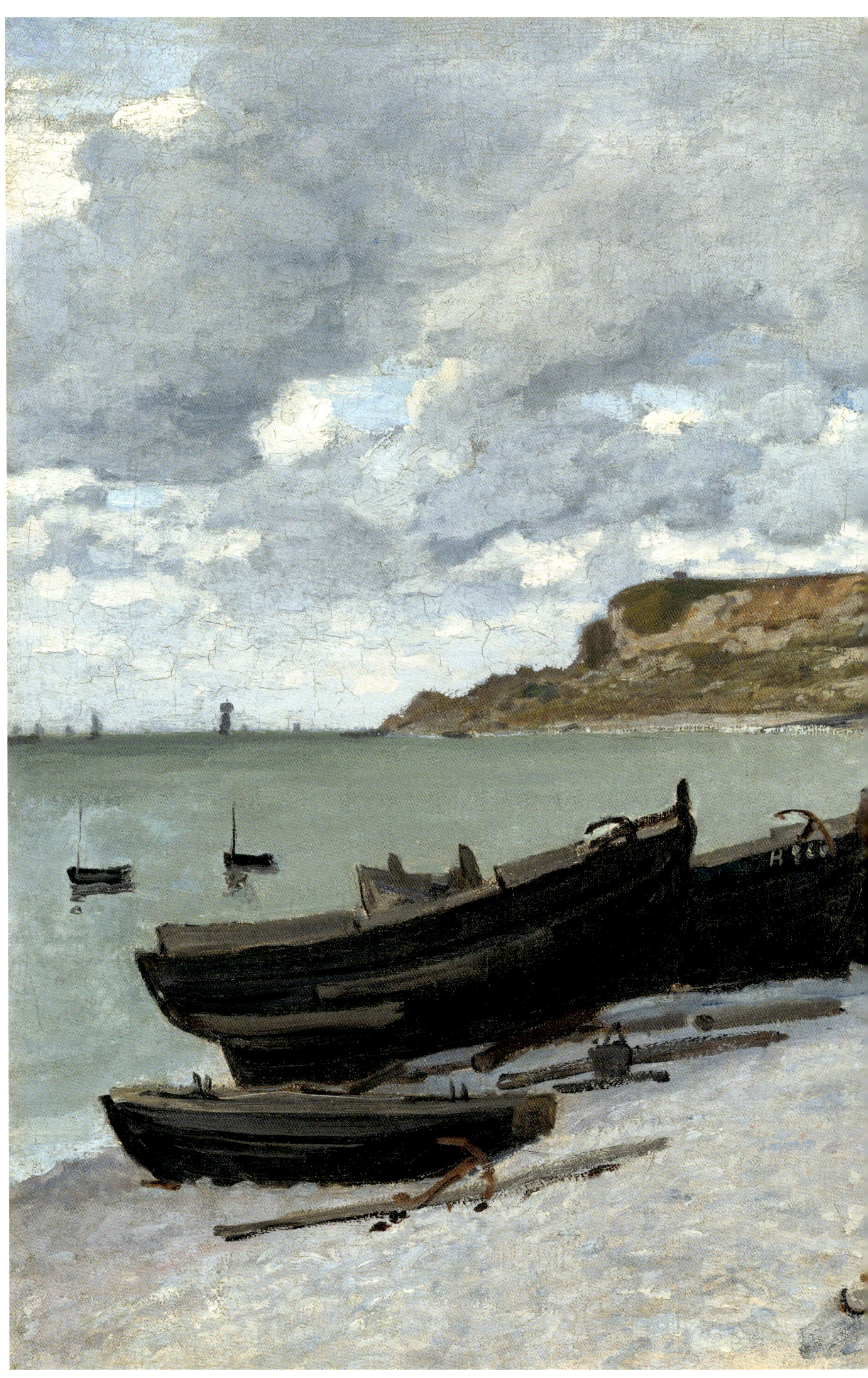

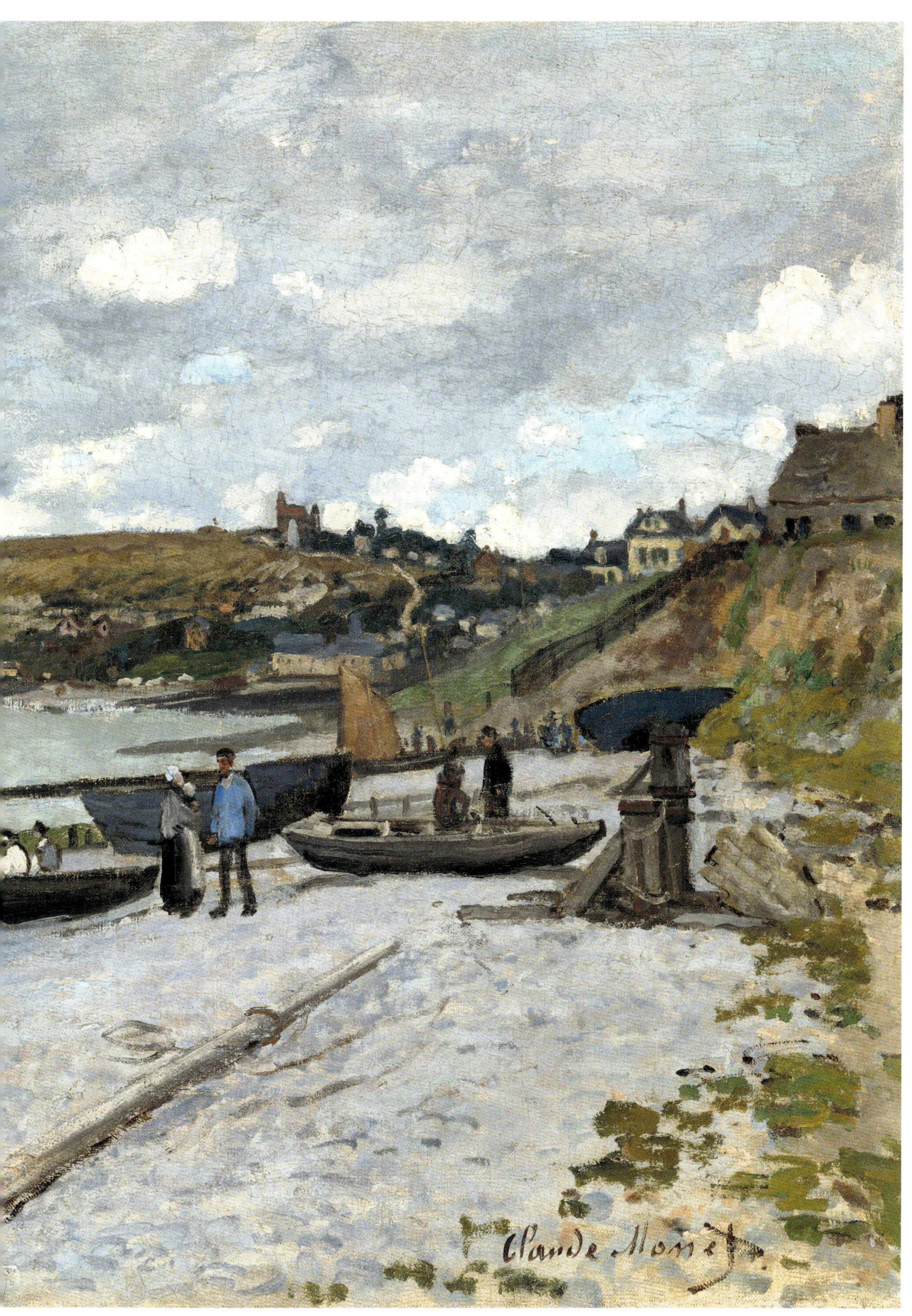
Claude Monet.

49 {cat.} – Eugène Boudin, *Lavandière près de Trouville* (*Washerwoman near Trouville*), c. 1872–1876. Oil on wood, 10¾ × 16¼ in. (27.6 × 41.3 cm). National Gallery of Art, Washington, D.C.

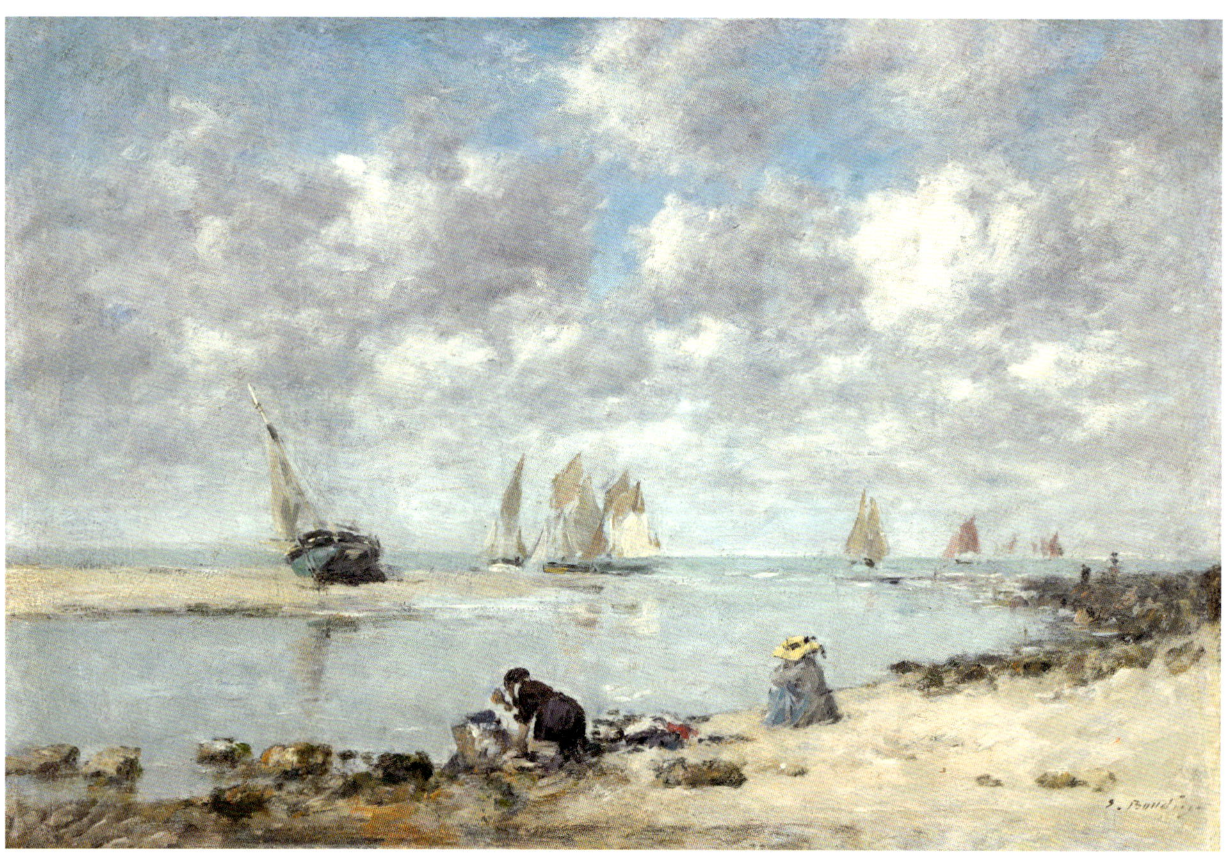

50 {cat.} – Eugène Boudin, *Normandes étendant du linge sur la plage* (Norman women drying laundry on the beach), 1865. Oil on canvas, 18 × 24 in. (46.2 × 61.3 cm). Musée d'Orsay, Paris, MNR 192.

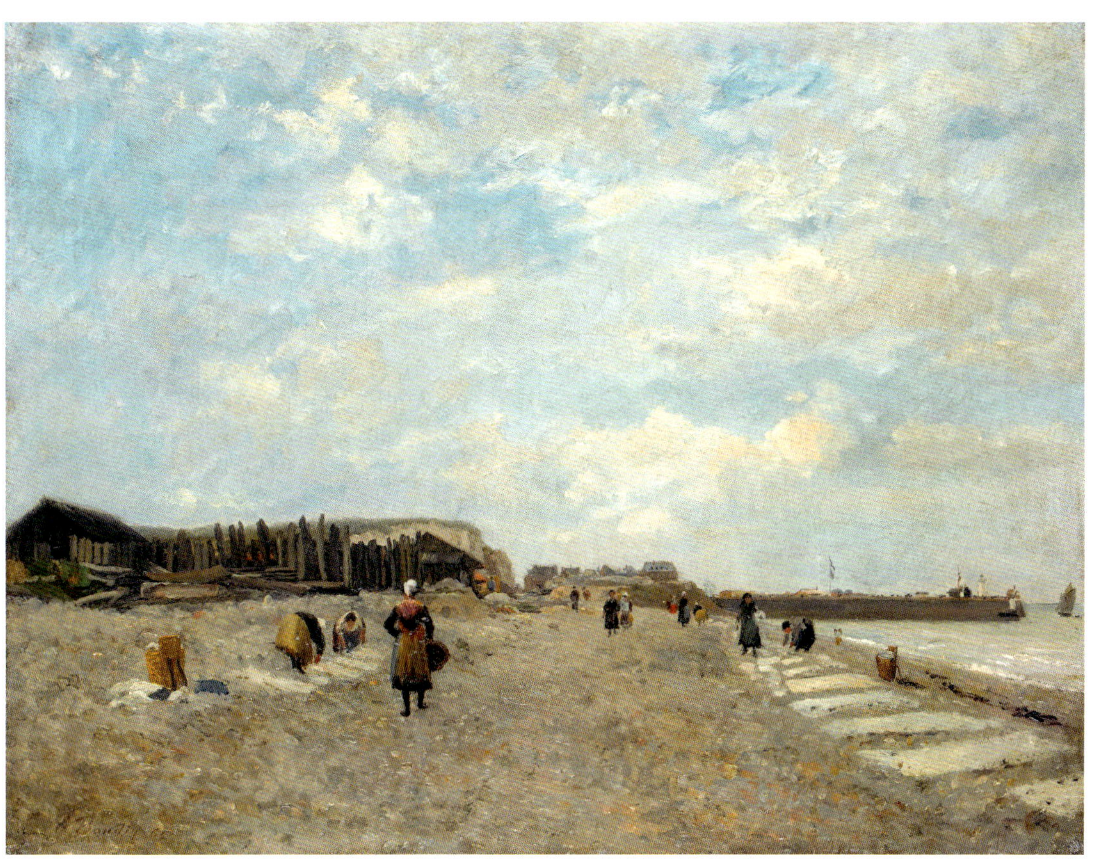

Best known for his seascapes and his depictions of skies, Boudin also experimented extensively with incorporating human figures into the landscape. The small town of Trouville, where he stayed each summer from the 1860s onward, offered him a wide variety of subjects, ranging from market scenes to the everyday activities of fishermen or washerwomen—a whole different class that contrasted with the elegant figures on the beach in Deauville, which Boudin also painted. In the 1850s, he turned his attention to the washerwomen on the edge of Touques, a motif that he would return to again and again up to the 1880s. On this Normandy beach at low tide, women in colorful clothes drape large white linen sheets on the shore.

THE CLIFFS OF NORMANDY

Impressionism was born in Normandy, in Le Havre, with Claude Monet's *Impression, soleil levant* (*Impression, Sunrise*), painted in 1872 and presented in 1874 at Nadar's studio in Paris. Inspired by the sea, the work is a milestone in modern art. Sensation is more important than a realistic view; this way of seeing the world enabled a generation of artists to depict the sea using a technique that favored immediacy. The paintings reproduced here give prominence to Monet, the movement's founder. From his early work in Sainte-Adresse, in 1867 {cat. 48}, to his view of Varengeville, painted in 1897 {cat. 52}, he continually depicted Normandy's coast. His fellow painters, including Courbet, Boudin, and Maufra, to name but a few, were inspired by his work and maintained a fruitful dialogue that extended along the Normandy coast. Jean Francis Auburtin, who was influenced by symbolism, also followed in Monet's footsteps and devoted several of his works to the imposing cliffs that are so characteristic of this stretch of coast. But rather than focusing on the fleeting effects of nature that were so important to his predecessor, Auburtin set out to paint the eternal and unchanging quality of the landscape {cats. 54 and 55}.

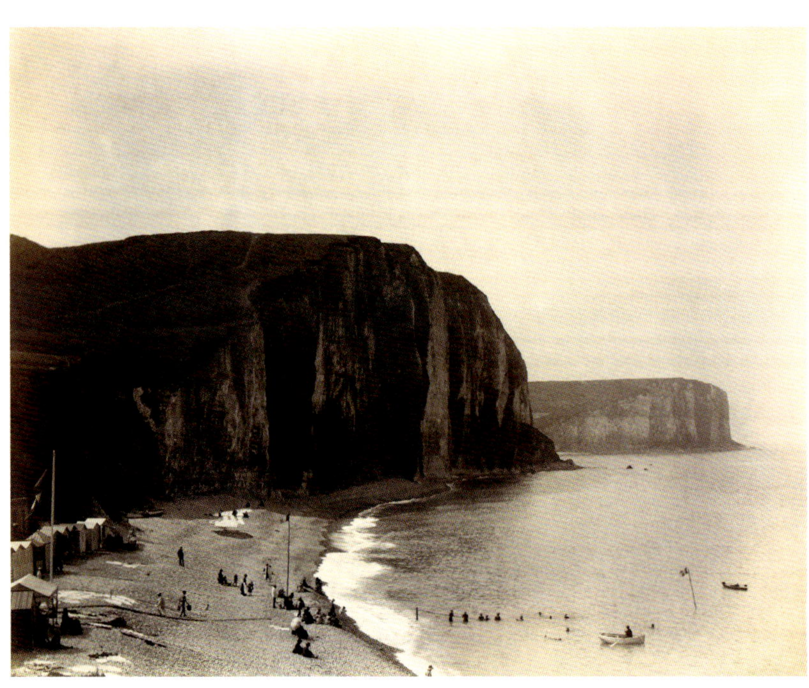

51 {fig.} – Gustave Eiffel, *La Plage des Petites Dalles et la falaise d'aval* (Les Petites Dalles beach and the cliffs above), 1885. Proof printed on paper. Musée d'Orsay, Paris.

52 {cat.} – Claude Monet, *La Pointe du Petit Ailly* (*The Pointe du Petit Ailly*), 1897.
Oil on canvas, 29 × 36½ in. (73.5 × 92.7 cm). Nahmad Collection.

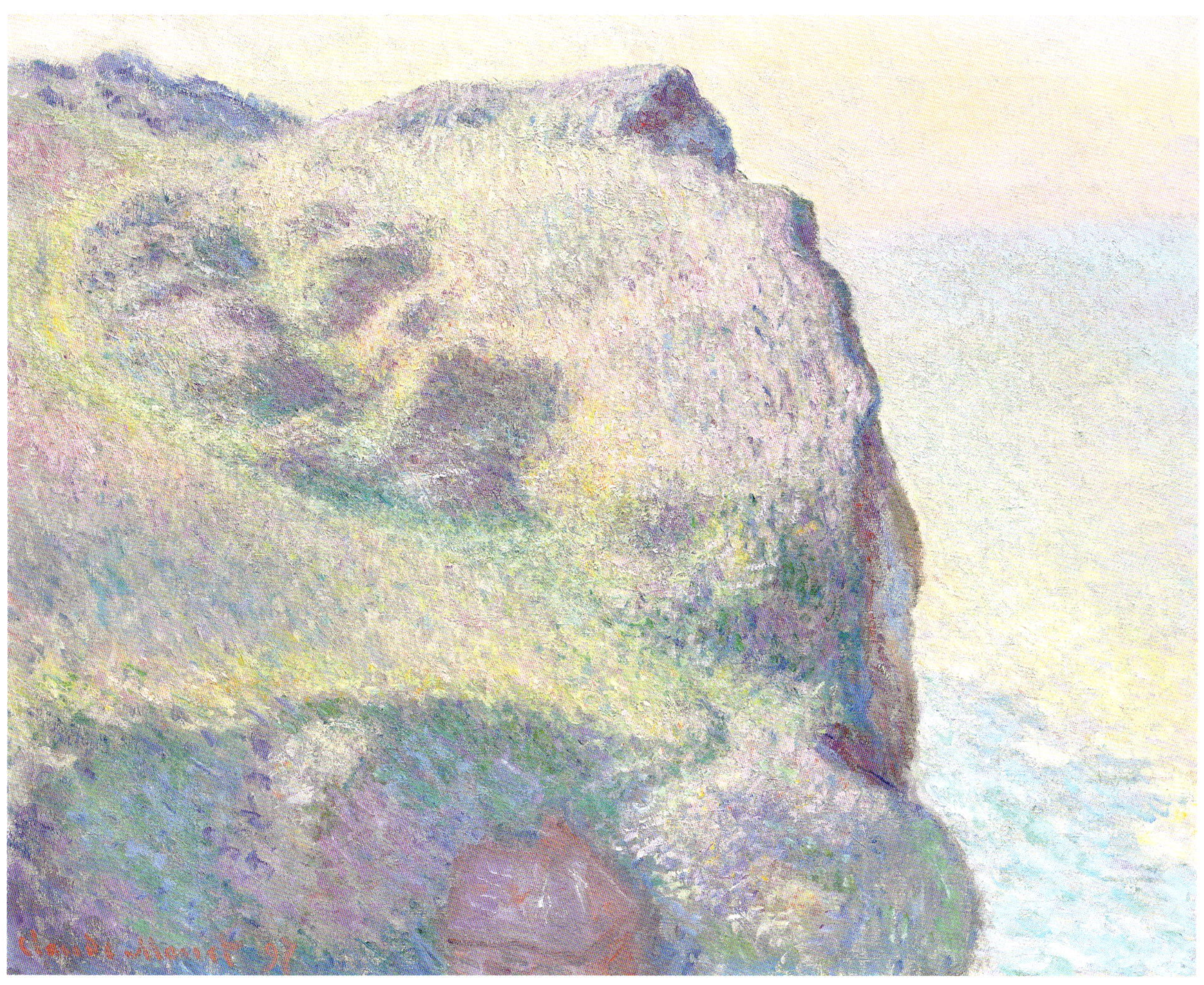

53 (cat.) – Claude Monet, *Falaises à Pourville* (*Cliffs at Pourville*), 1882.
Oil on canvas, 1 ft. 11½ in. × 3 ft. 3 in. (60 × 100 cm). National Gallery of Art, Washington, D.C.

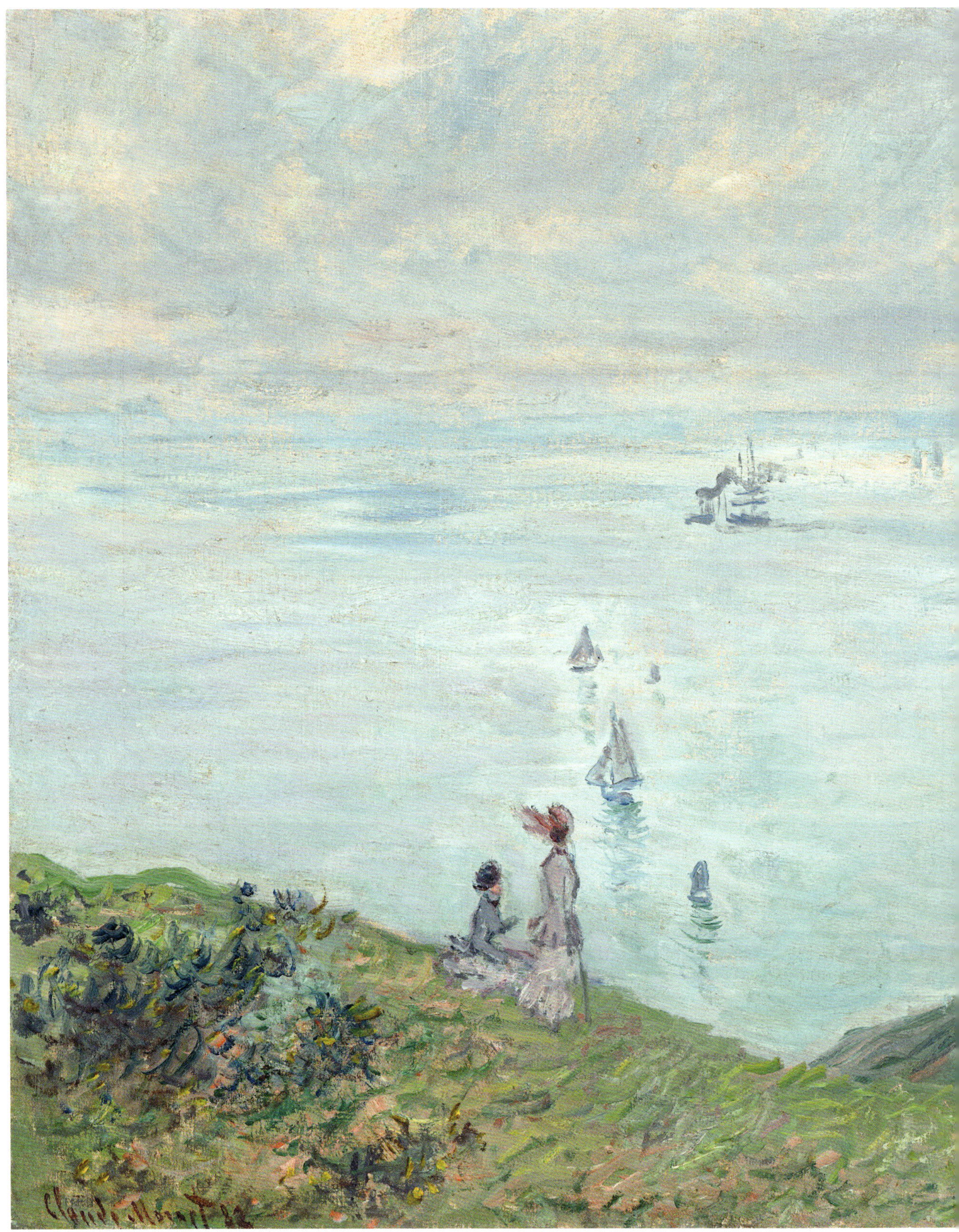

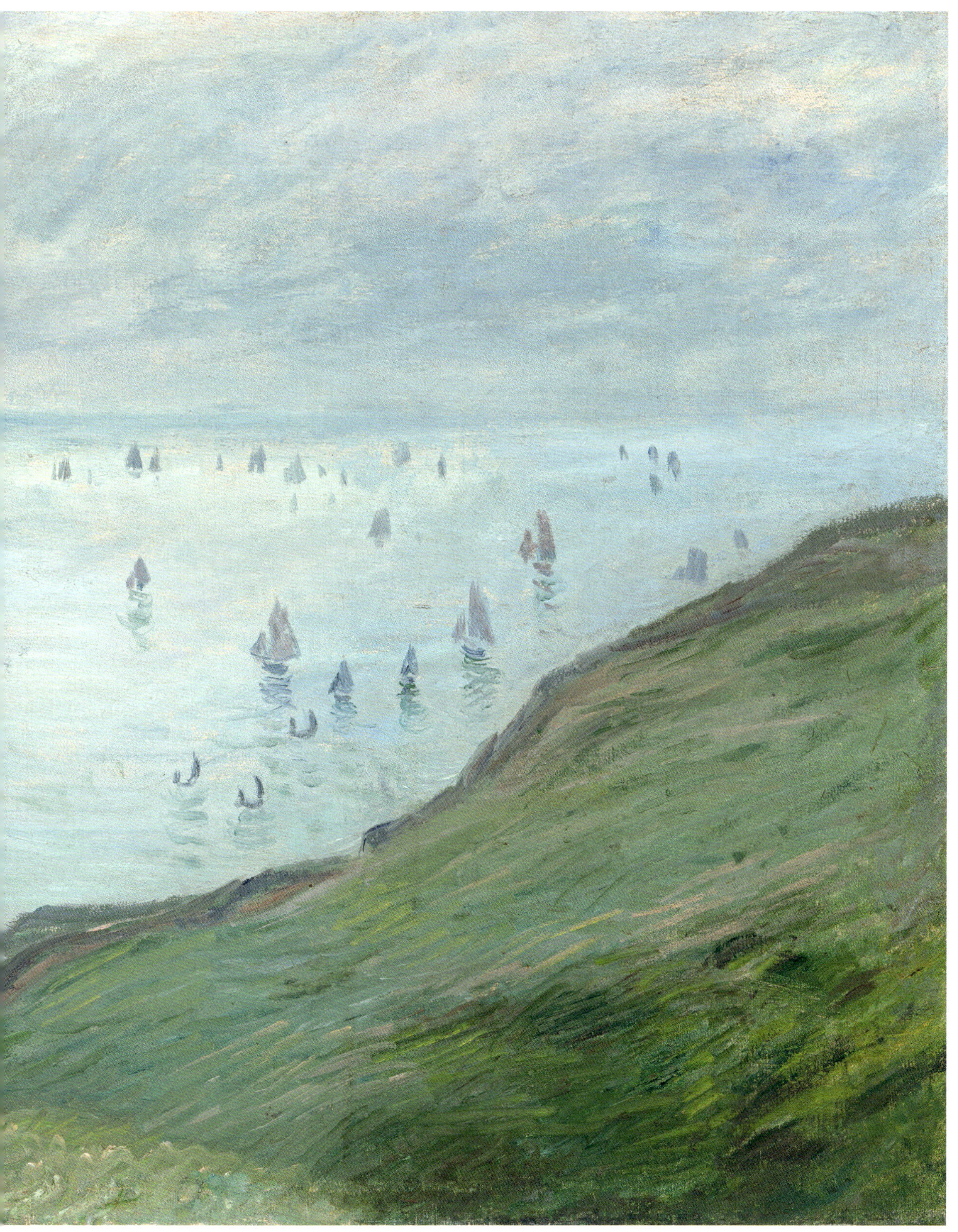

54 {cat.} – Jean Francis Auburtin, *Les Pêcheries. Falaises de Pourville* (Fishing grounds: Cliffs at Pourville), n.d.
Oil on canvas, 2 ft. 7 in. × 4 ft. 3 in. (78.4 × 130.4 cm). Musée des Impressionnismes, Giverny.

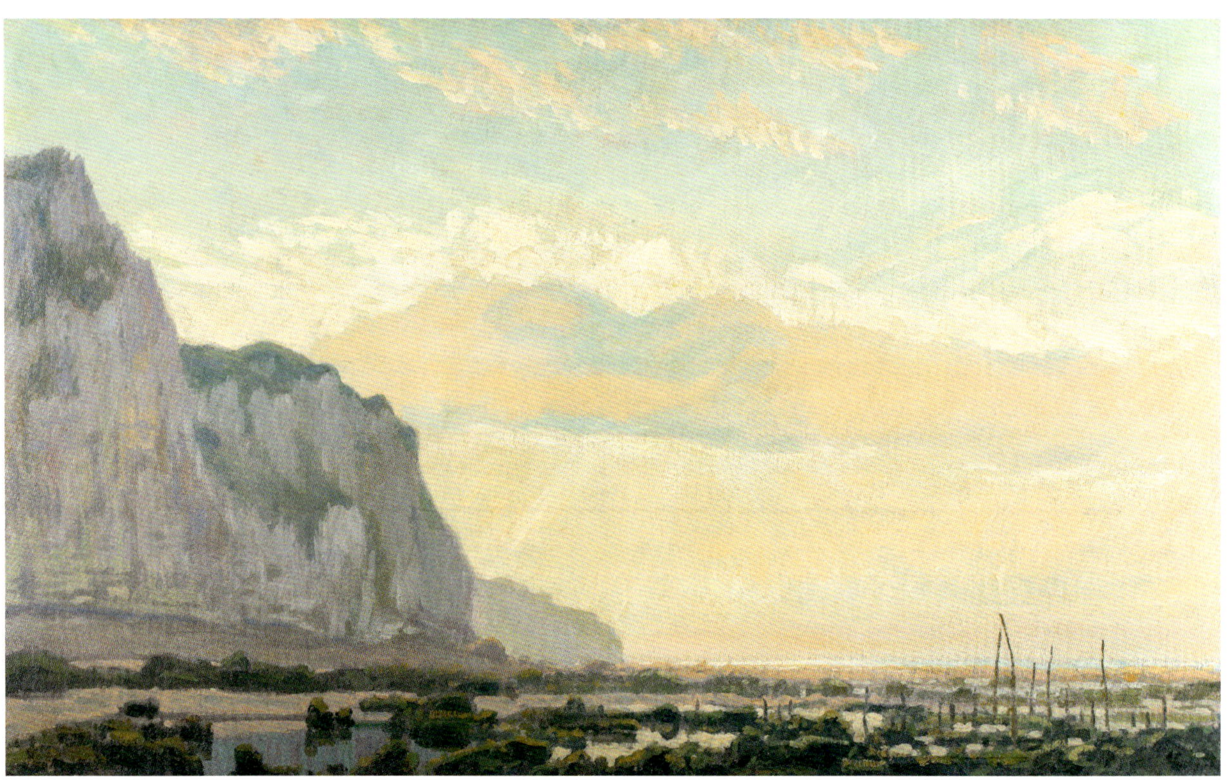

55 {cat.} – Jean Francis Auburtin, *Varengeville. Rayons jaunes aux falaises de Mordal* (Varengeville: Yellow light on the cliffs at Mordal), n.d. Oil on board, 2 ft. 1½ in. × 3 ft. (65 × 92 cm). Musée des Impressionnismes, Giverny.

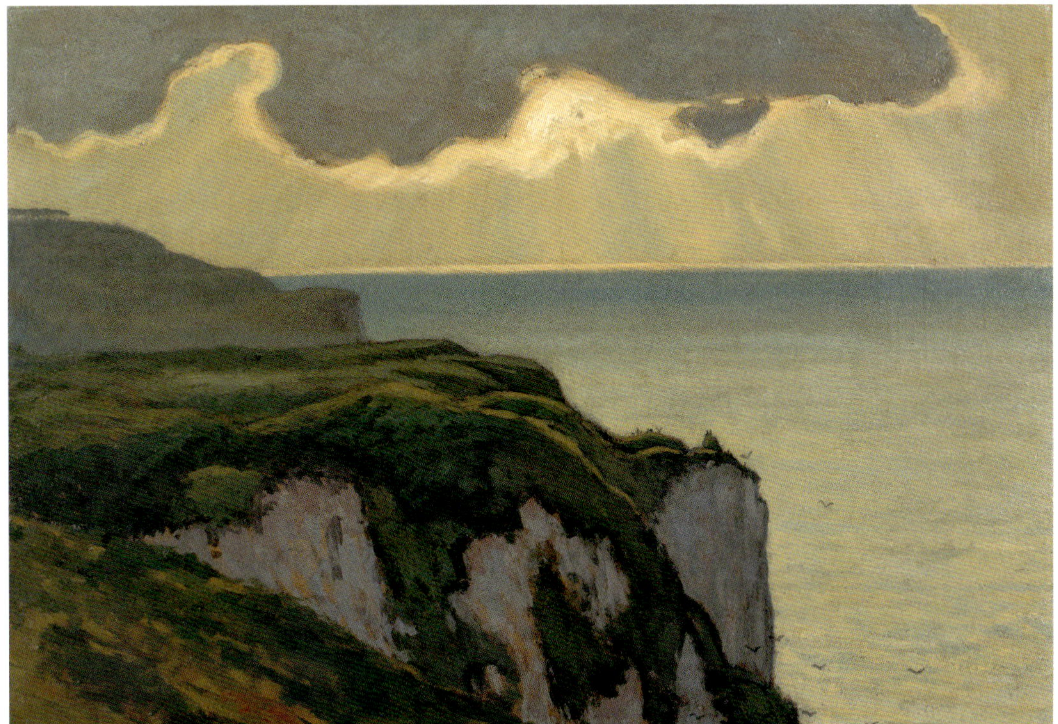

STORMS AND SHIPWRECKS

Following the work of Joseph Vernet in the late eighteenth century, the popularity of storms and shipwrecks as a theme grew considerably. It was a favorite with Romantic artists like Victor Hugo, Eugène Delacroix, Paul Huet, and Théodore Géricault. Théodore Gudin began specializing in these kinds of scenes in the period from 1830 to 1850, and met with great success. From the following generation, around 1870, Gustave Courbet produced a series of *Vagues* (*Waves*) depicting a raging, troubling sea. His friend Eugène Boudin also explored the subject in his dramatic painting *Un grain* (Squall) {cat. 58}, which depicts a ship struggling against the elements under a dark sky. A short time later, Maxime Maufra produced a set of paintings inspired by the works of Monet and his Belle-Île-en-Mer series: *Le Bateau à la côte; Morgat* (Grounded boat at Morgat) {cat. 64} and *La Tempête à Quiberon* (Gale in Quiberon) {cat. 63} owe much to Monet, while *L'Orage* (The storm) {cat. 105} reflects the influence of Gauguin and Paul Sérusier, in the spirit of the Pont-Aven School. Many artists in search of new sources of creativity migrated to Brittany in the late nineteenth century, to draw inspiration from these most unusual sites.

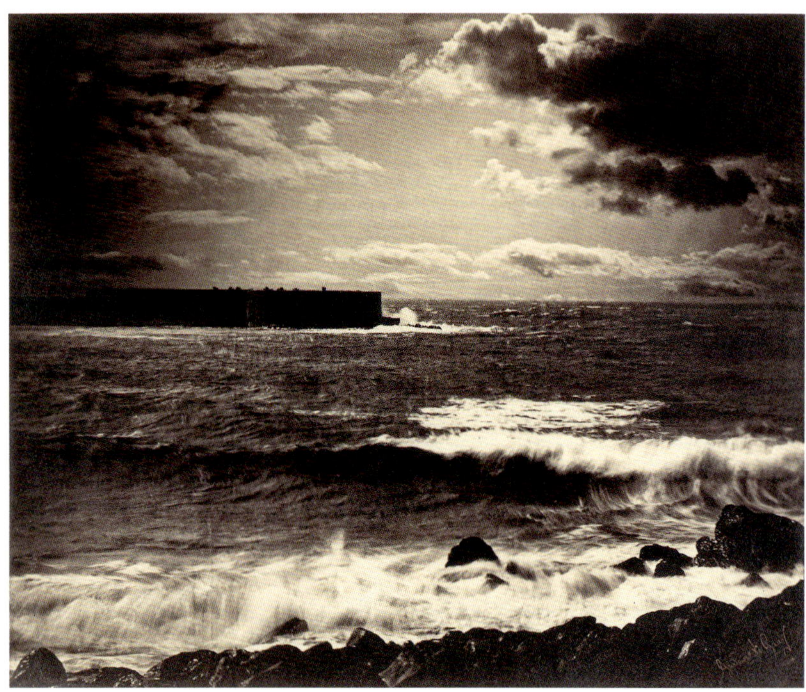

56 {fig.} Gustave Le Gray, *Grande vague, Sète – nº 17* (*The Great Wave, Sète, no. 17*), c. 1857. Albumen silver print from a collodion-on-glass negative, 13 × 16 in. (34.2 × 42 cm). BNF, Paris.

57 {cat.} – Gustave Courbet, *La Vague* (*The Wave*), c. 1871–1873.
Oil on canvas, 21½ × 25½ in. (55 × 65 cm). De Bueil & Ract-Madoux Collection, Paris.

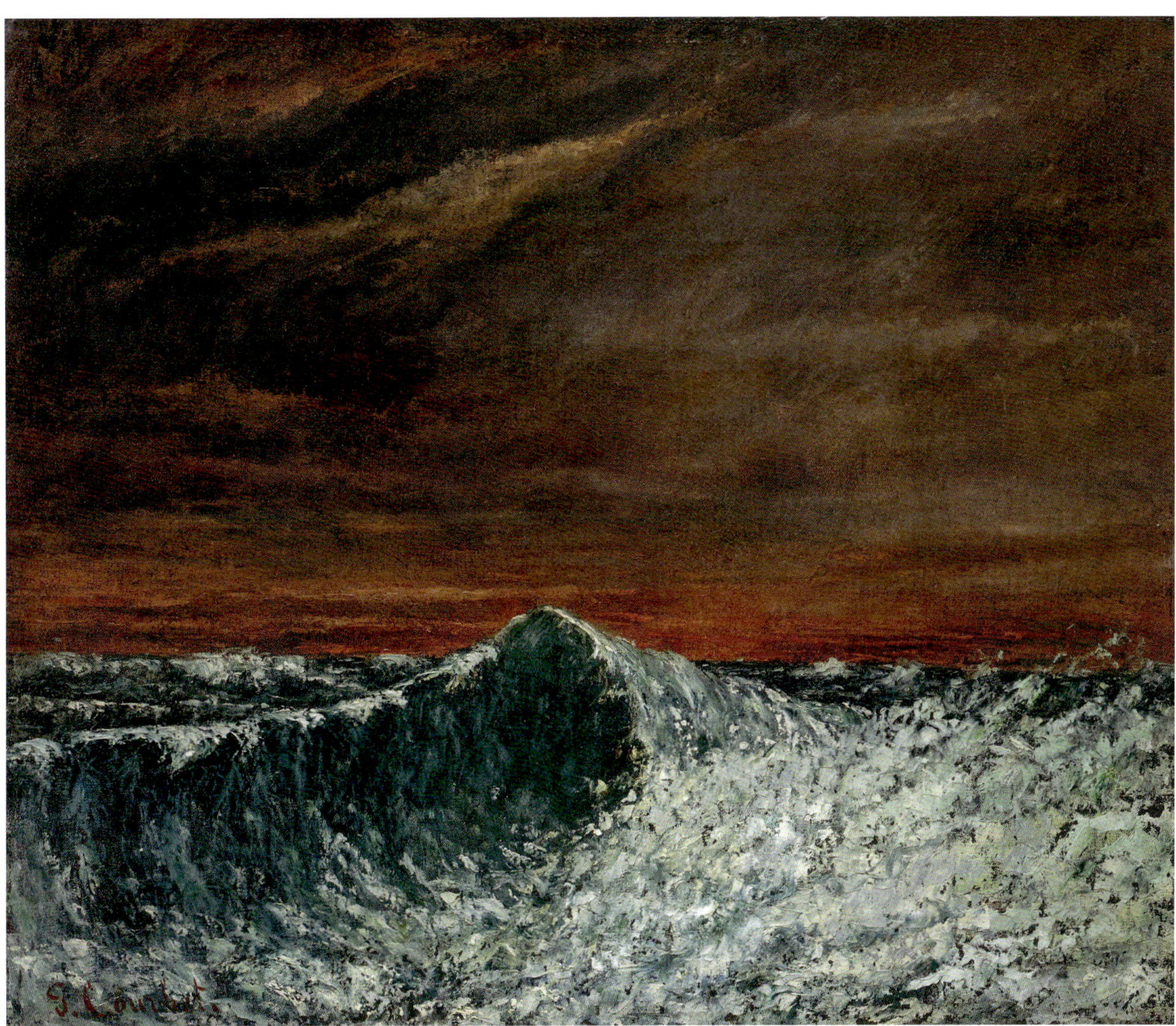

58 (cat.) – Eugène Boudin, *Un grain* (Squall), 1886.
Oil on canvas, 3 ft. 10 in. × 5 ft. 3 in. (117 × 160 cm). Collection of the Musée des Jacobins, Morlaix.

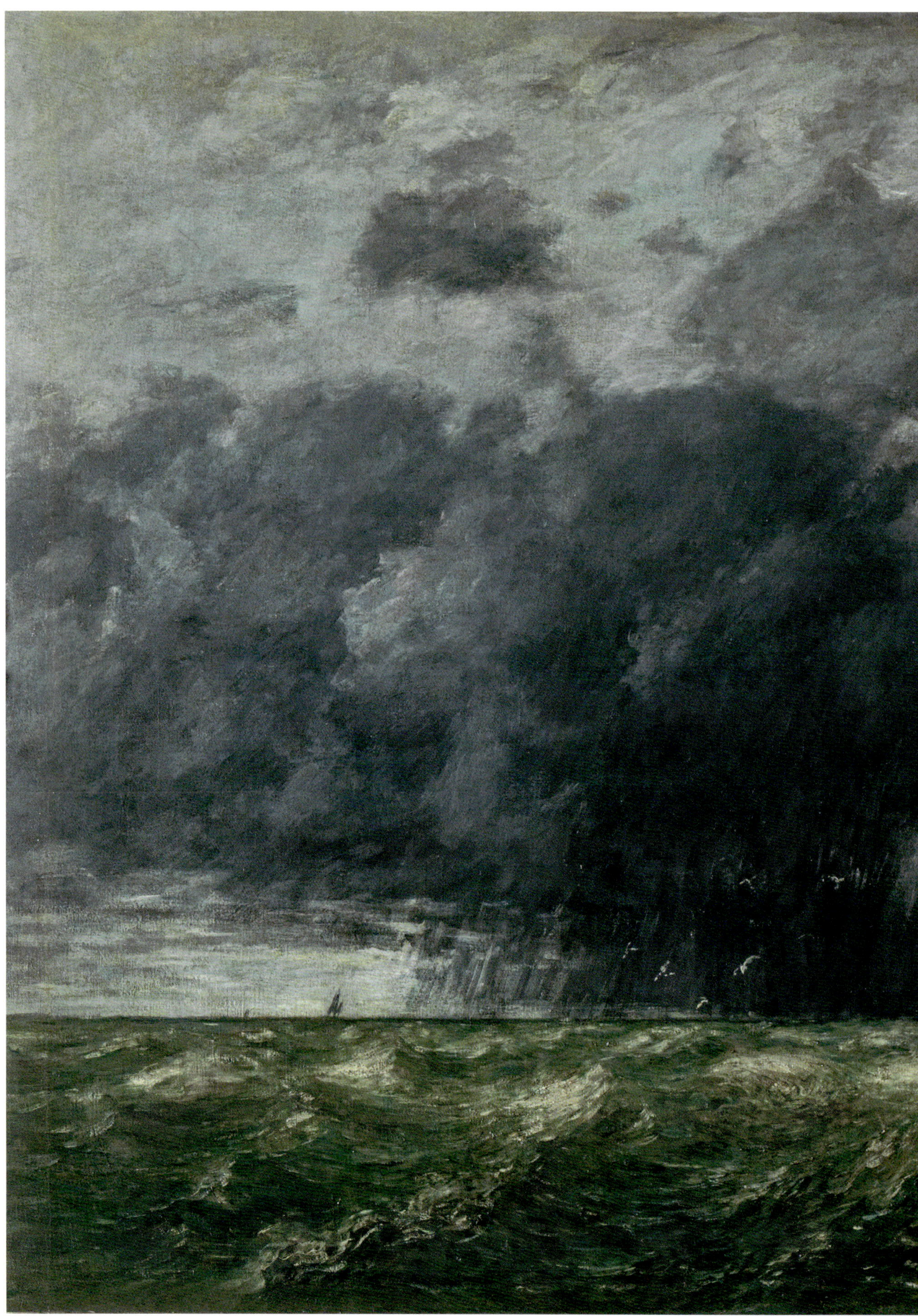

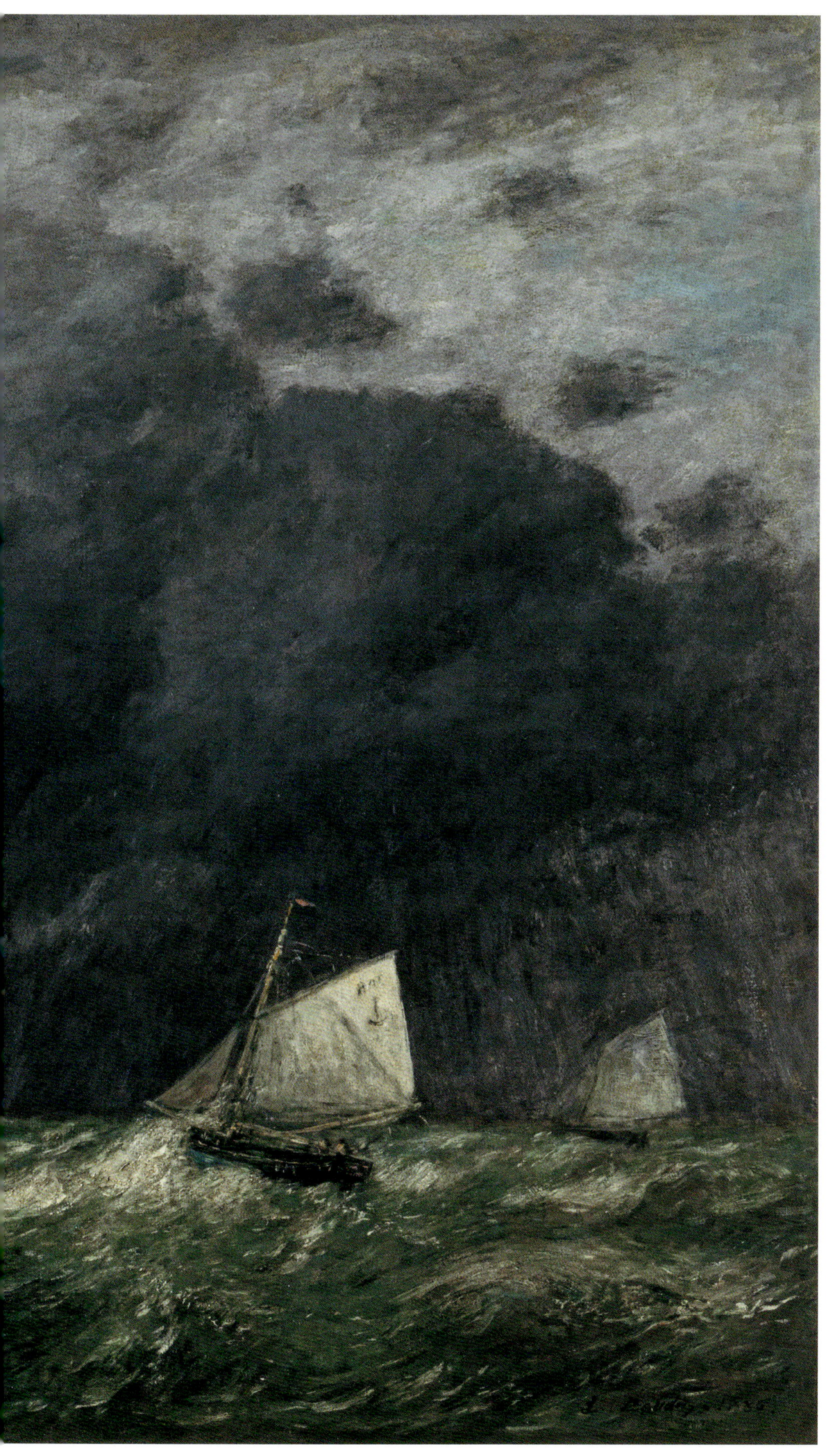

59 {cat.} – Alexandre Marcette, *En route. Bateaux sur la mer du Nord* (En route: Boats on the North Sea), n.d. Gouache on paper on canvas, 26½ × 37½ in. (67 × 95 cm). Musée d'Orsay, Paris.

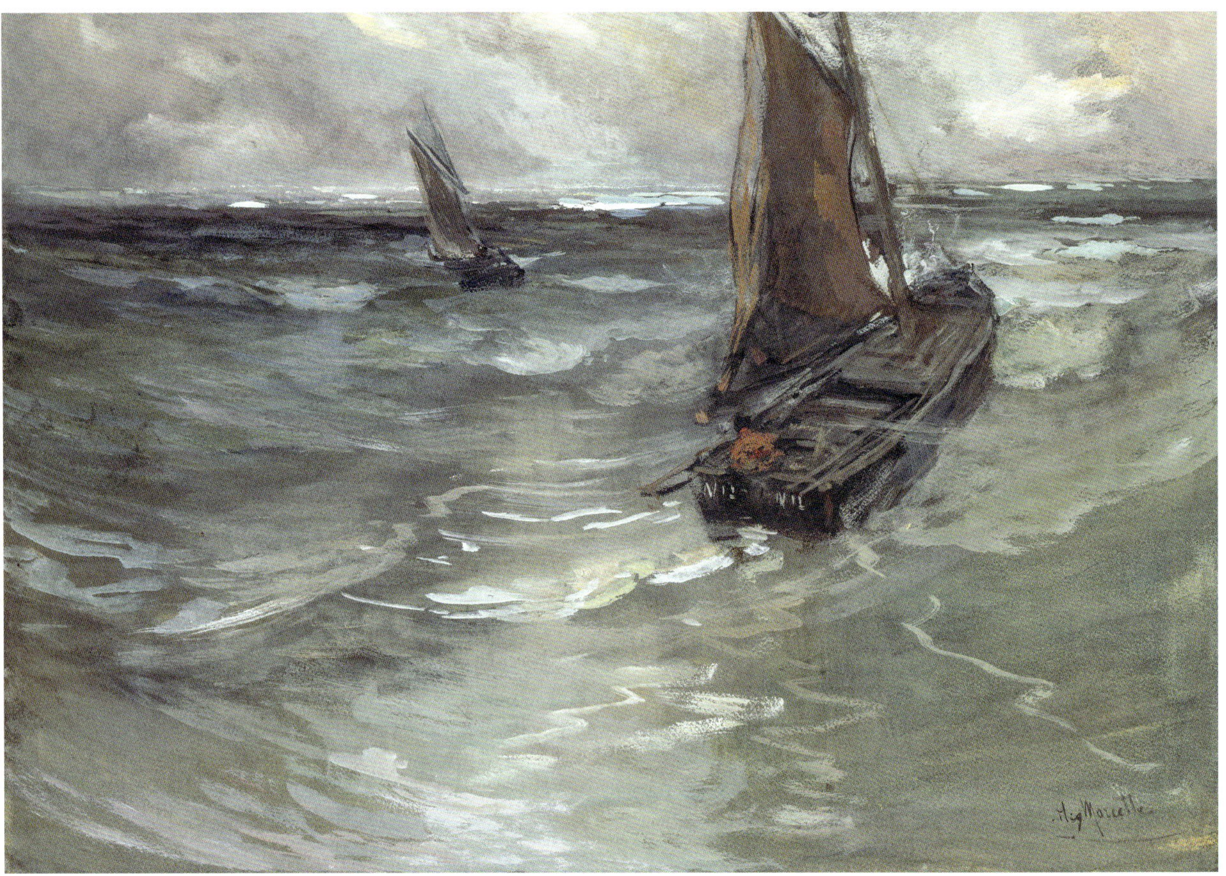

60 {cat.} – Gustave Courbet, *La Vague* (*The Wave*), 1870.
Oil on canvas, 35 in. × 3 ft. 6 in. (88.4 × 107.2 cm). Musée des Beaux-Arts, Orléans.

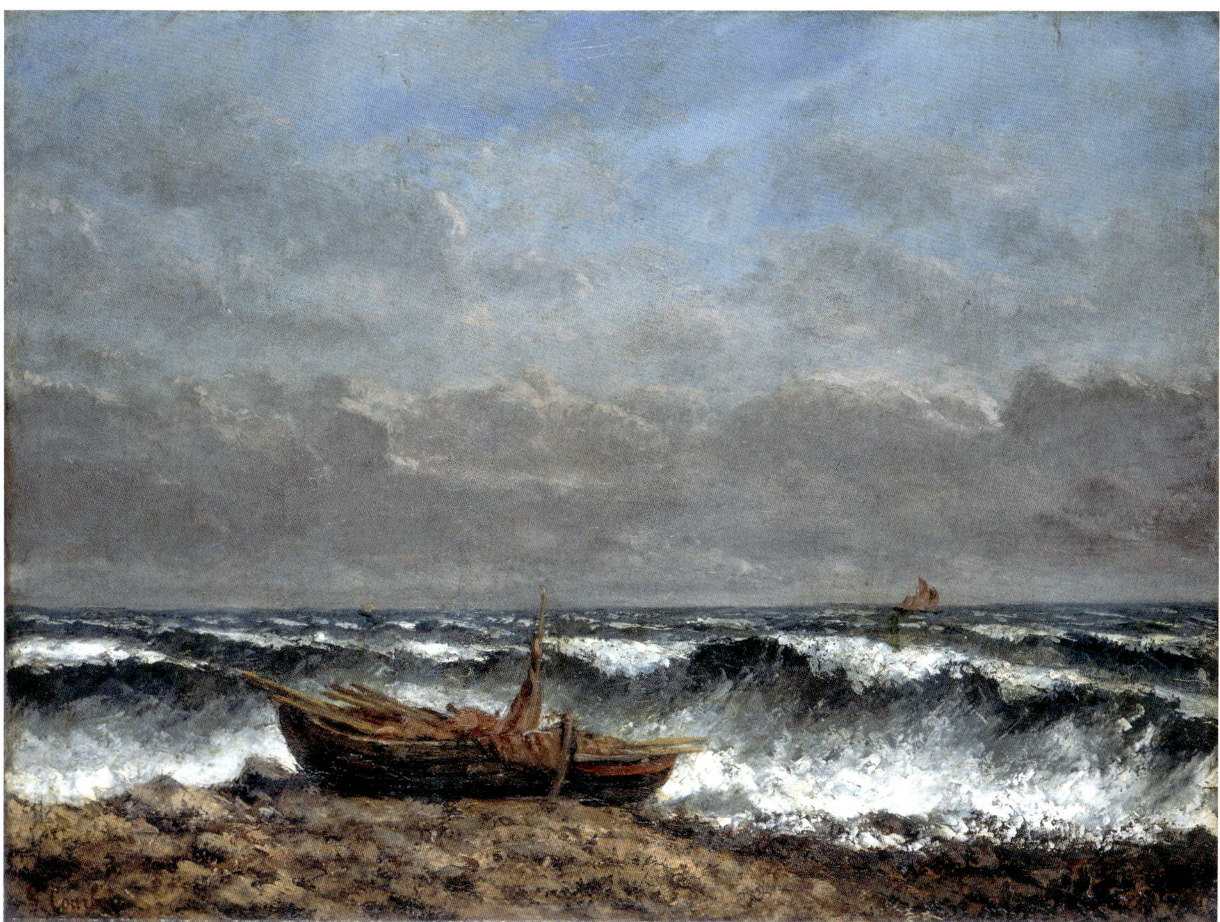

61 {cat.} – Maxime Maufra, *Côte de Goulphar* (The coast at Goulphar), 1900.
Oil on canvas, 25½ × 32 in. (65.5 × 81 cm). Musée des Beaux-Arts, Rennes.

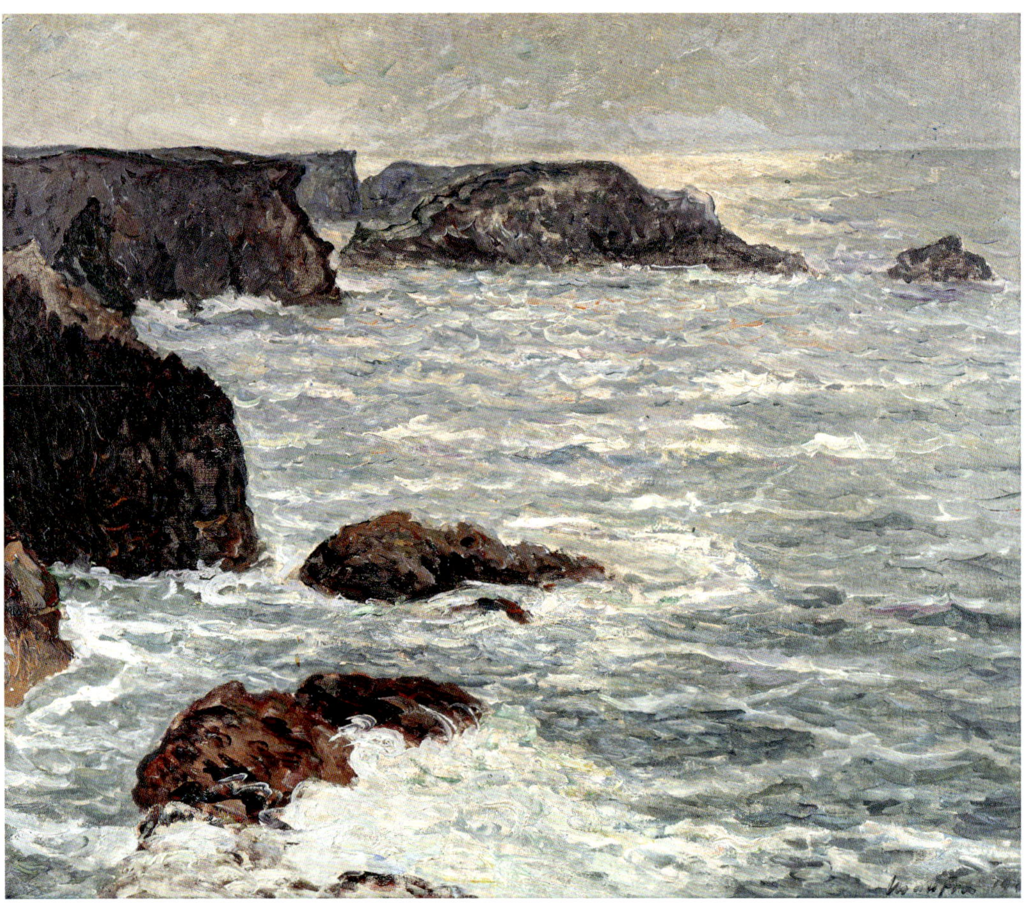

62 {cat.} – Armand Guillaumin, *Rocher à la pointe de la Baumette* (Rock at Pointe de la Baumette), 1893. Oil on canvas, 13 × 18 in. (33 × 46 cm). Wallraf-Richartz Museum & Fondation Corboud, Cologne.

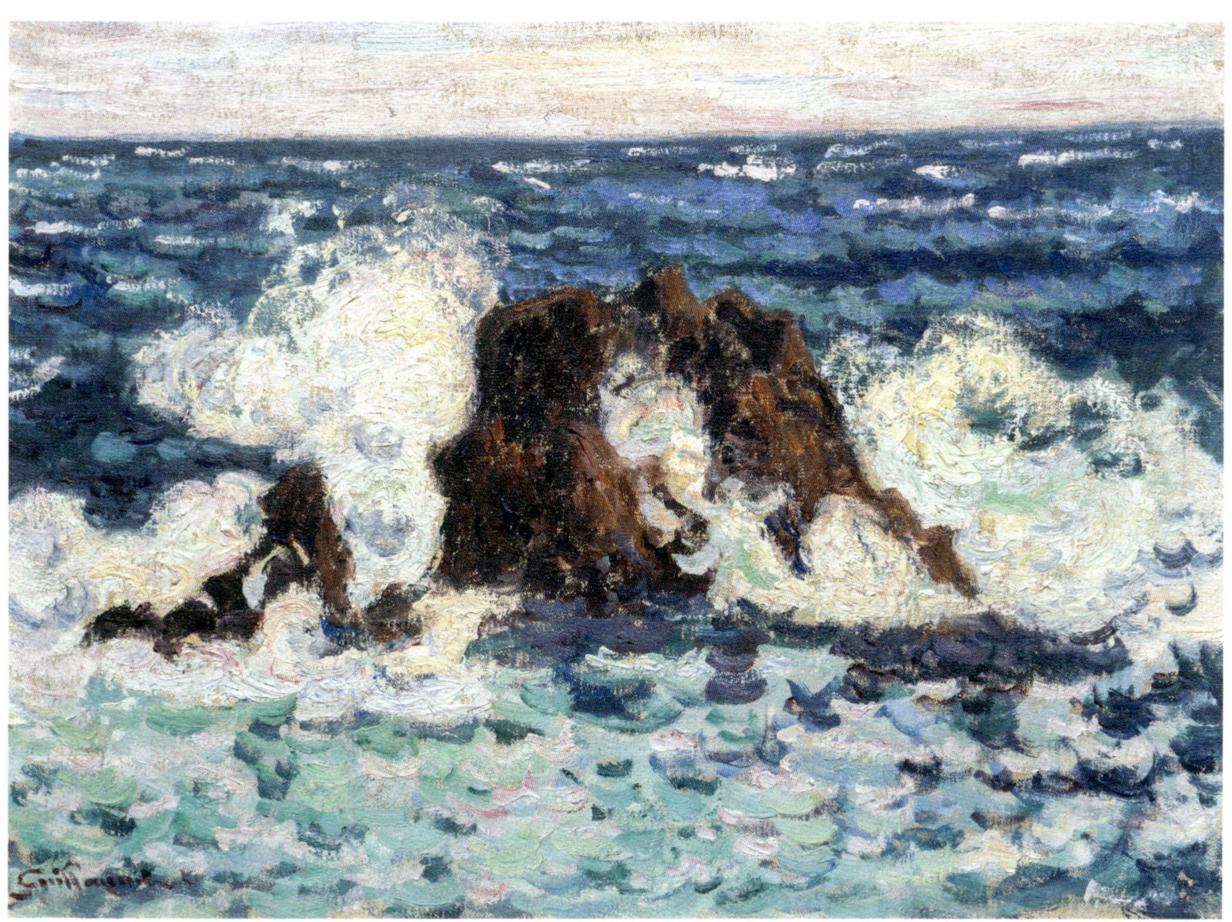

"The sea rises to the invisible mouth; a mound of water is formed; the swell increases, and the waterspout appears; the Prester of the ancients, stalactite above, stalagmite below, a whirling double-inverted cone … the embrace of two mountains—a mountain of foam ascending, a mountain of vapour descending."
Victor Hugo, *Toilers of the Sea*, 1866

63 {cat.} – Maxime Maufra, *La Tempête à Quiberon* (Gale in Quiberon), 1900.
Oil on canvas, 2 ft. 8 in. × 3 ft. 3 in. (81.2 × 100 cm). Musée des Beaux-Arts, Reims.

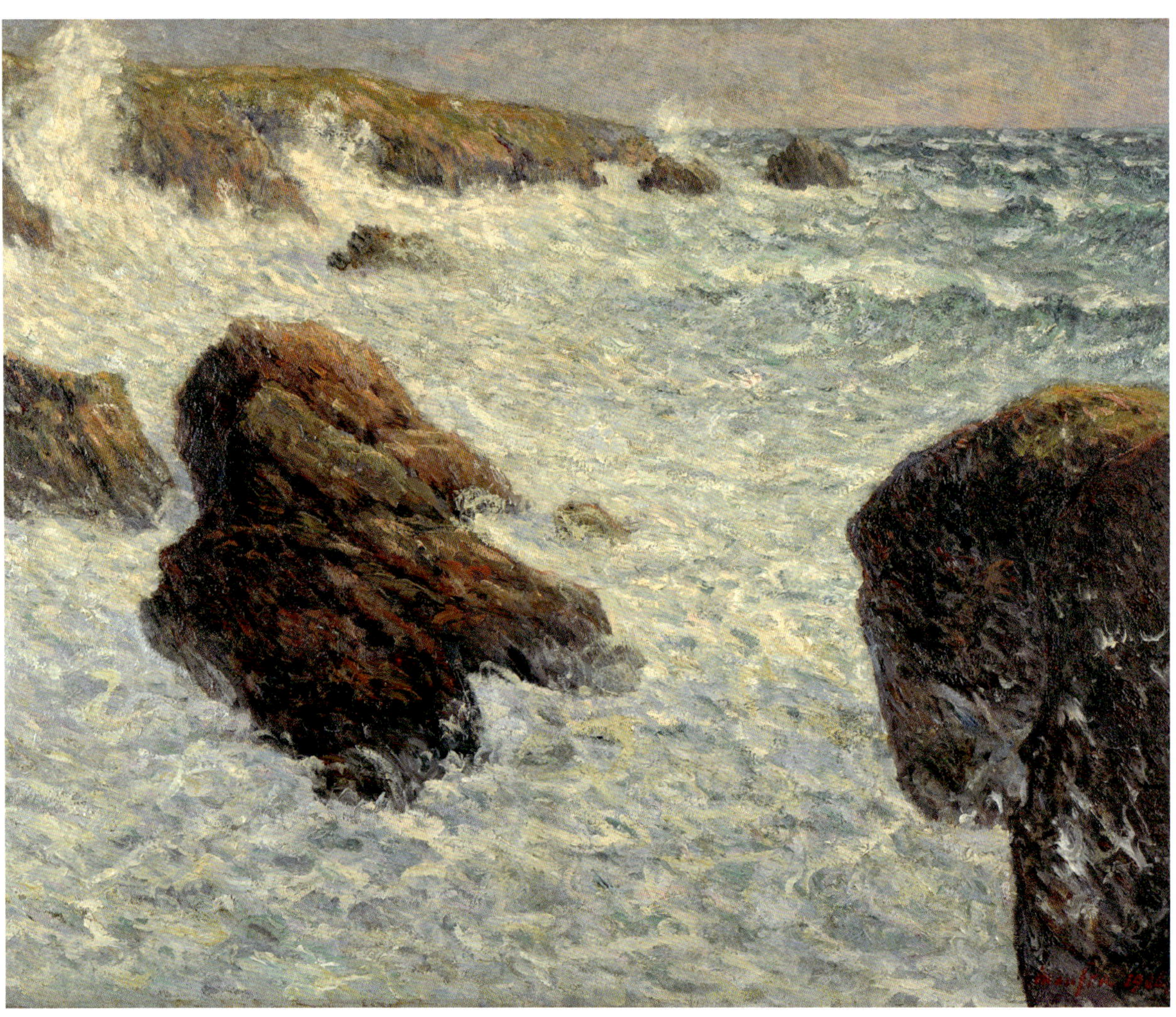

64 {cat.} – Maxime Maufra, *Le Bateau à la côte; Morgat* (Grounded boat at Morgat), 1902. Oil on canvas, 2 ft. 8 in. × 3 ft. 3 in. (81.5 × 100 cm). MuMA, Le Havre.

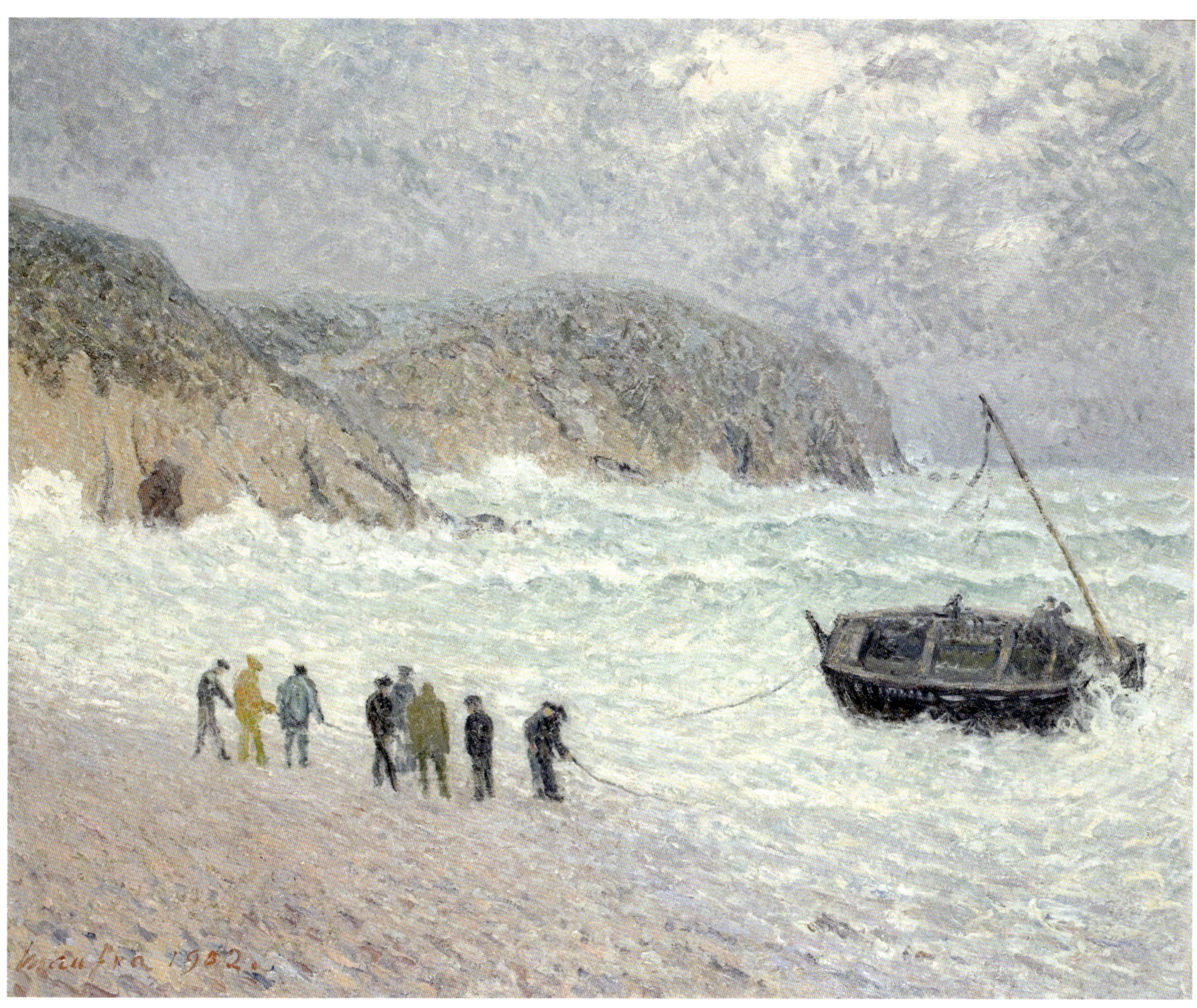

Paul Gauguin, who moved to Pont-Aven in July 1886, would reinvigorate French painting by infusing it with a "primitivism" that he sought in Breton traditions. The same year, from September to November, Claude Monet wandered the shores of Belle-Île-en-Mer. The two artists pointed the way to two different creative paths. *Le Talisman* (*The Talisman*; 1888, Musée d'Orsay, Paris), painted by Paul Sérusier with Gauguin's guidance, would breathe new life into landscape painting. Members of the Nabis movement—Pierre Bonnard, Édouard Vuillard, and Maurice Denis among them—followed suit, as did a whole generation of Breton painters. Ferdinand du Puigaudeau, along with Henry Moret and Maxime Maufra, bridged the gap between Gauguin's art and Monet's legacy. Brittany became a new center of artistic creation where the methods of the future were conceived. Artistic production shifted from Normandy to Brittany, focusing on views of rock formations and storms depicted in a pointillist manner that retained Monet's impressionist influence. Inspired by Monet's example, both Armand Guillaumin and Maufra depicted the dramatic coasts of Belle-Île-en-Mer. At the same time, Gauguin trailed Maufra and Moret in his wake, but they hesitated, leaning at times toward Monet and at others toward Gauguin. This second Breton impressionist school continued into the 1920s.

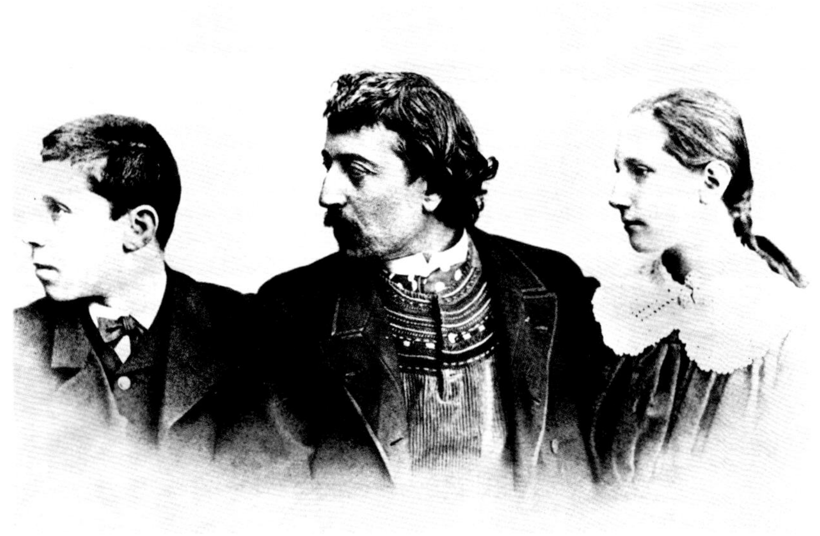

65 {fig.} – *Paul Gauguin Wearing a Breton Jacket, with His Children Émile and Aline, in Copenhagen before Leaving for Tahiti*, March 1891.

66 {cat.} – Paul Gauguin, *Sur la plage de Bretagne* (On the beach in Brittany), 1889.
Oil on canvas, 23½ × 28½ in. (60 × 73 cm). Nasjonalmuseet for Kunst, Arkitektur og Design, Oslo.

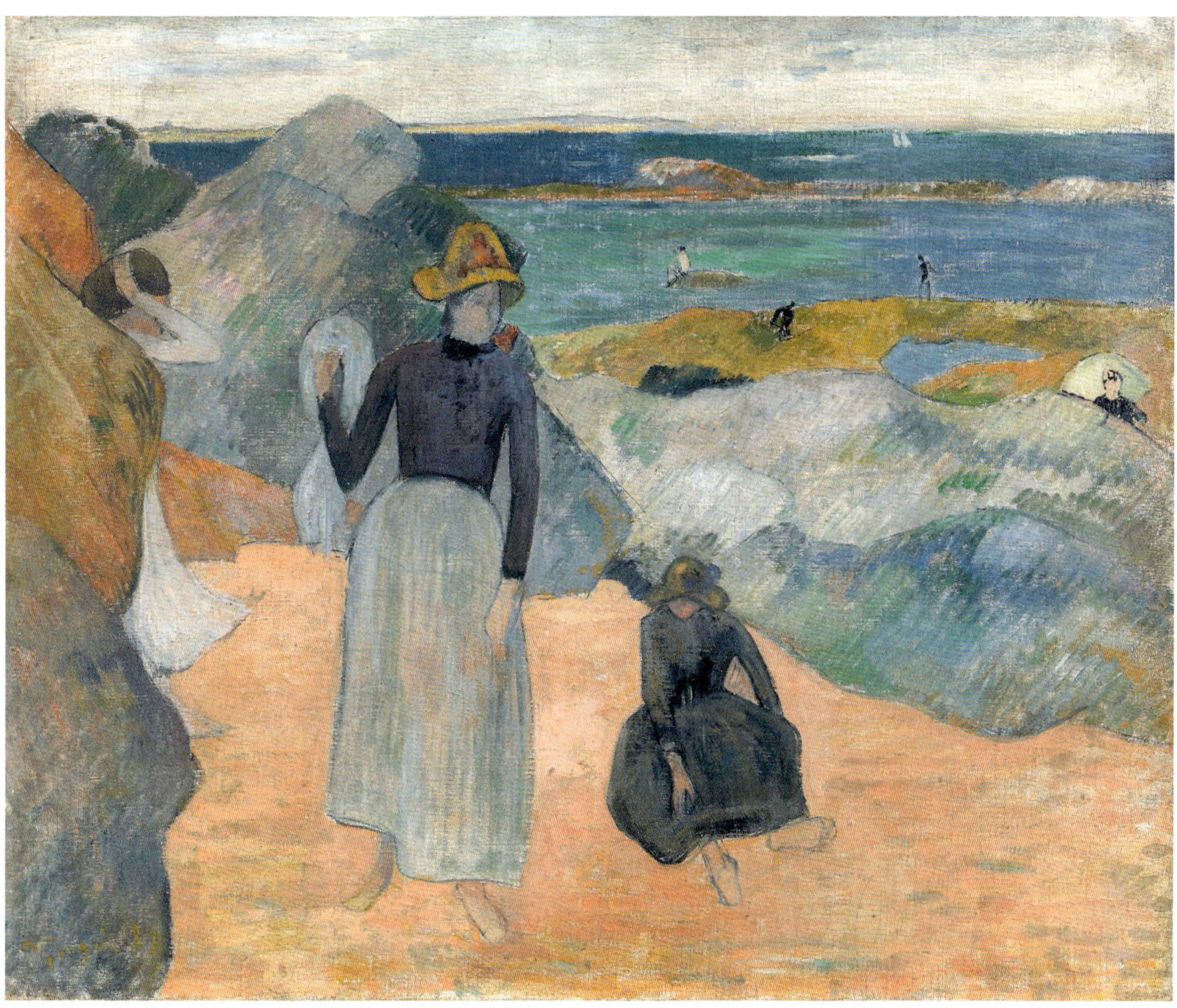

67 (cat.) – Henry Moret, *Gros temps à Doëlan* (Rough weather at Doëlan), n.d.
Oil on canvas, 31½ × 23½ in. (80 × 60 cm). Musée des Beaux-Arts, La Cohue, Vannes.

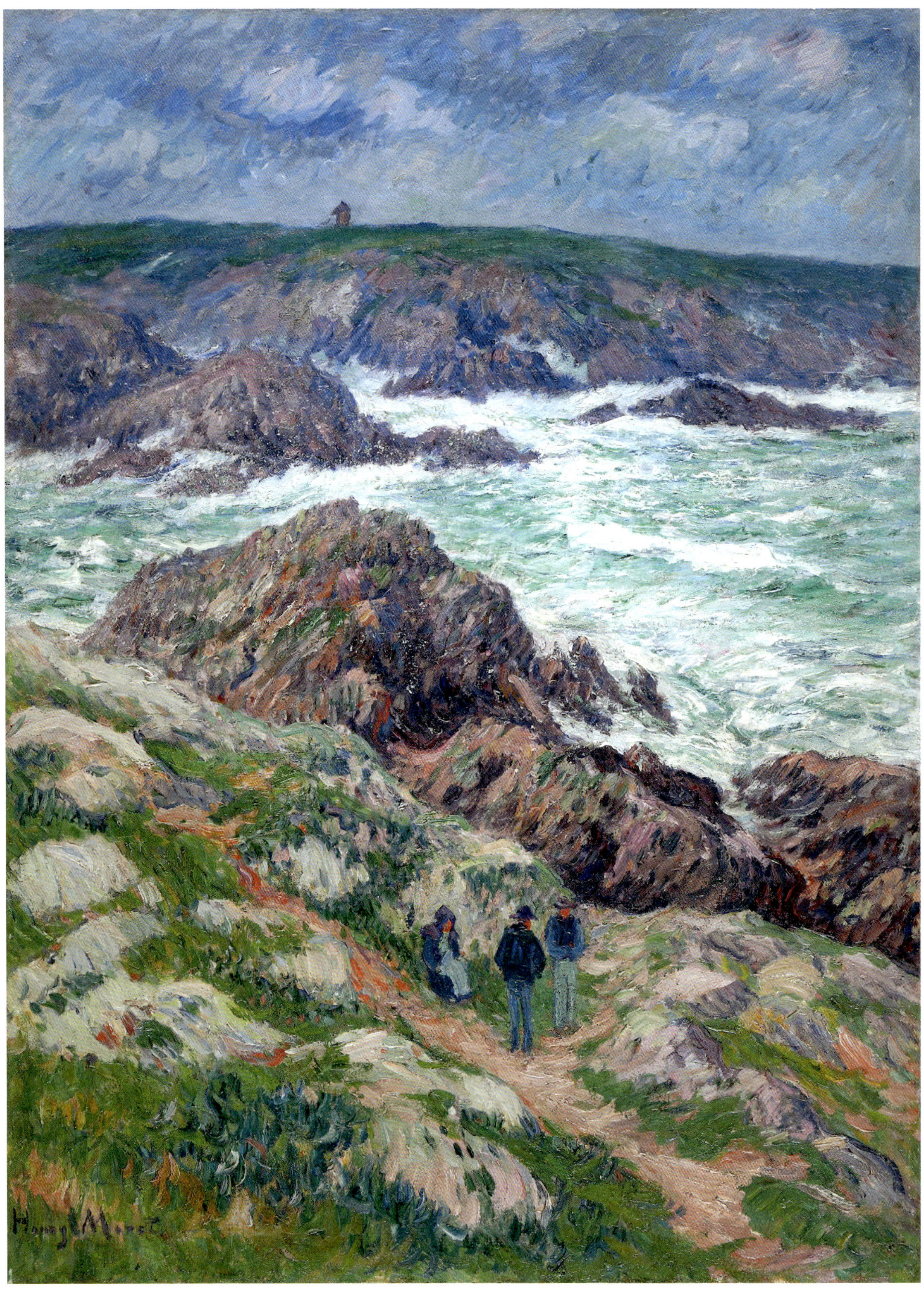

68 {cat.} – Claude Monet, *Les Rochers de Belle-Île, la Côte sauvage* (Rocks on Belle-Île, Côte Sauvage), 1886. Oil on canvas, 25½ × 32 in. (65.5 × 81.5 cm). Musée d'Orsay, Paris.

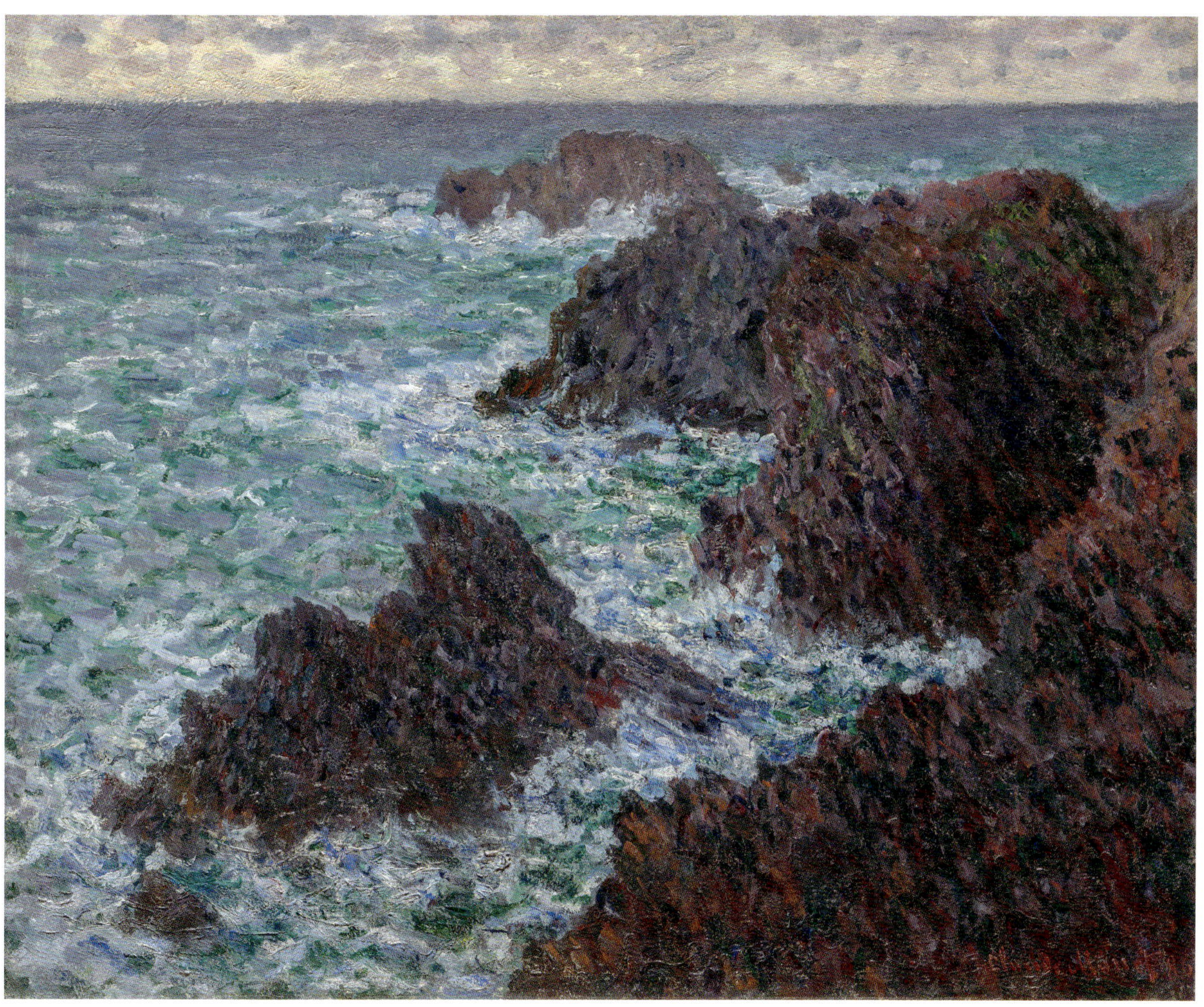

69 {cat.} – Henry Moret, *L'Île d'Ouessant, la chaussée Keller* (Ushant island, Keller's causeway), 1897. Oil on canvas, 23½ × 28½ in. (60 × 73 cm). Musée Lambinet, Versailles.

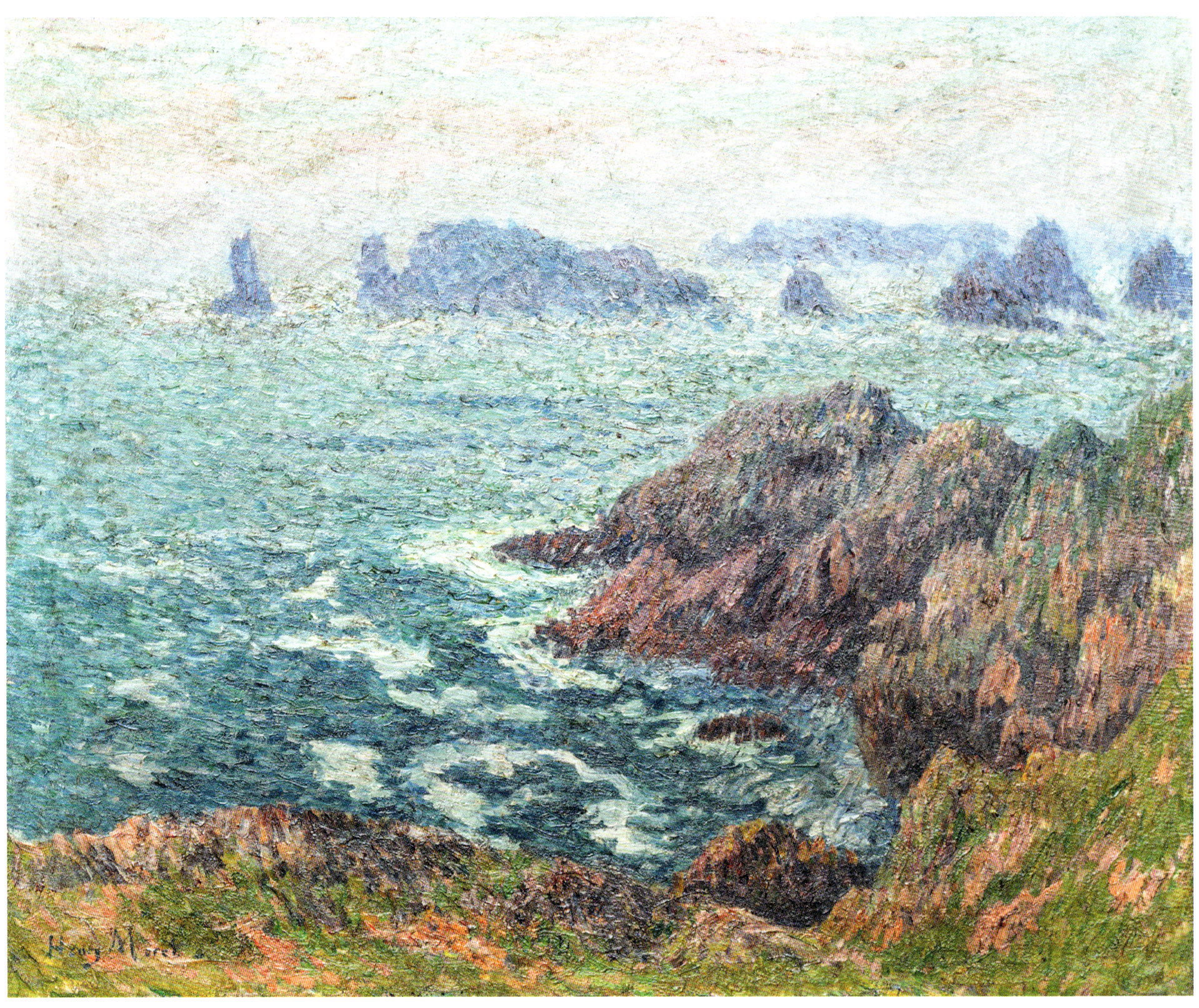

70 {cat.} – Henry Moret, *Île de Groix, paysage côtier* (Groix island, coastal landscape), c. 1893.
Oil on canvas, 3 ft. × 2 ft. 1 in. (92 × 64 cm). Musée de la Compagnie des Indes – Musée d'Art et d'Histoire de la Ville de Lorient, Lorient.

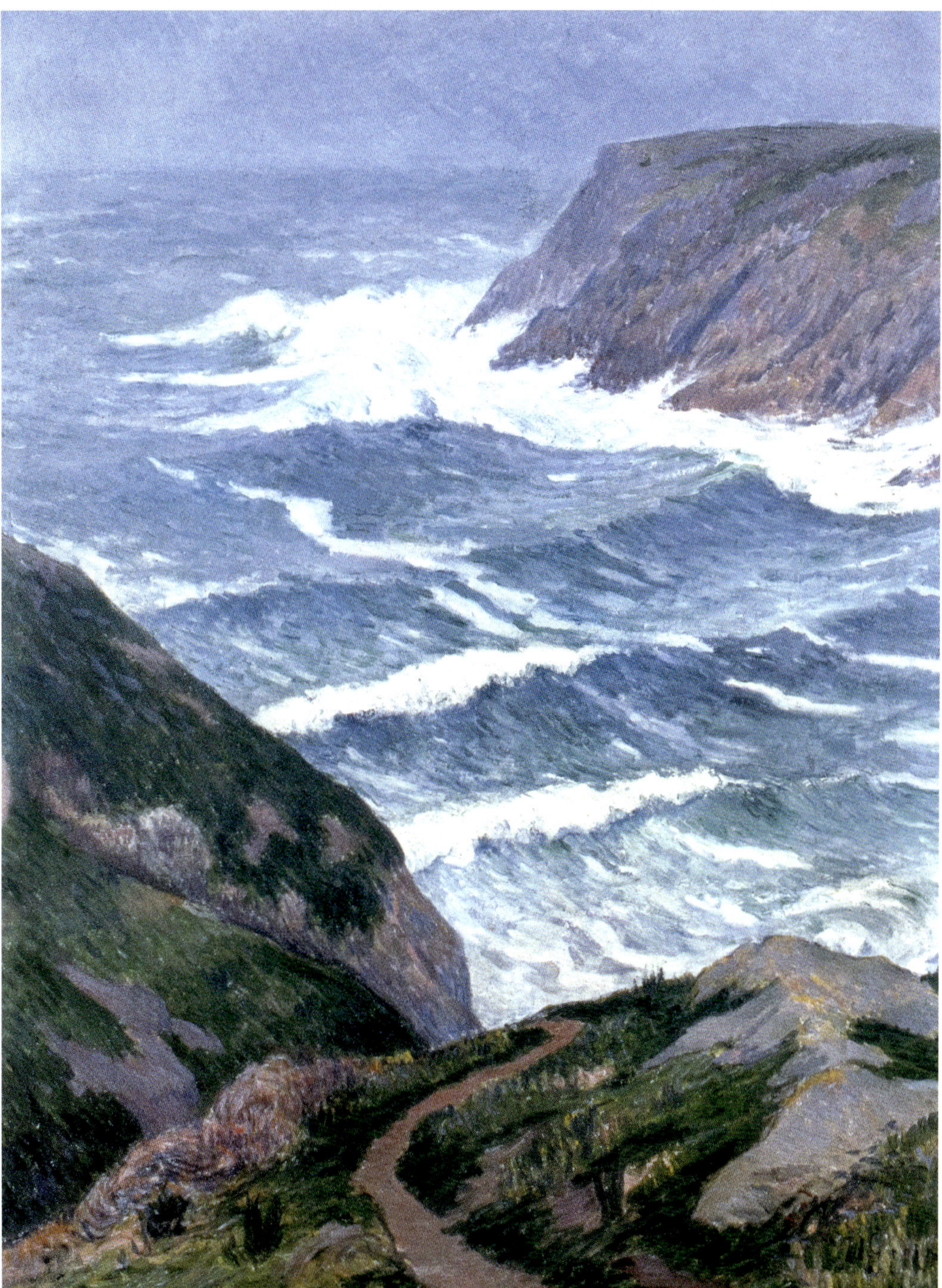

71 {cat.} – Armand Guillaumin, *Rochers sur la côte bretonne* (Rocks off the coast of Brittany), c. 1895.
Oil on canvas, 23½ × 29 in. (60 × 73.5 cm). Musée d'Art et d'Archéologie, Guéret.

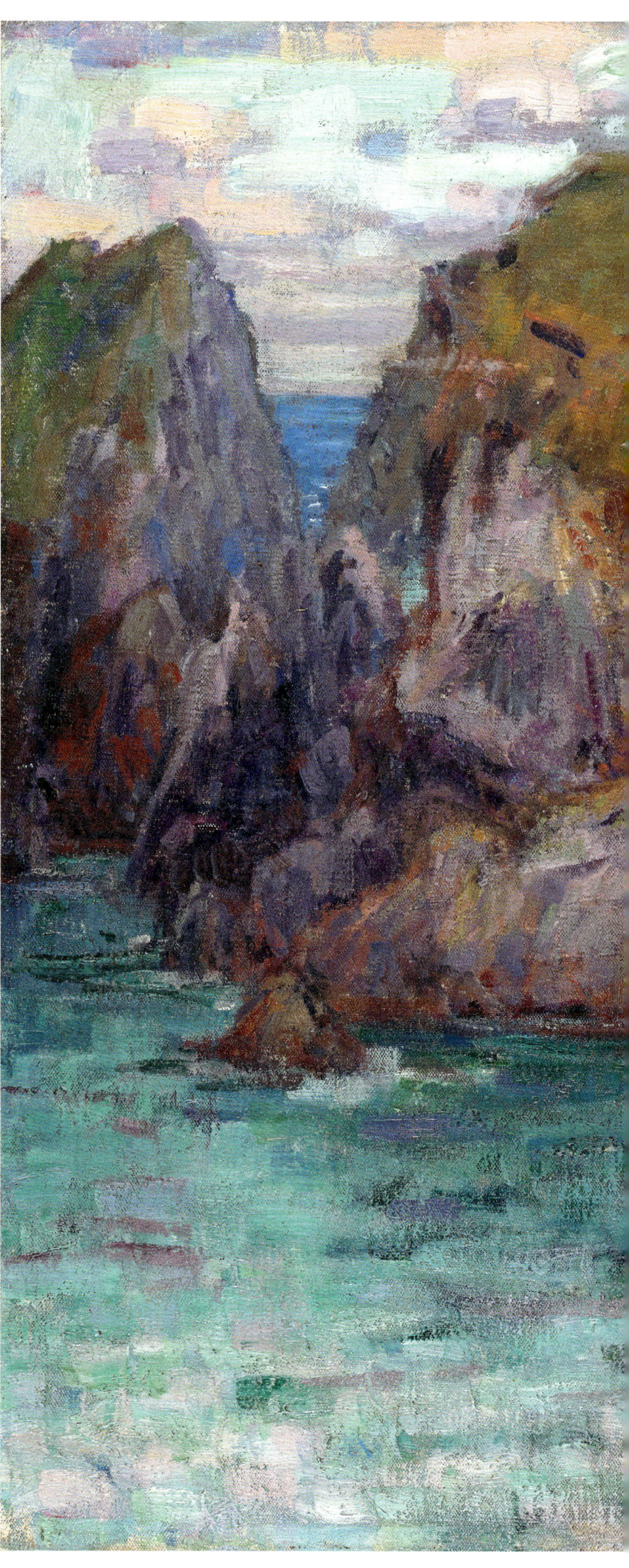

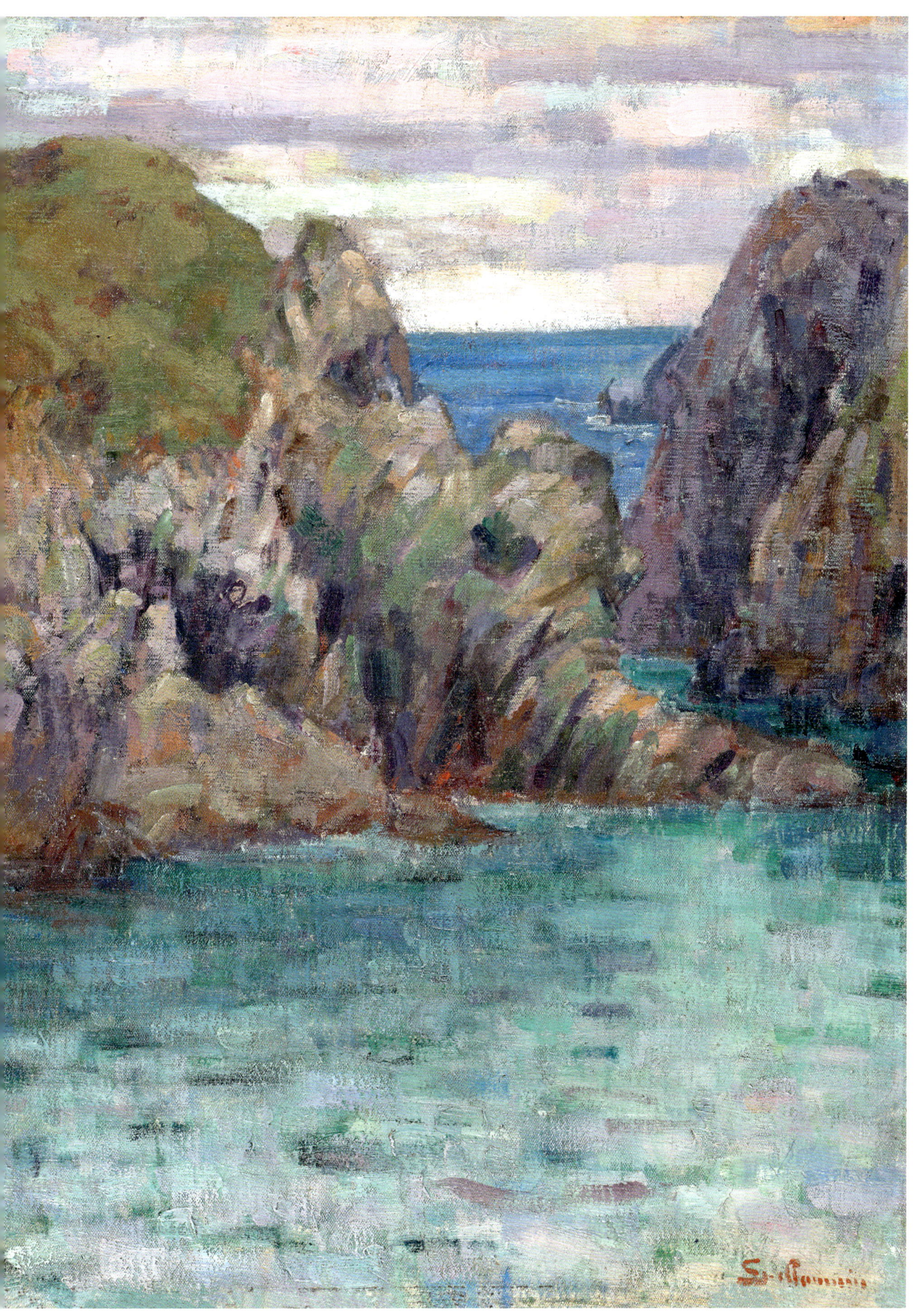

72 {cat.} – Maxime Maufra, *Entrée du port de Port Goulphar, Belle-Île-en-Mer* (*Entrance to the Port on Port-Goulphar, Belle-Île-en-Mer*), 1909. Oil on canvas, 20 × 25½ in. (51 × 65.5 cm). Museo Nacional Thyssen-Bornemisza, Madrid.

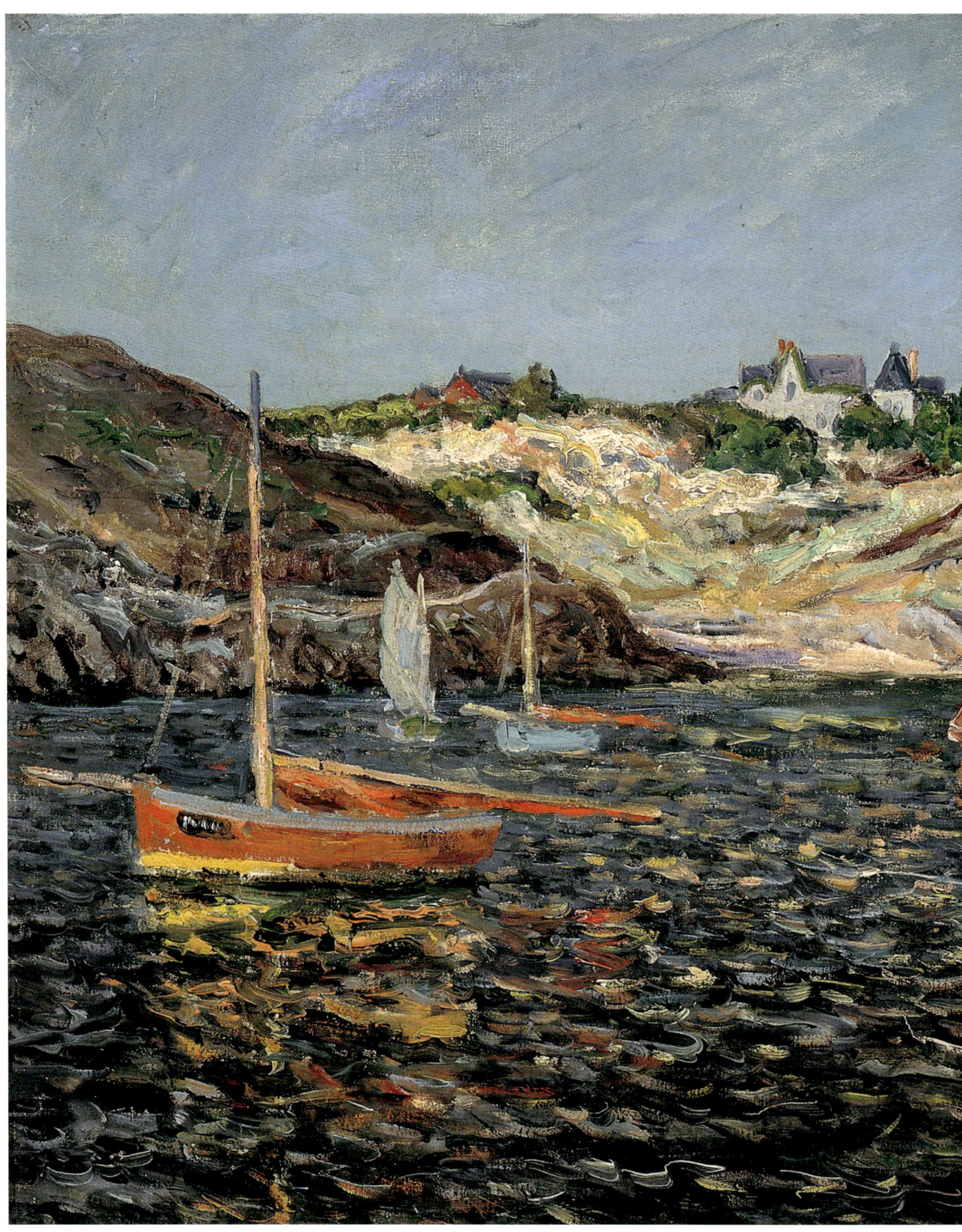

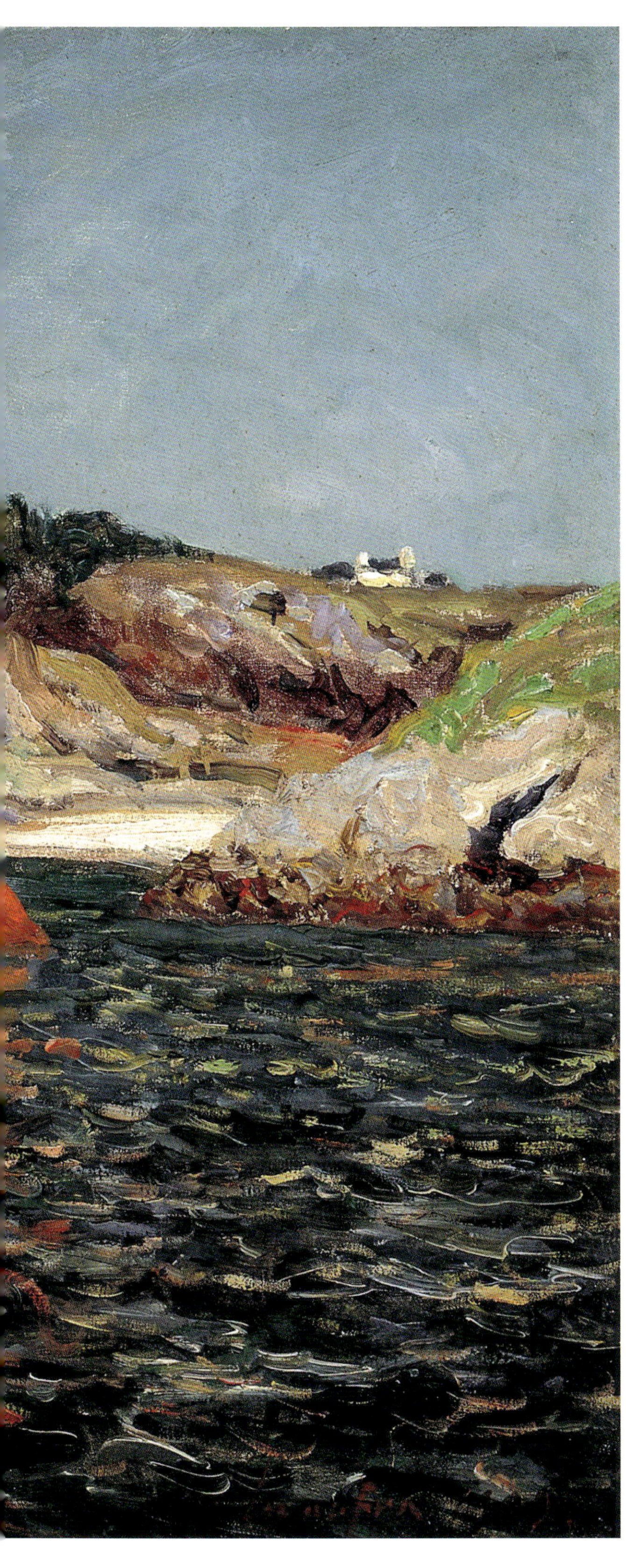

73 {fig.} – Constant Puyo, *Lavandières et voiliers près de Penmarc'h, Bretagne* (Washerwomen and sailboats near Penmarc'h, Brittany), c. 1890–1900. Aristotype, 7½ × 2½ in. (19 × 6 cm). Musée d'Orsay, Paris.

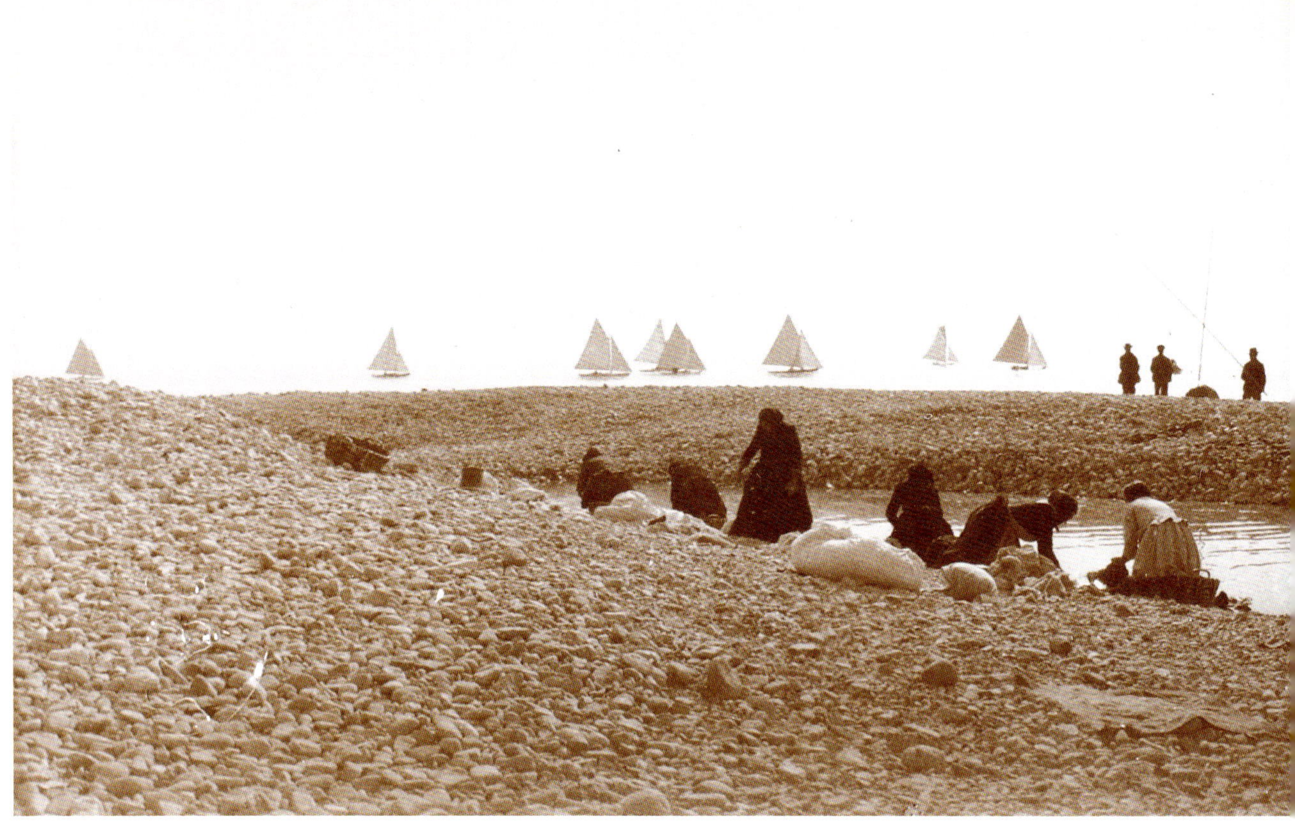

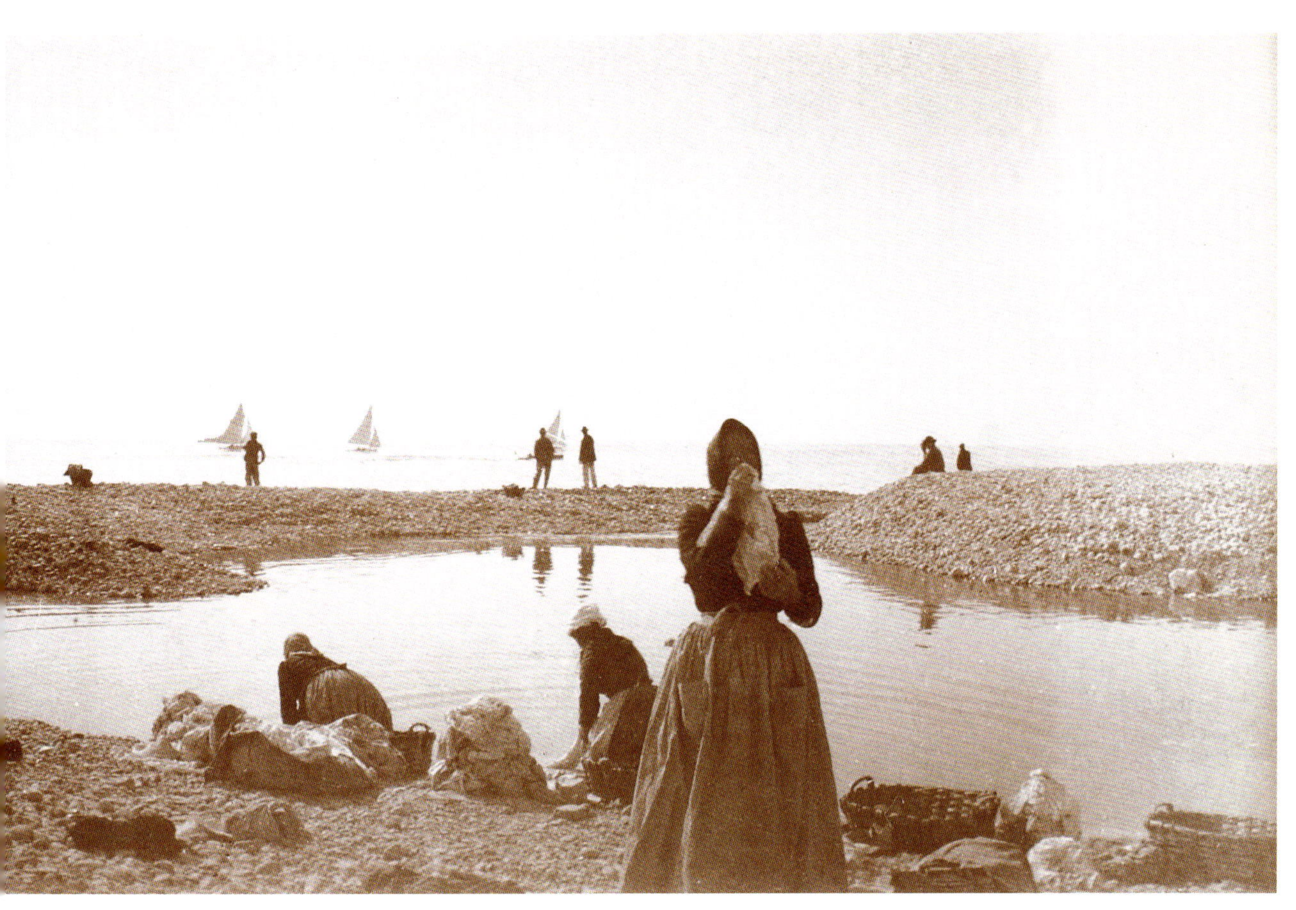

74 {cat.} – Maxime Maufra, *La Plage du Pouldu, rivage breton à marée basse. Finistère* (The beach at Le Pouldu, shoreline at low tide: Finistère), 1891.
Oil on canvas, 16 × 22½ in. (41.2 × 57.2 cm). Musée des Impressionnismes, Giverny.

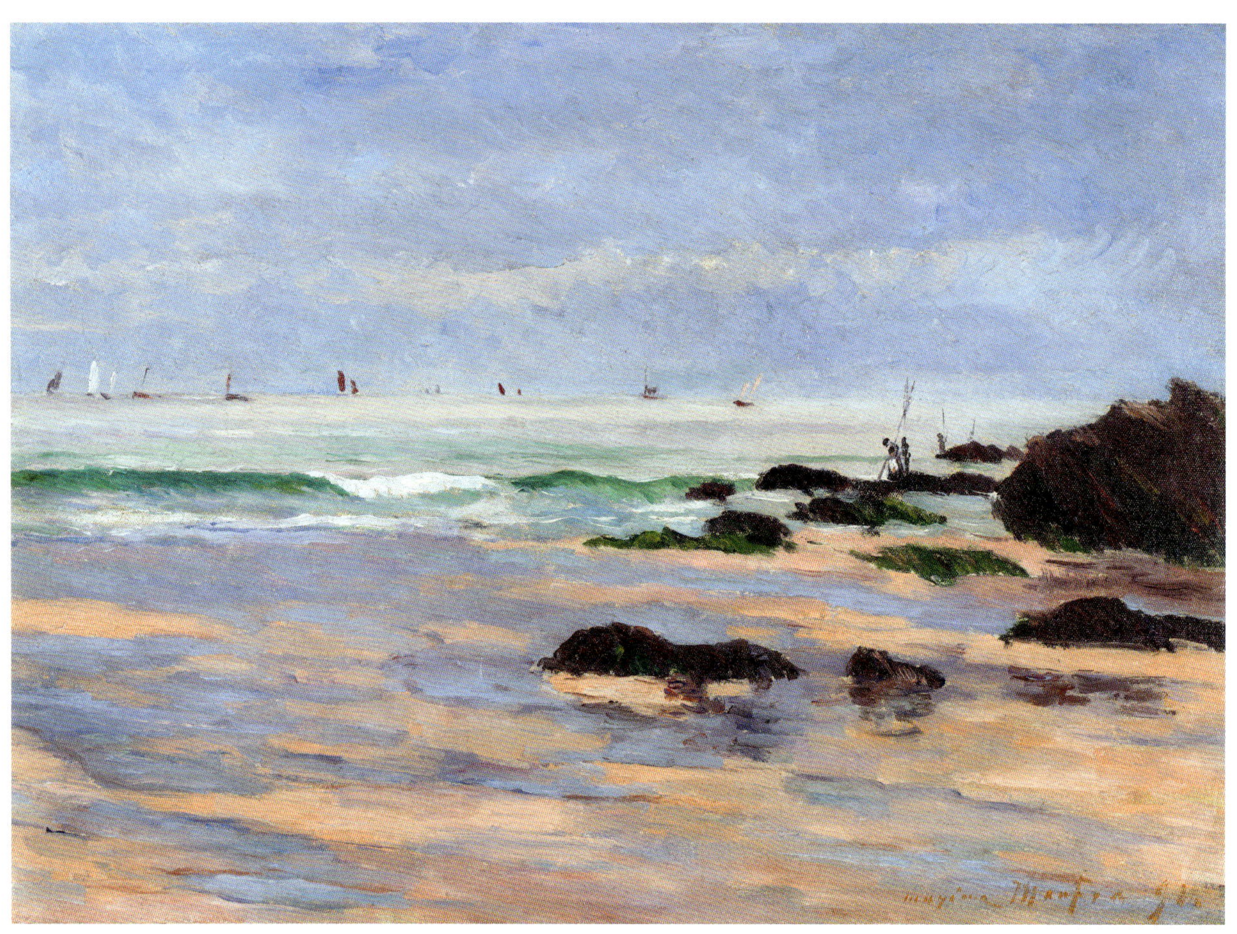

Born into a family from Nantes, Maufra was originally destined for a life in commerce. His father sent him to England, where he discovered the works of J.M.W. Turner and decided he wanted to focus on painting. Initially, he painted landscapes in the Loire and in Nantes, before traveling through Brittany. He met Gauguin in 1890 in Pont-Aven. The beach at Le Pouldu, famous for inspiring works by Paul Gauguin, Paul Sérusier, and Émile Bernard, was a meeting place for painters of the Pont-Aven School.

75 {cat.} – Maxime Maufra, *Rochers au soleil couchant; L'Anse du port Lonnec* (Rocks at sunset: The cove at Port Lonnec), 1899. Oil on canvas, 21½ × 28½ in. (54.1 × 73.1 cm). Musée des Beaux-Arts, Reims.

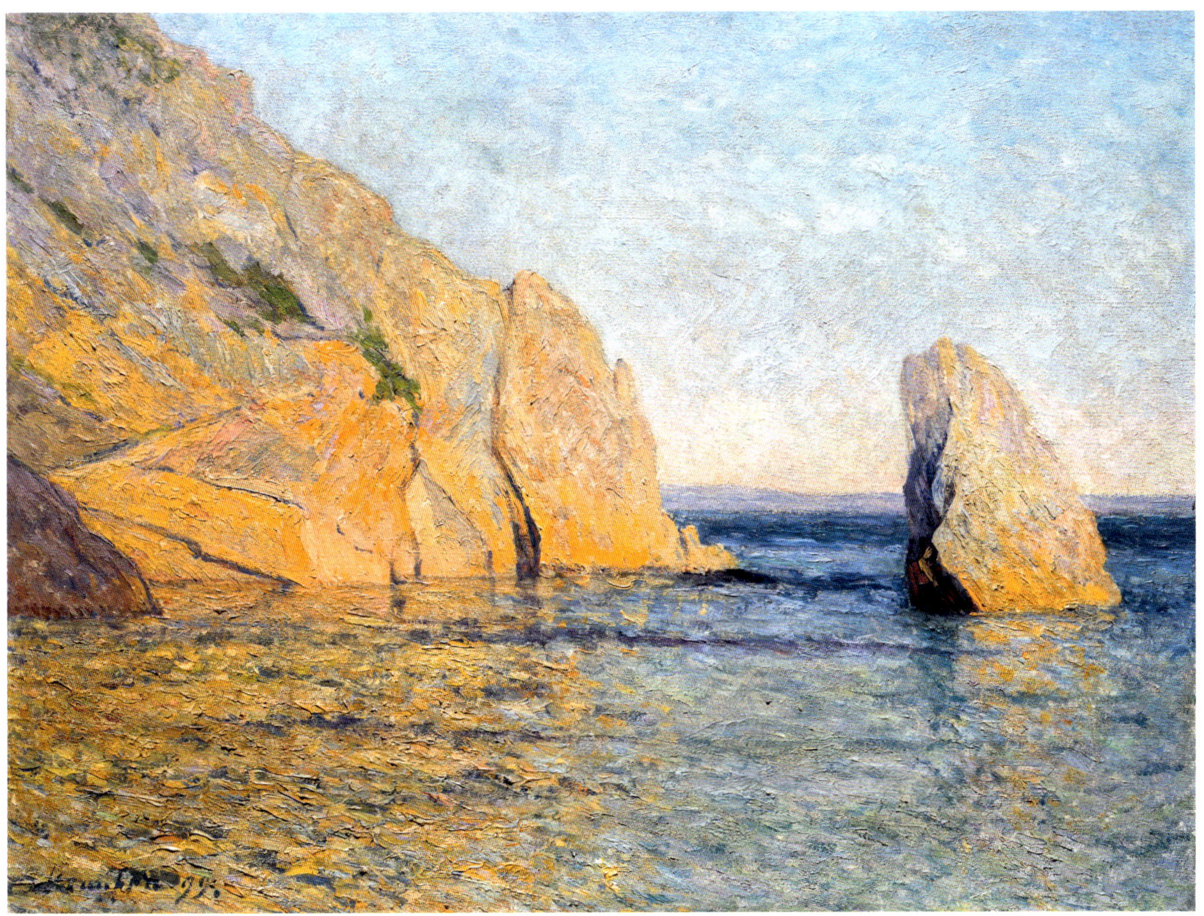

SEASIDE RESORTS

The seaside provided an ideal setting for social life to unfold, drawing crowds of summer vacationers who sought the benefits of sea air and beach games. The impressionists, more interested in the water's reflections than in the people walking along the shore, nevertheless used friends or family as models. Édouard Manet, Edgar Degas, and Claude Monet sometimes painted portraits of family members on the beach, while Eugène Boudin specialized in portrayals of strollers in Deauville and Trouville. In fact, he created a whole genre of it: the "crinoline" was named for the lighter garments worn by elegant women at the beach. During Napoleon III's Second Empire, Boudin successfully captured the unique atmosphere: bathers, children, dandies, and the aristocratic elite mingle on the sand. Philip Wilson Steer went further and painted the archetypal "elegant woman" dreaming of elsewhere (*Jeune femme sur la plage* [*Young Woman on the Beach*] {cat. 77}). In the nineteenth century, the theme of escape and travels to exotic locales took root, as portrayed by Maxime Maufra in *Transatlantique sortant du port* (Transatlantic liner leaving port) {cat. 93}, one of the first depictions of an ocean liner.

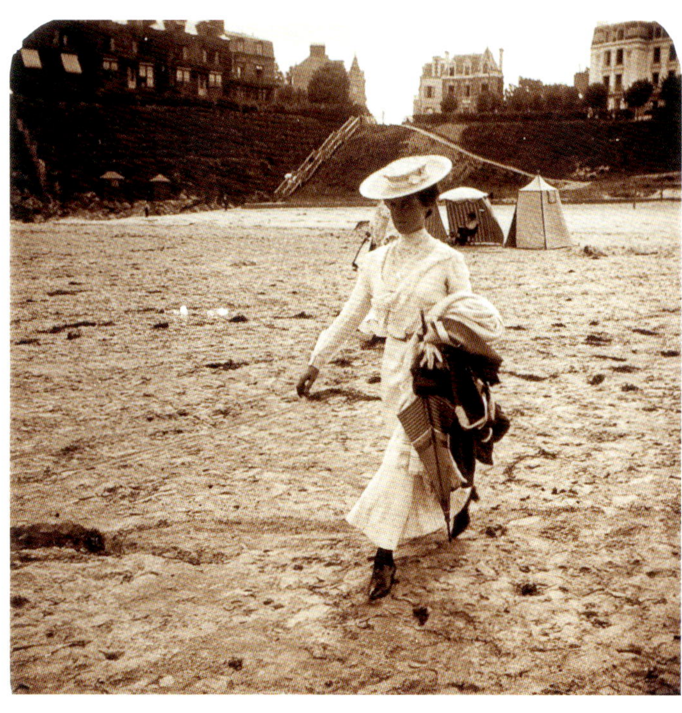

76 {fig.} – Jean Binot, *Dinard*, 1904. Musée du Quai Branly – Jacques Chirac, Paris.

77 {cat.} – Philip Wilson Steer, *Jeune femme sur la plage* (*Young Woman on the Beach*), 1888.
Oil on canvas, 4 ft. 1 in. × 3 ft. (125.5 × 92 cm). Musée d'Orsay, Paris.

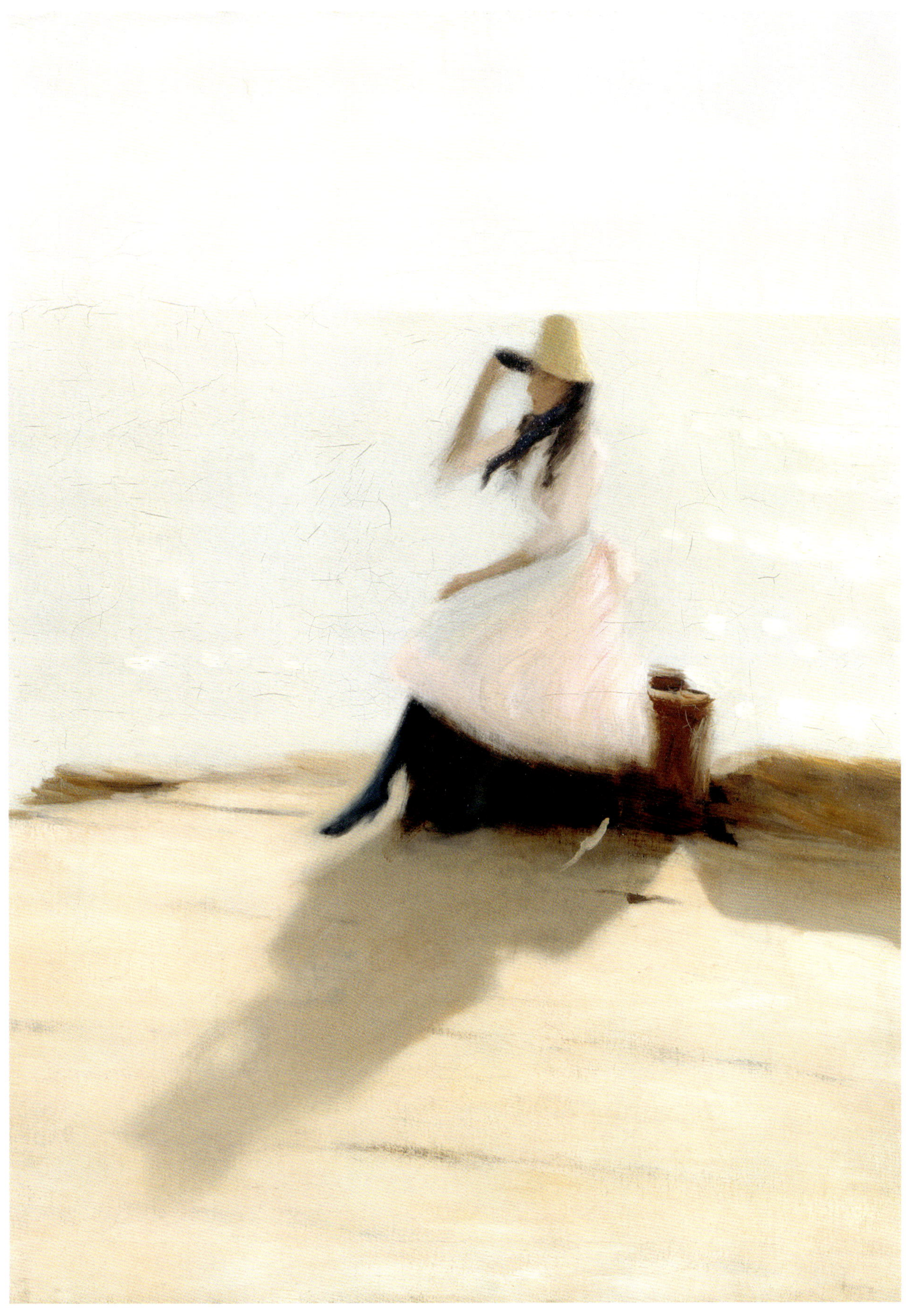

78 {cat.} – Eugène Boudin, *Élégants et crinolines sur la plage* (Dandies and crinolines on the beach), 1864. Watercolor on paper, 7 × 10½ in. (18.3 × 27.1 cm). Private collection.

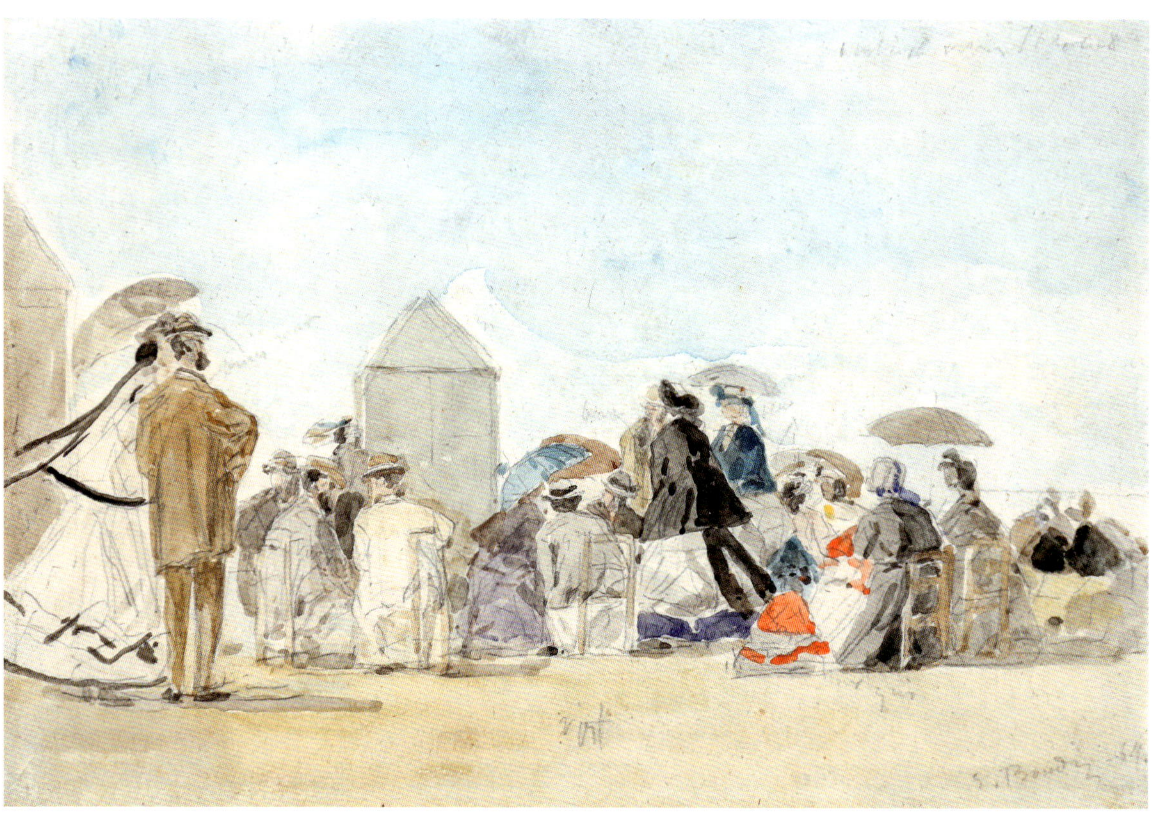

79 {cat.} – Eugène Boudin, *La Plage* (The beach), c. 1863–1866.
Pastel on paper, 10 × 16 in. (25.5 × 40.5 cm). Private collection.

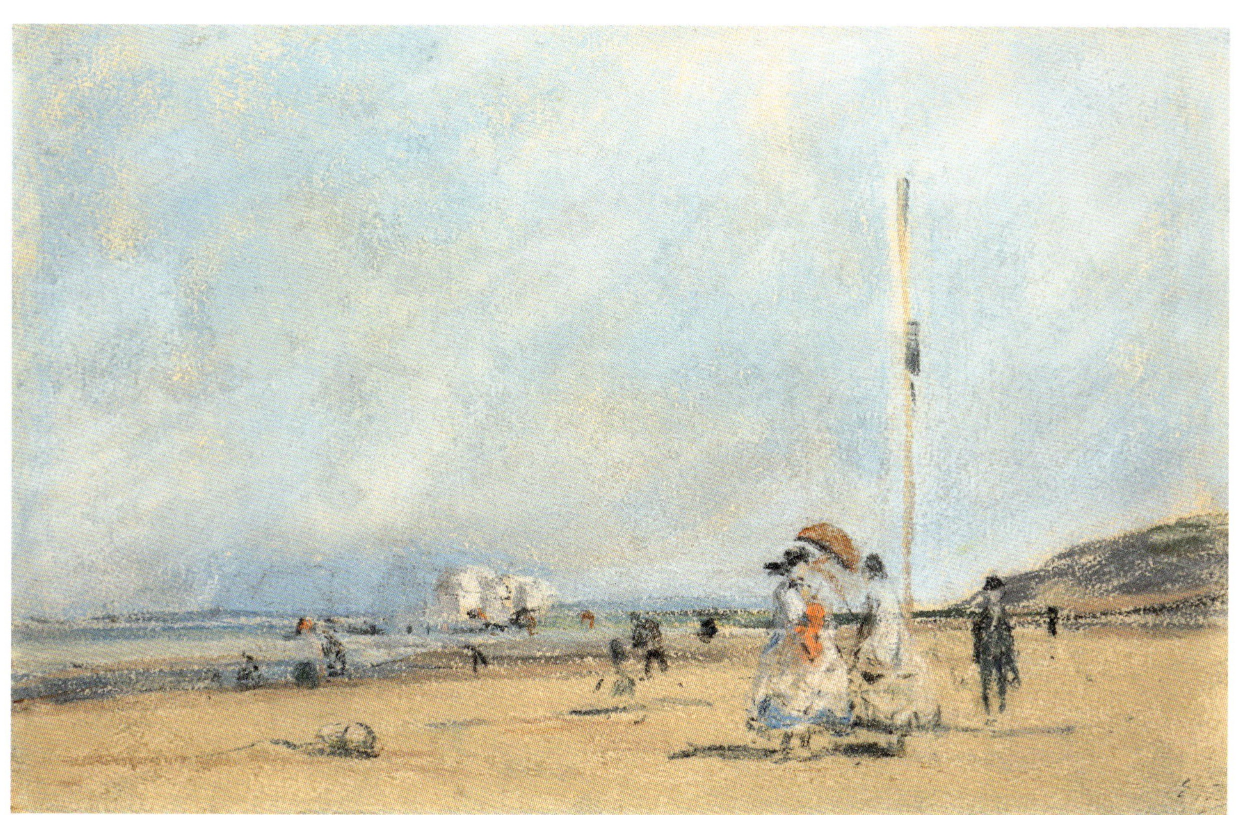

80 {fig.} – Jean Binot, *Dinard*, 1904. Musée du Quai Branly – Jacques Chirac, Paris.

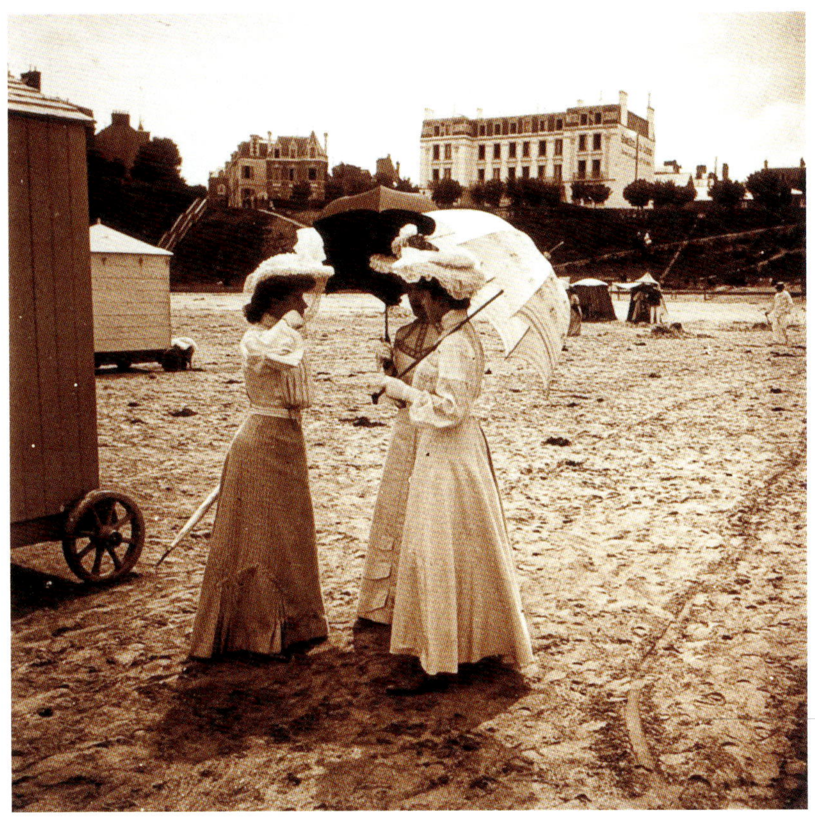

Top: 81 {cat.} – Eugène Boudin, *Sur la plage* (On the beach), n.d. Watercolor on paper, 5 × 9 in. (13 × 23.4 cm). Private collection. Bottom: 82 {cat.} – Eugène Boudin, *Scène de plage* (Beach scene), 1866. Watercolor on paper, 5½ × 10½ in. (14.3 × 26.6 cm). Private collection.

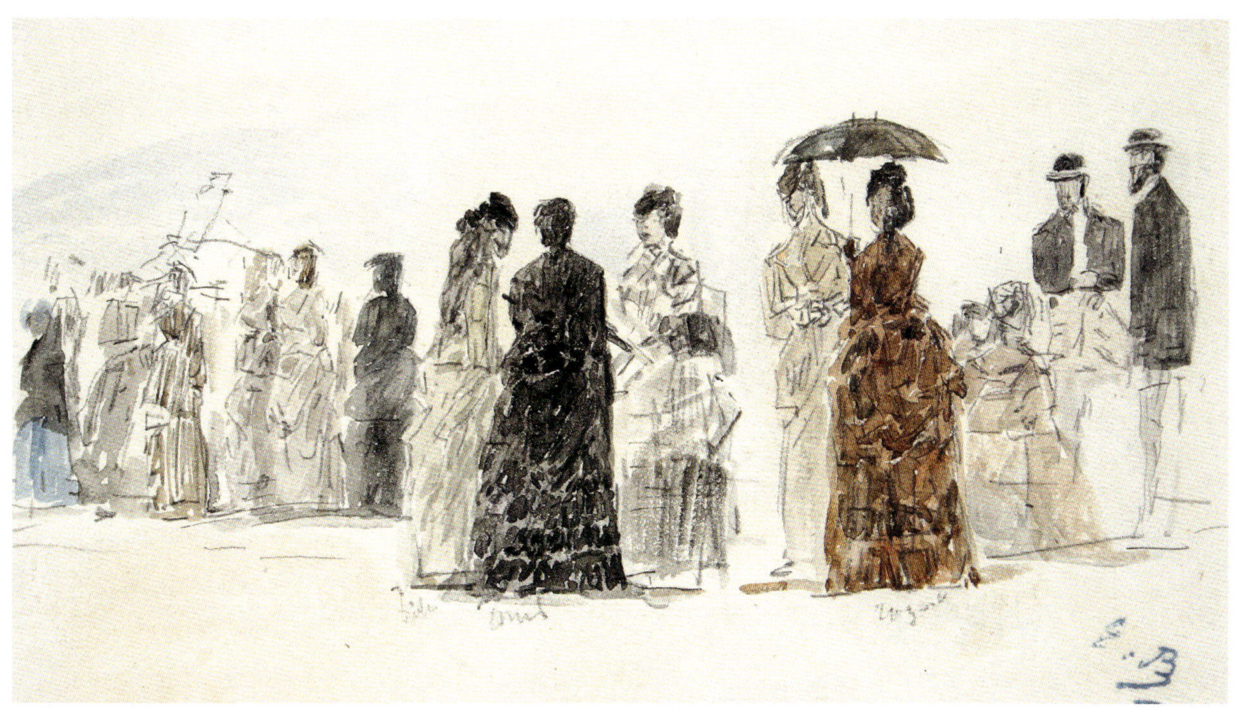

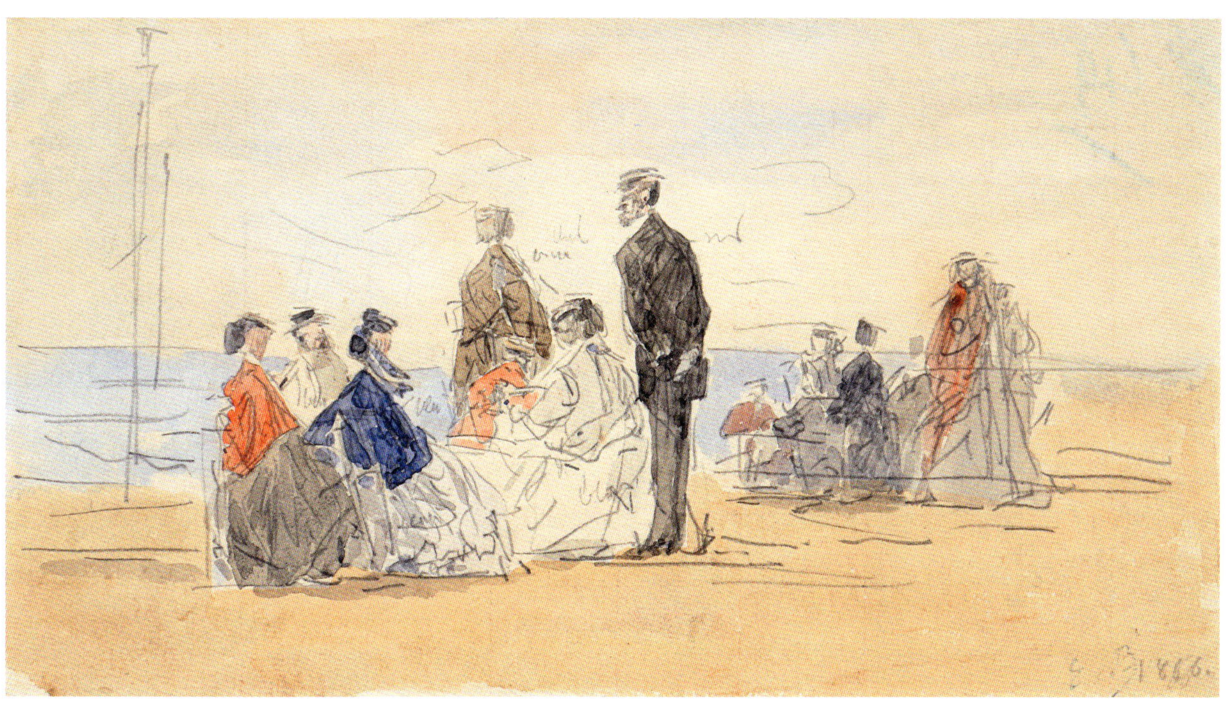

83 (cat.) – Eugène Boudin, *La Plage de Trouville* (The beach at Trouville), 1865.
Oil on board, 10½ × 15½ in. (26.5 × 40.3 cm). Musée d'Orsay, Paris.

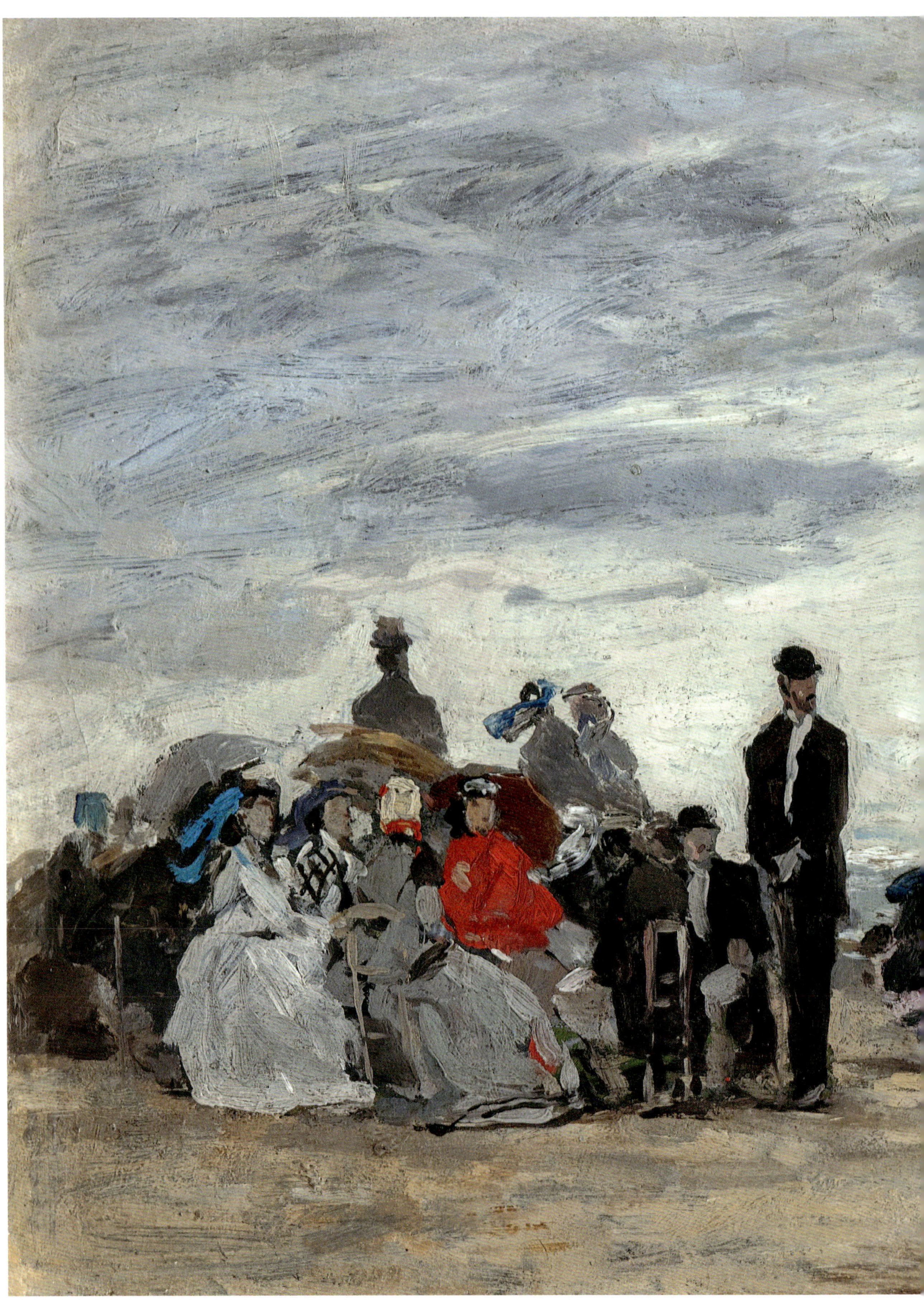

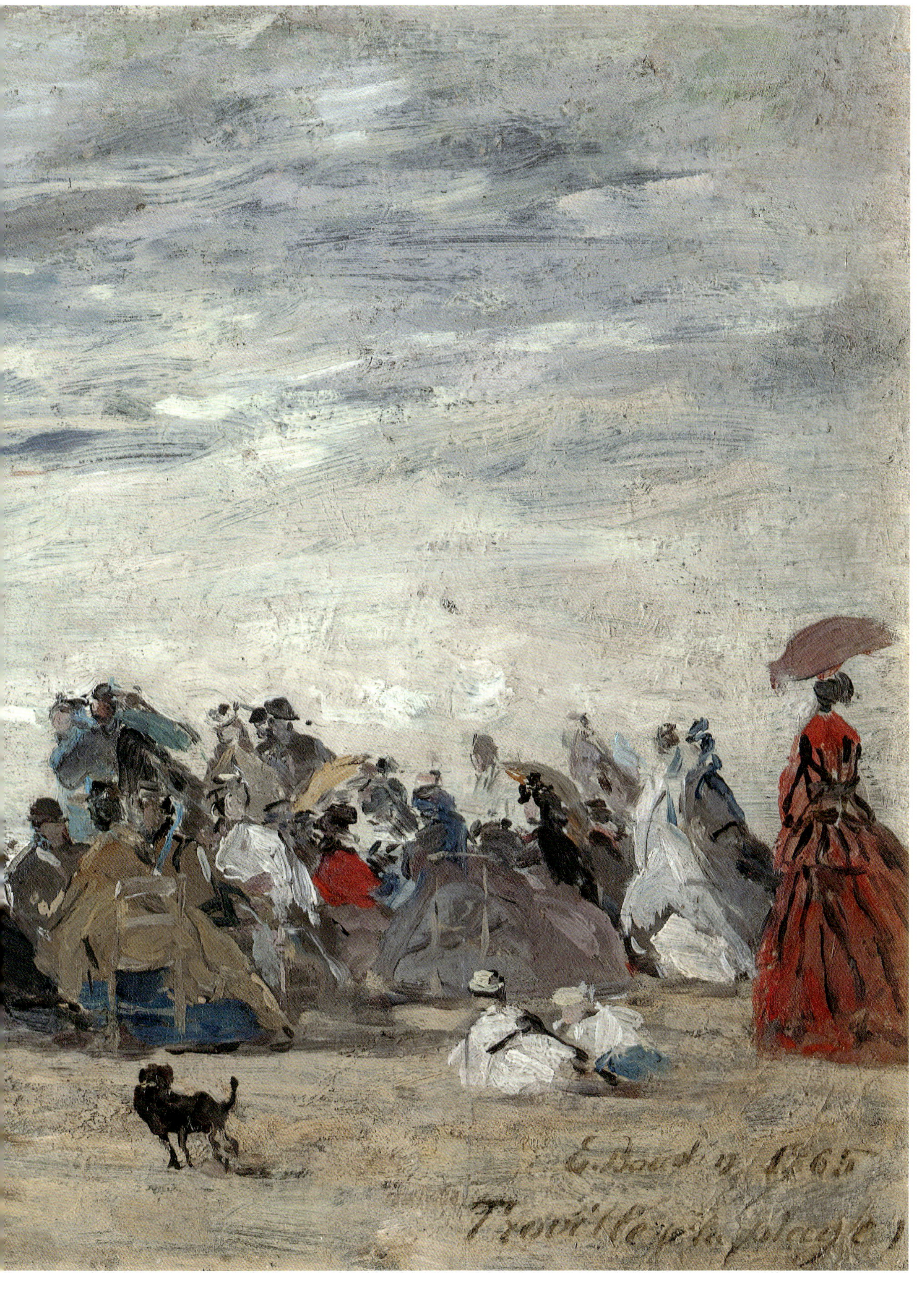

84 {cat.} – Eugène Boudin, *La Plage de Trouville* (The beach at Trouville), 1867.
Oil on wood, 12 × 19 in. (31 × 48 cm). Musée d'Orsay, Paris.

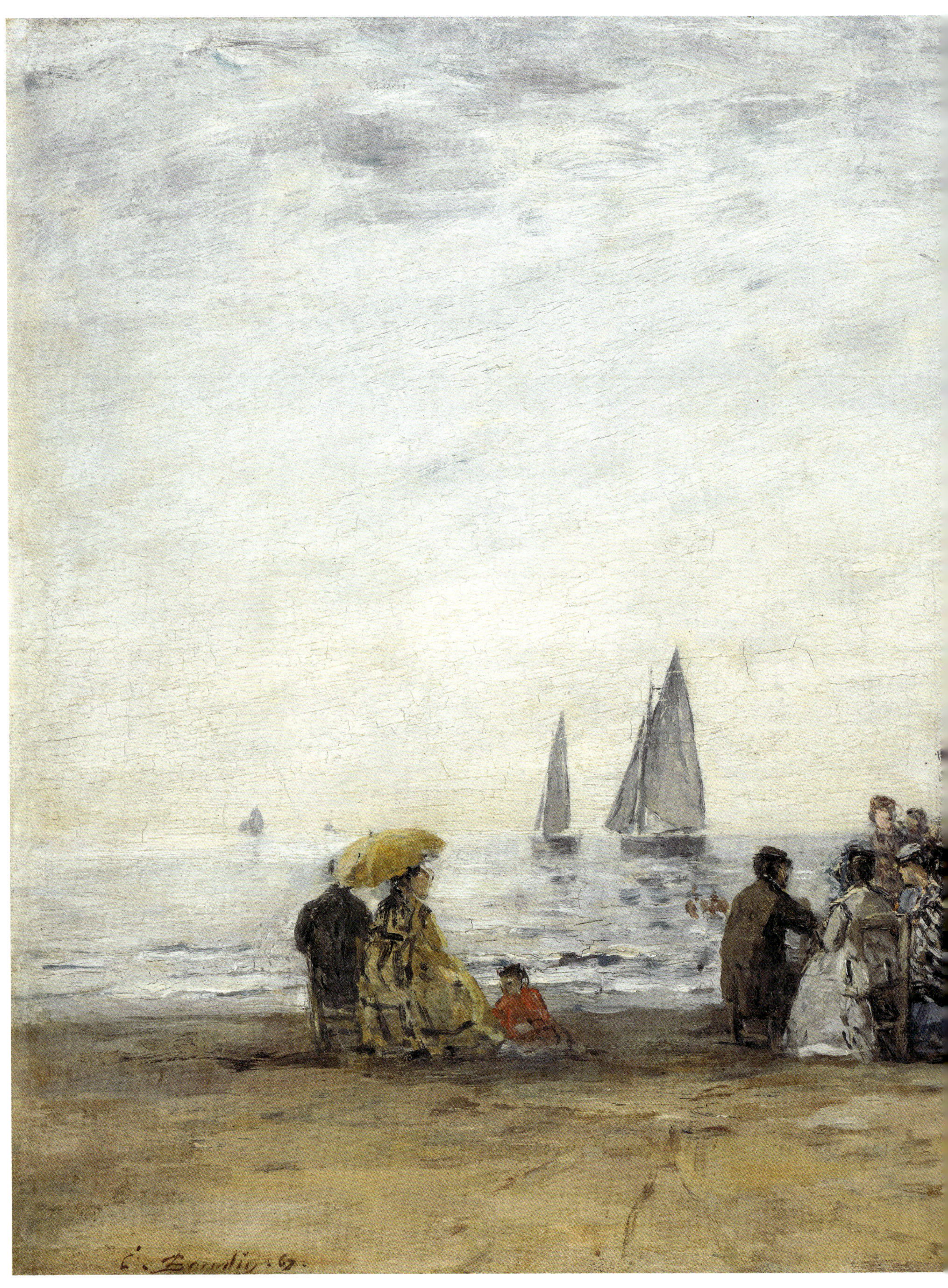

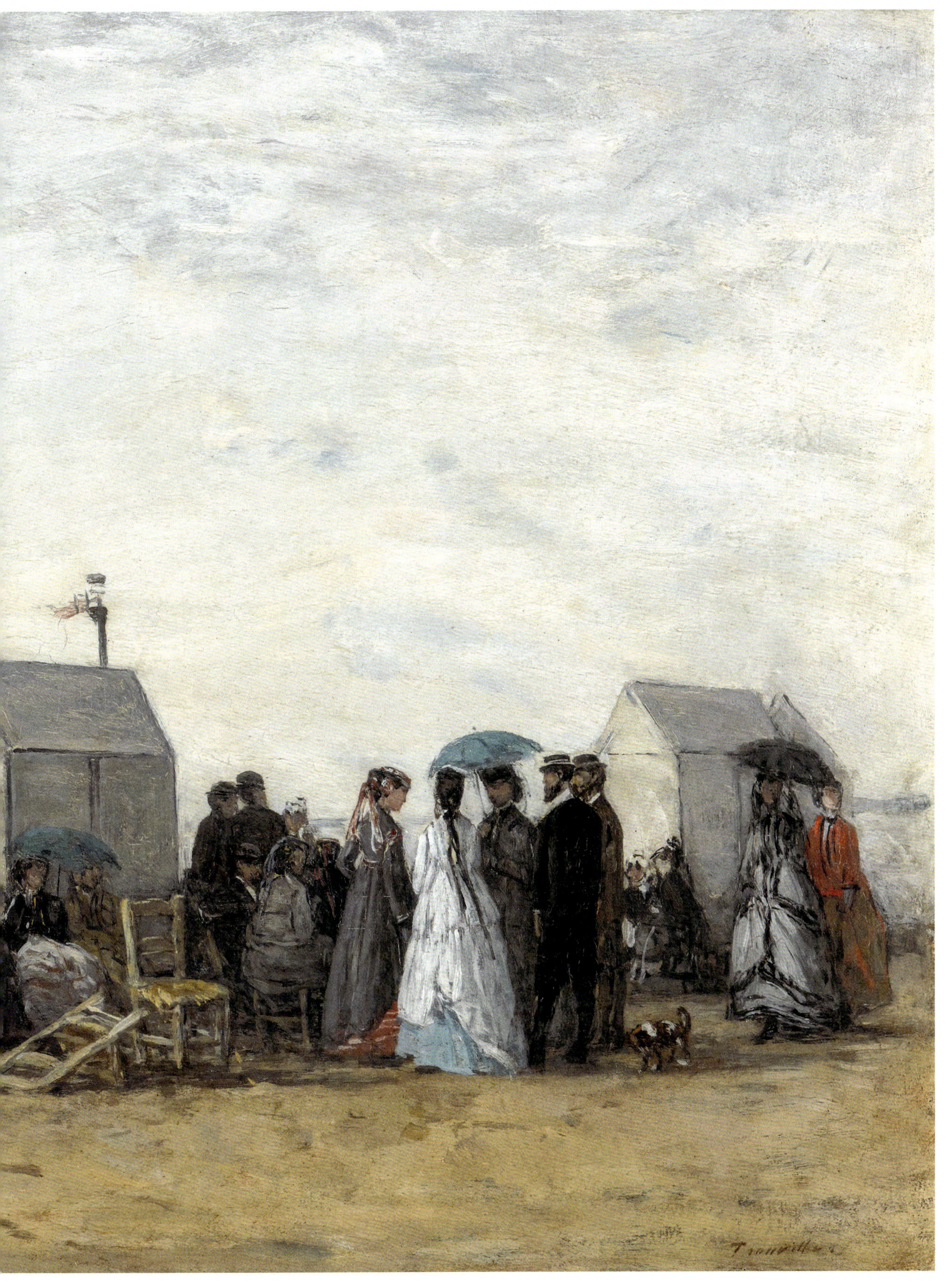
Trouville

85 {cat.} – Eugène Boudin, *Scène de plage* (Beach scene), 1869.
Oil on panel, 7 × 12½ in. (18 × 32.5 cm). Private collection.

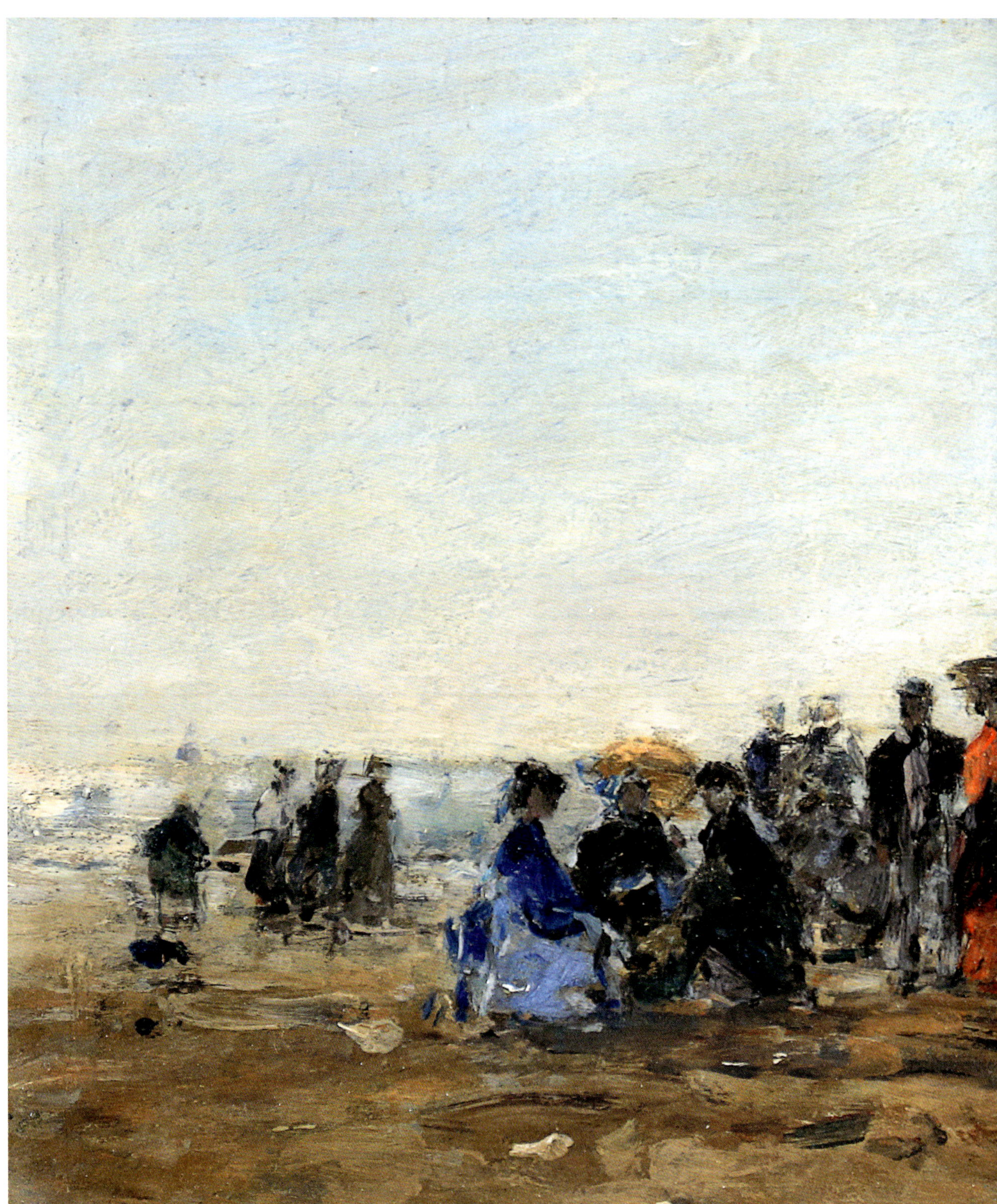

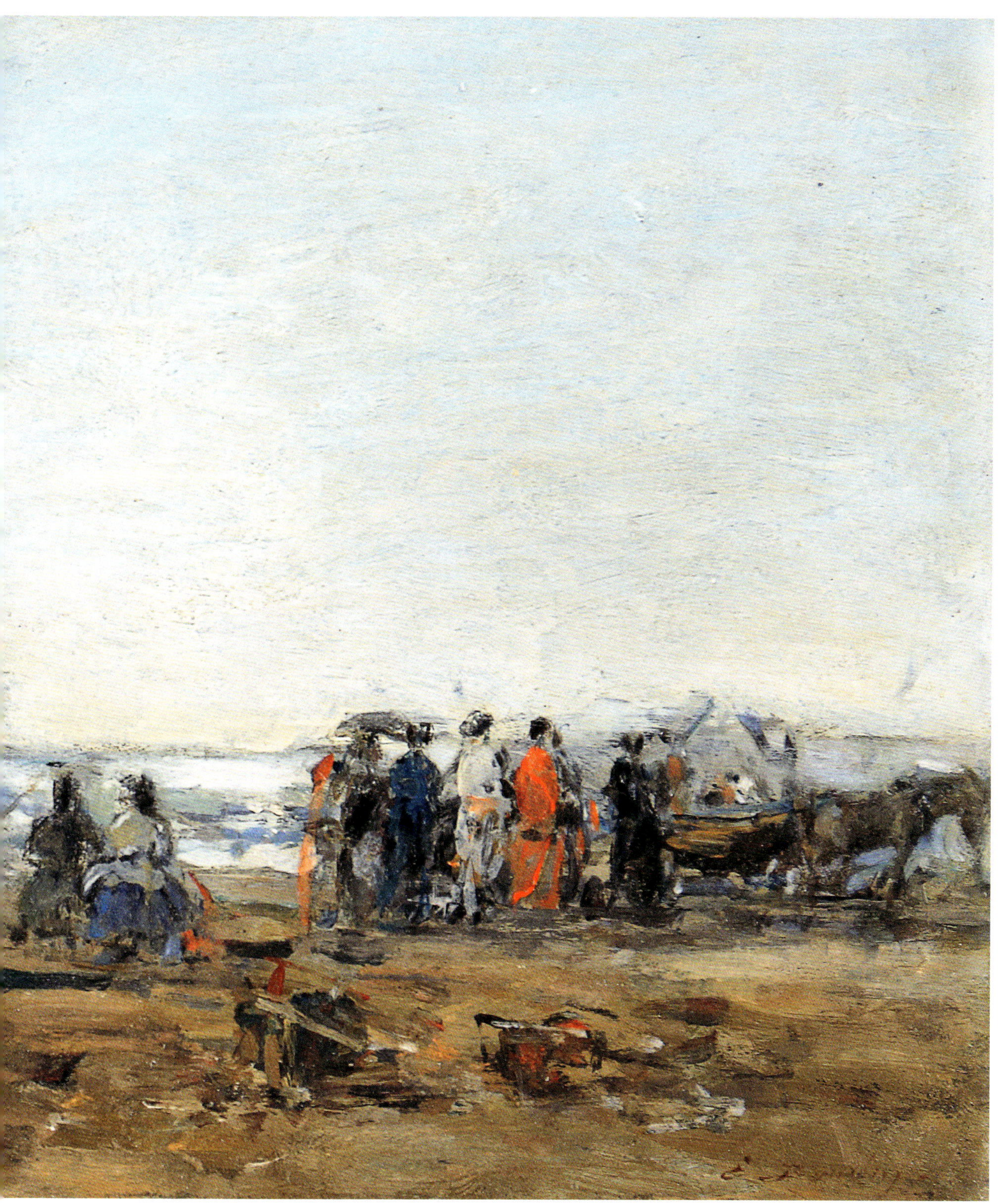

86 {cat.} – Eugène Boudin, *Berck, pêcheuses sur le rivage* (Fisherwomen on the shore, Berck), 1880–1885. Oil on panel, 5½ × 6½ in. (13.5 × 17 cm). Private collection.

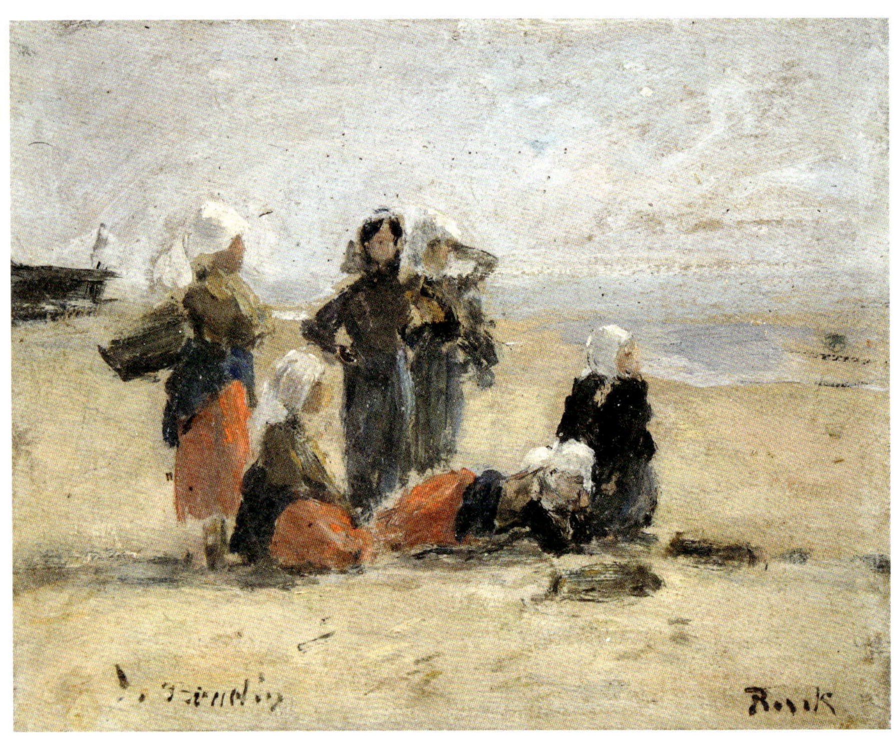

87 {cat.} – Eugène Boudin, *La Plage* (The beach), 1868.
Watercolor on paper, 6 × 10 in. (15 × 26 cm). Private collection.

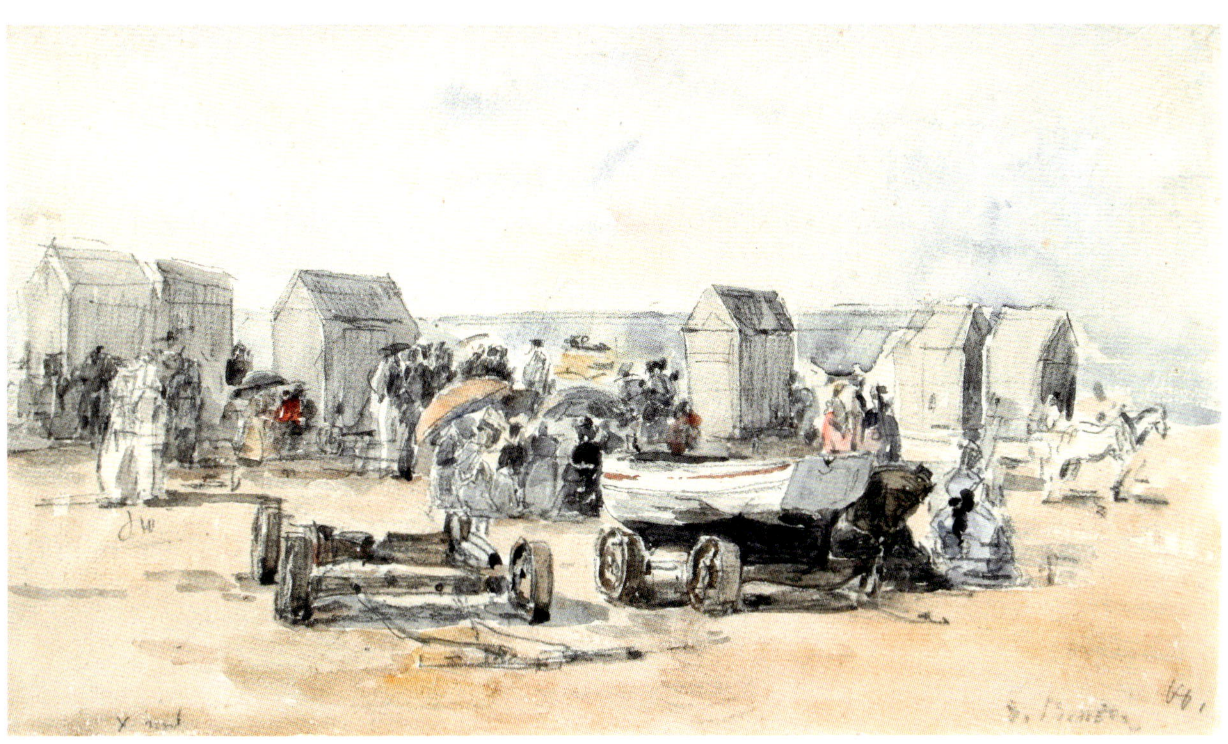

88 {fig.} – Jean Binot, *Dinard*, 1904. Musée du Quai Branly – Jacques Chirac, Paris.

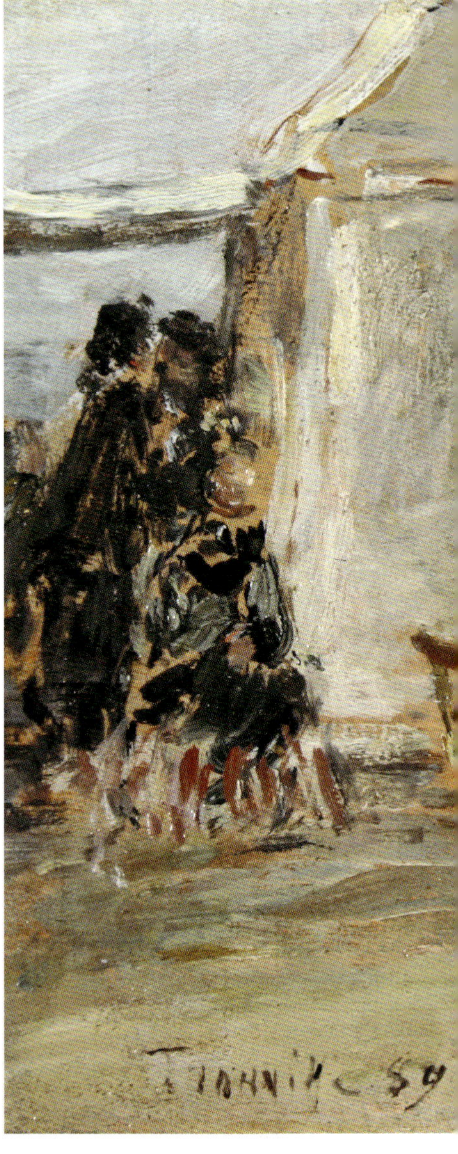

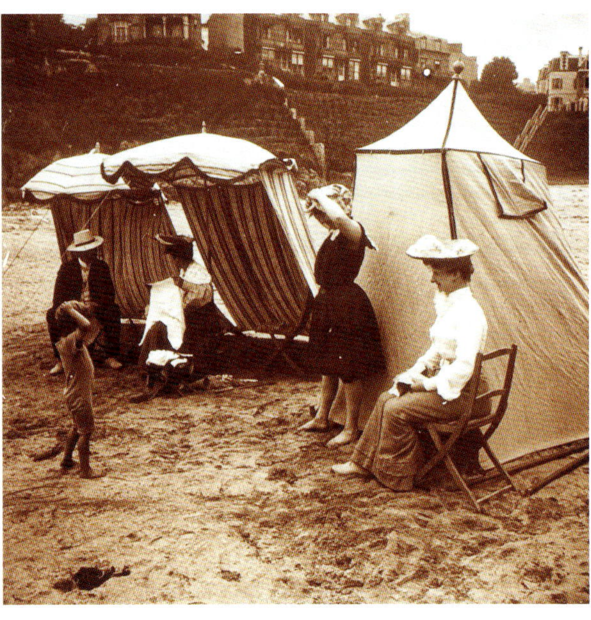

89 {cat.} – Eugène Boudin, *Les Crinolines à Trouville* (Crinolines at Trouville), 1889.
Oil on board, 5½ × 9 in. (14 × 22.8 cm). Private collection.

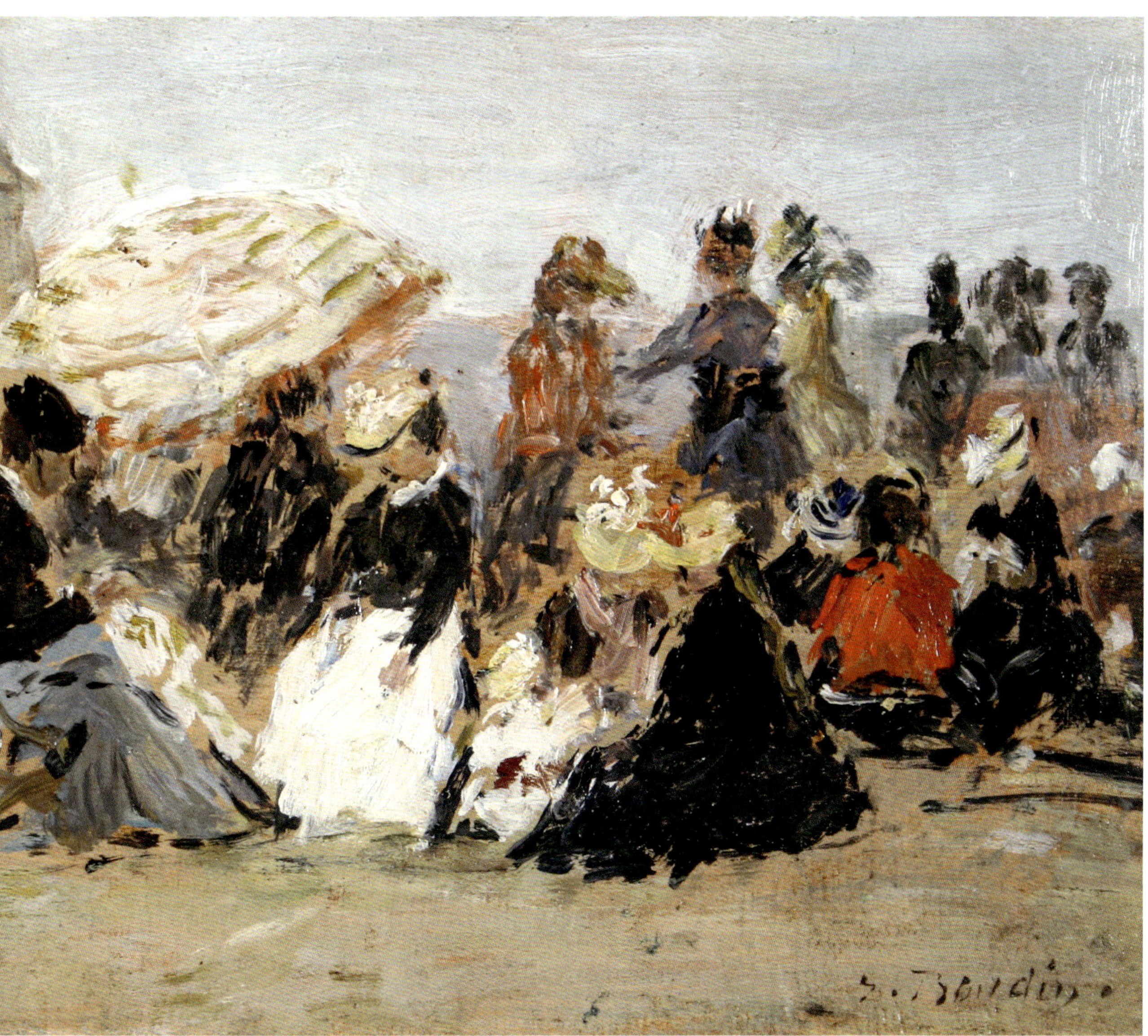

90–91 {cats.} – Société des Établissements Gaumont, *Deauville–Trouville: The Beach and Seafront*, 1912. Chronochrome film, 6 min. 30 sec.

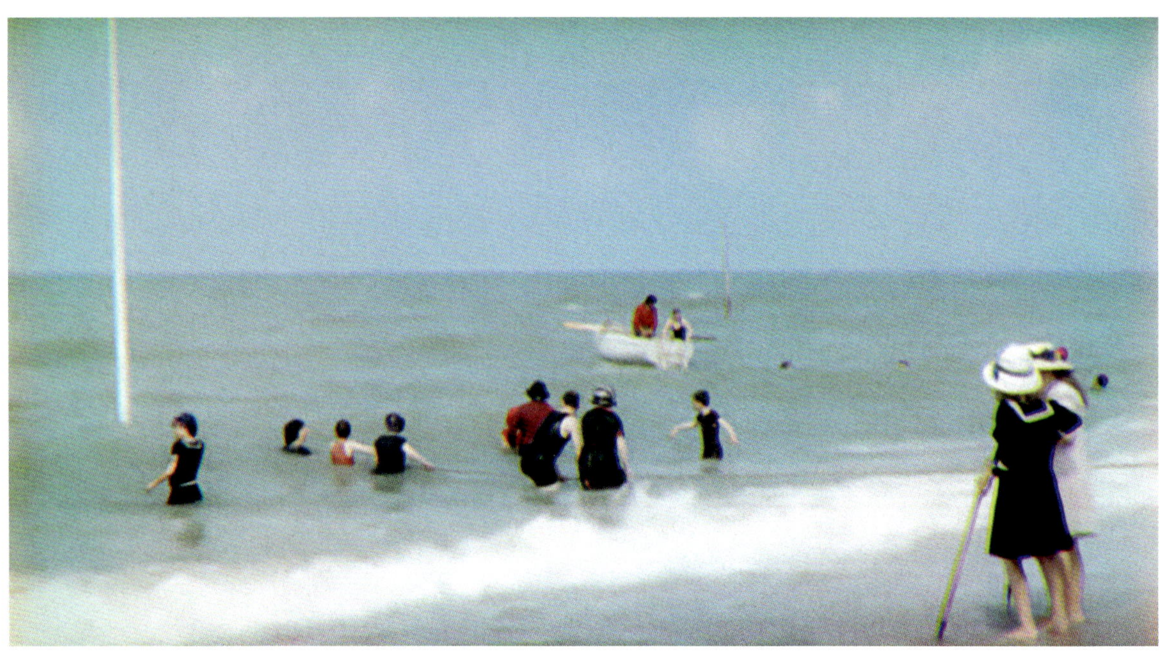

The Chronochrome process, patented by Léon Gaumont in 1911, made it possible to produce movies in natural colors using a camera equipped with a triple lens fitted with red, green, and blue filters. During projection, colors were reproduced on screen using additive color synthesis. The process, which proved to be too costly and complex, was discontinued in the early 1920s. Among the first sequences presented to the public in 1912 were views of Deauville, Trouville, and Honfleur, which capture the bustling activity of these locations in the early twentieth century.

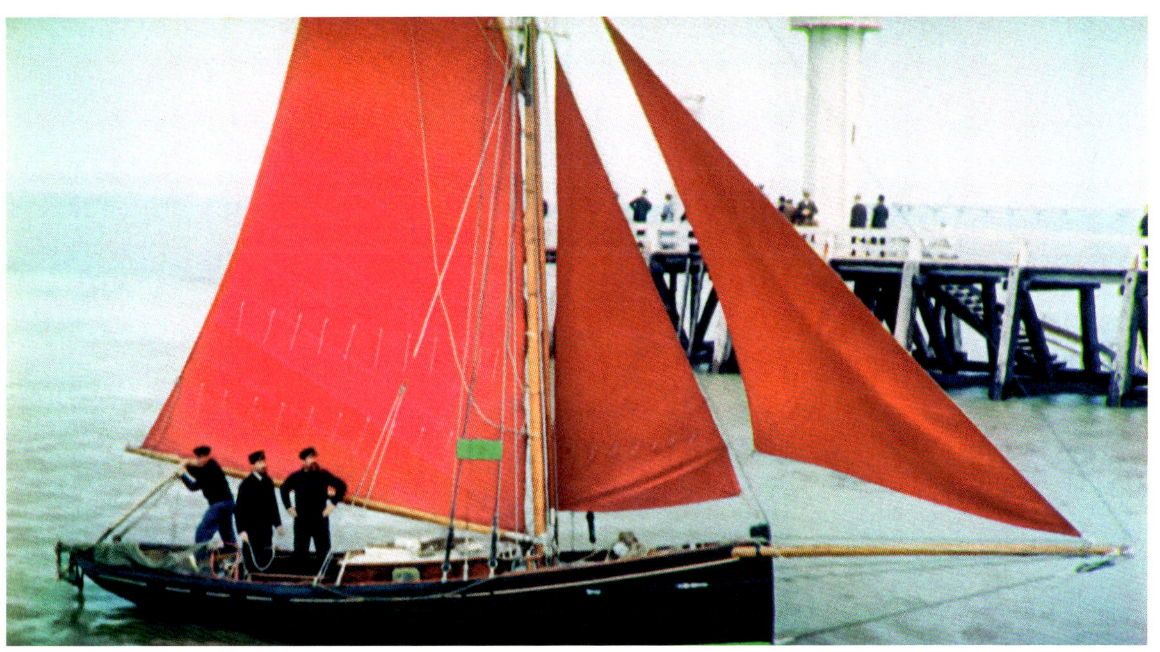

92 {cat.} – Société des Établissements Gaumont, *Deauville–Trouville: The Beach and Seafront*, 1912. Chronochrome film, 6 min. 30 sec.

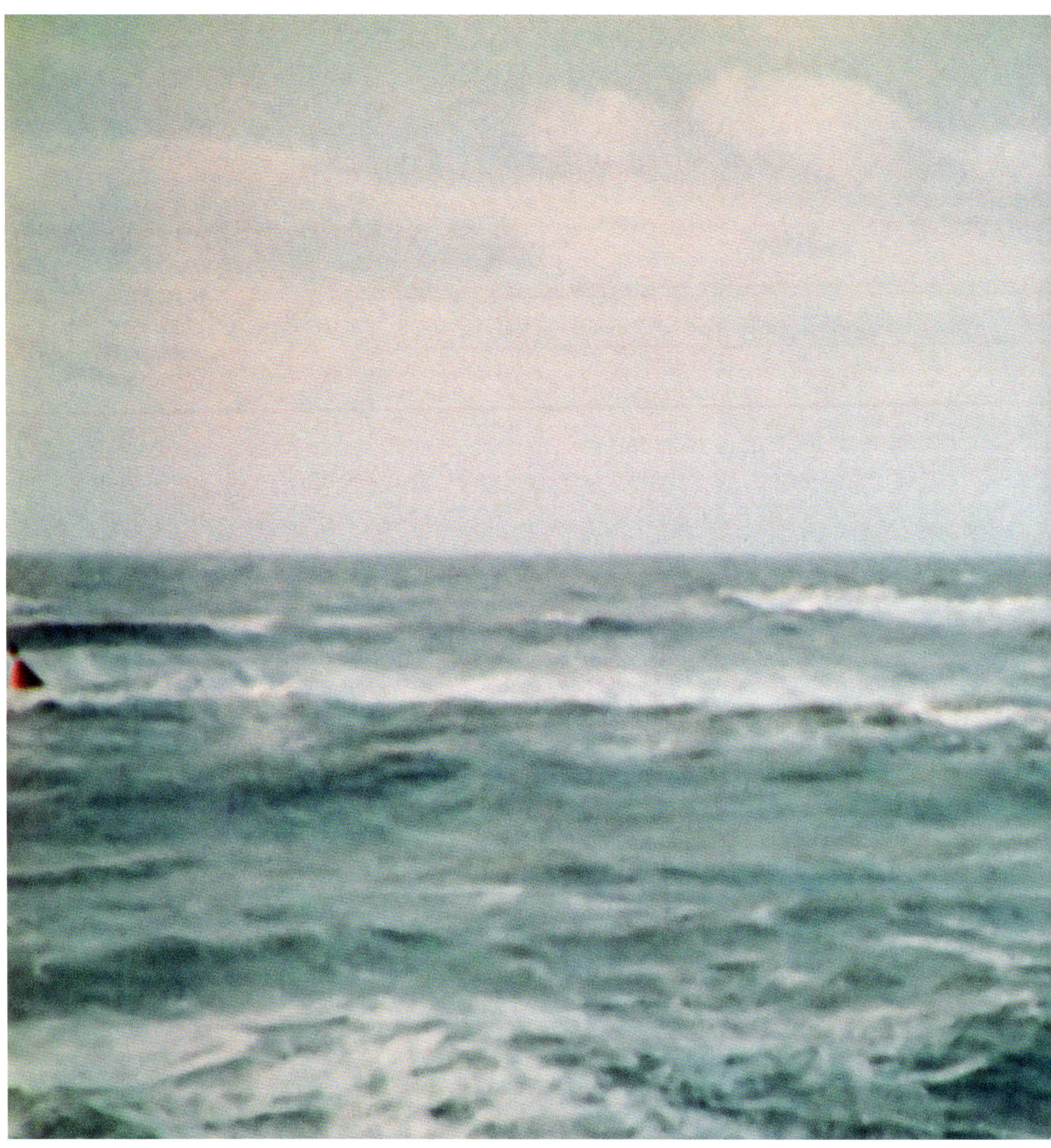

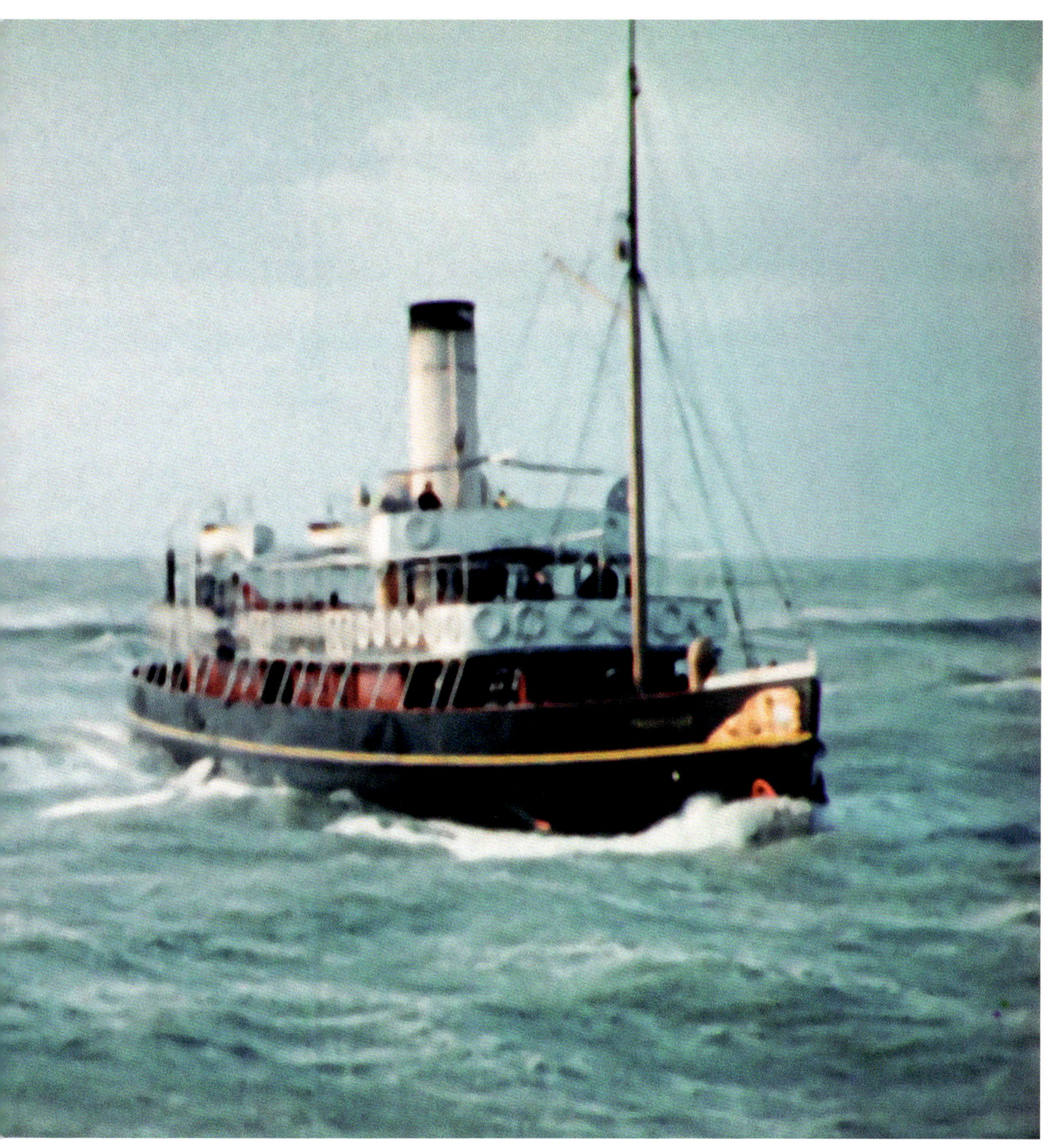

93 {cat.} – Maxime Maufra, *Transatlantique sortant du port* (Transatlantic liner leaving port), 1905. Oil on canvas, 25½ × 32 in. (65.5 × 81 cm). MuMA, Le Havre.

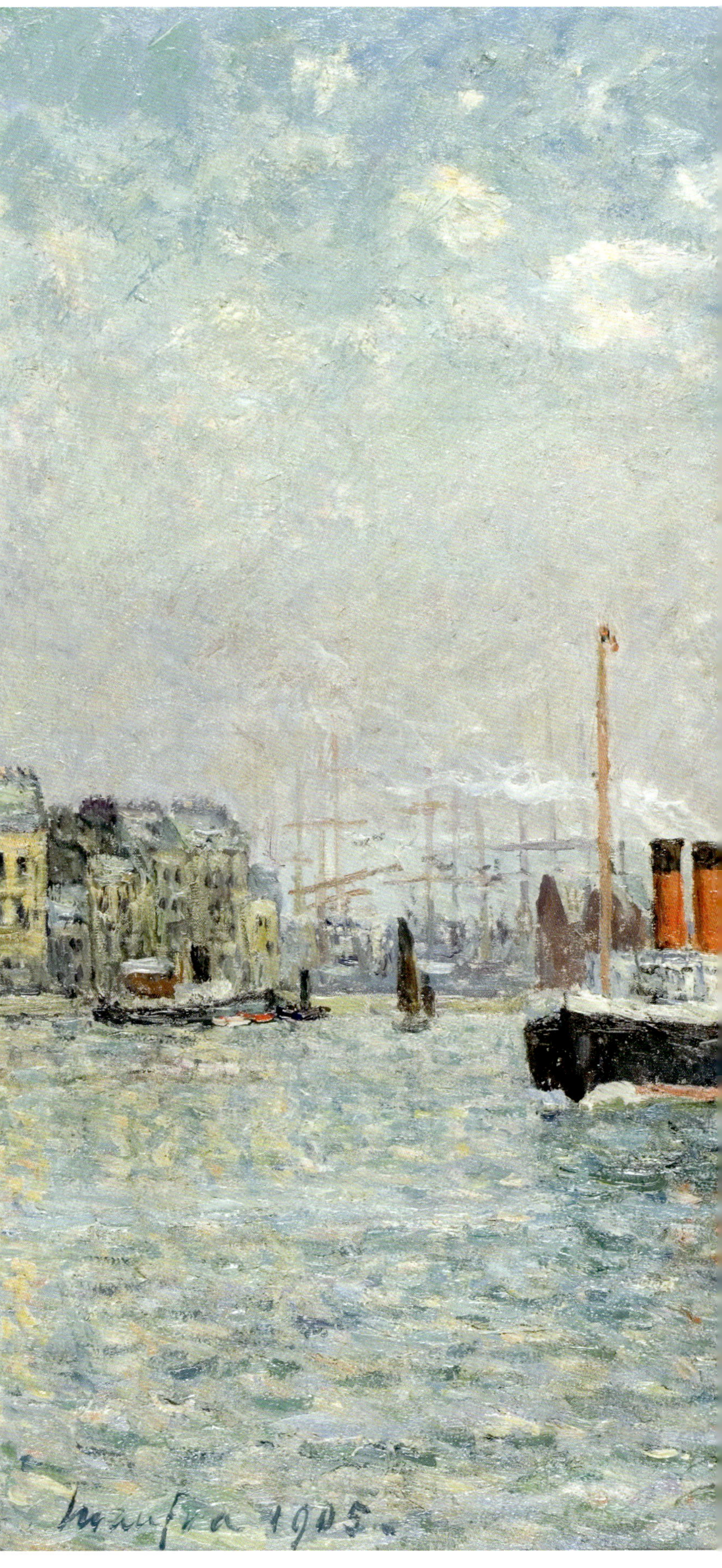

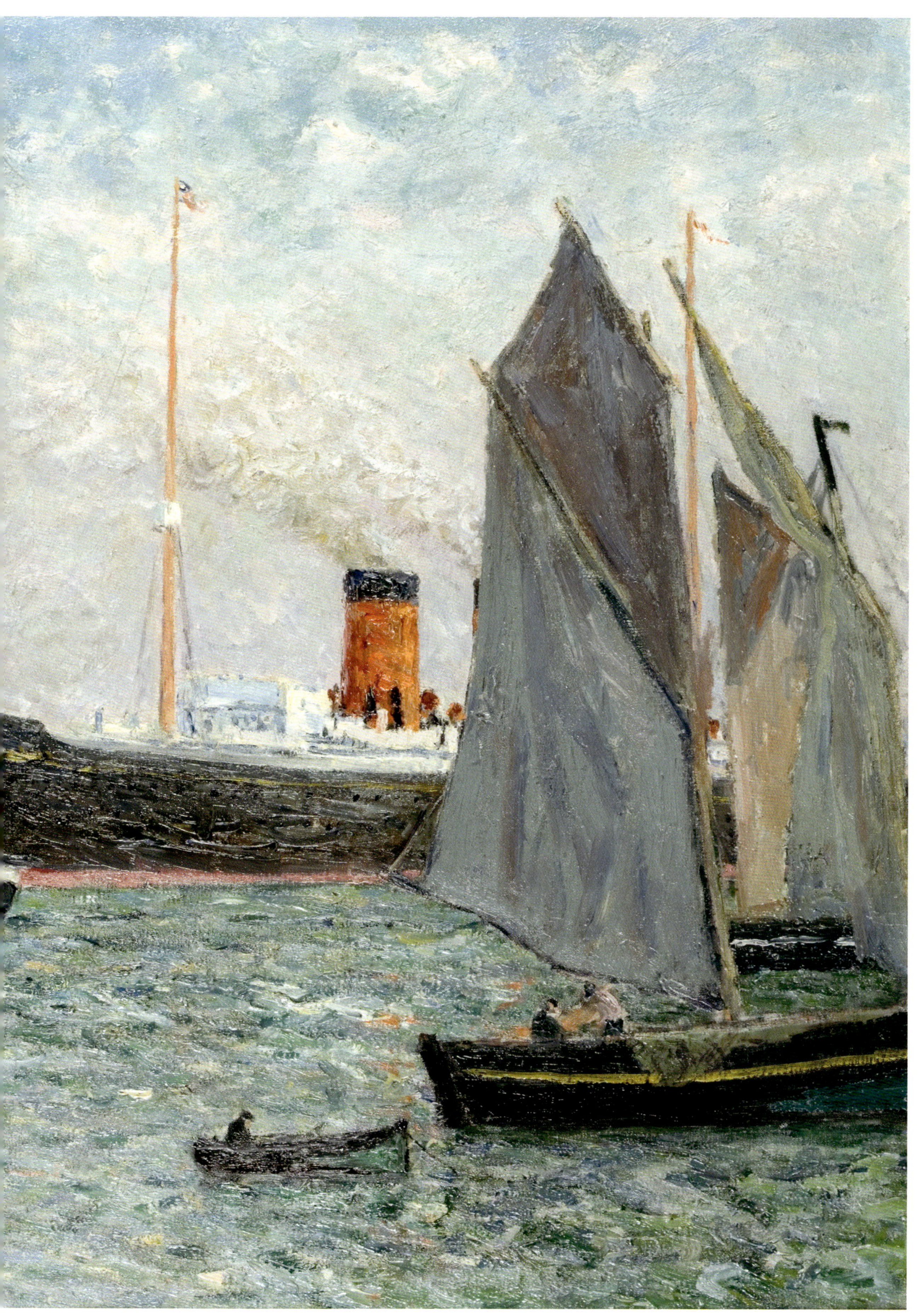

94 {cat.} – Marie-Auguste Flameng, *Marine* (Seascape), c. 1880. Oil on wood, 15 × 11 in. (38 × 27.8 cm). Private collection.

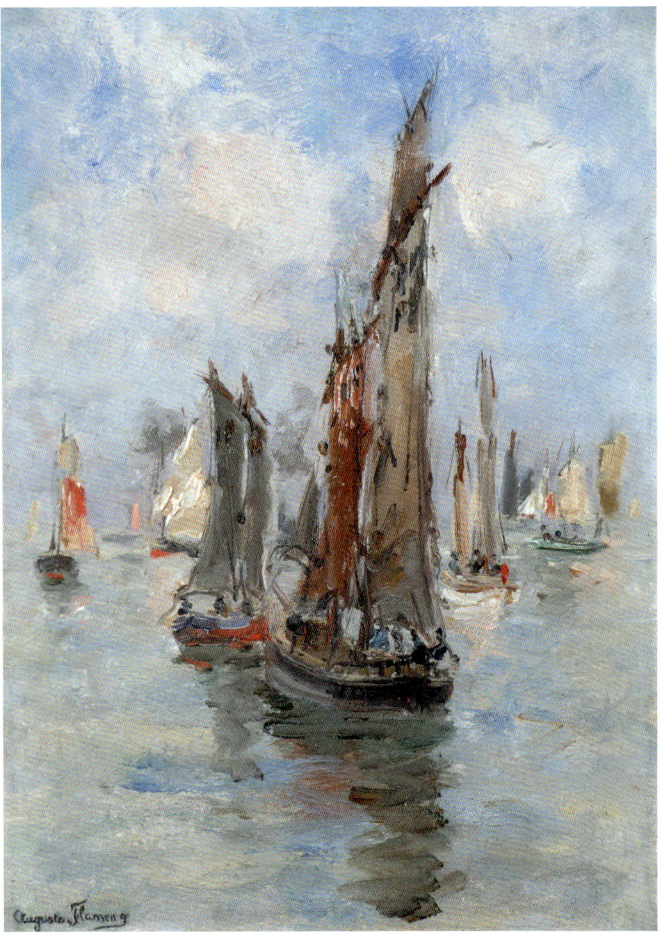

Left: 95 {cat.} – Marie-Auguste Flameng, *Marine* (Seascape), c. 1880. Oil on wood, 15 × 11 in. (38 × 27.8 cm). Private collection. Right: 96 {cat.} – Marie-Auguste Flameng, *Marine* (Seascape), c. 1880. Oil on wood, 21½ × 12½ in. (55 × 32.7 cm). Private collection.

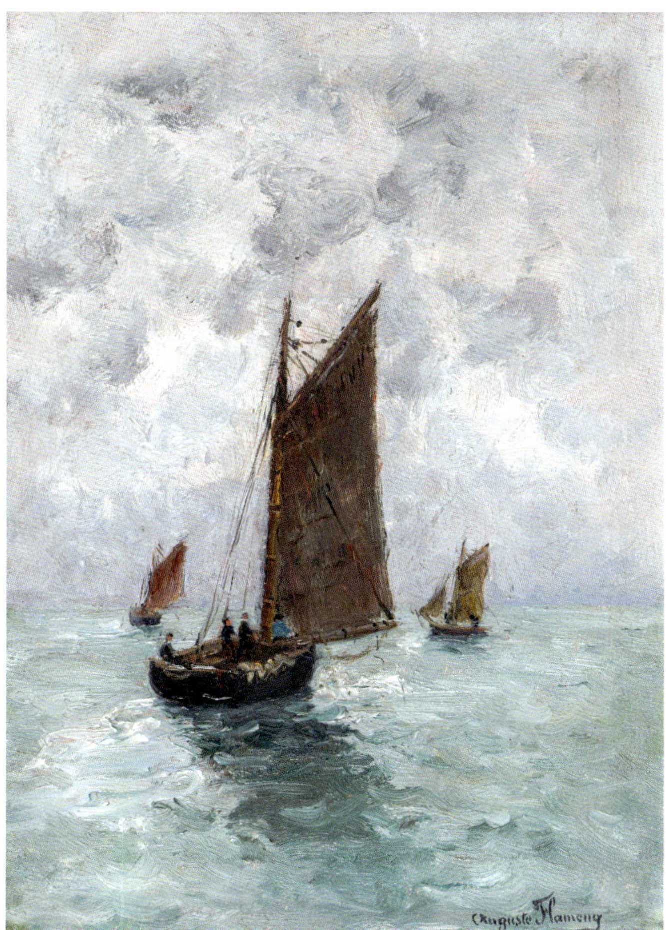

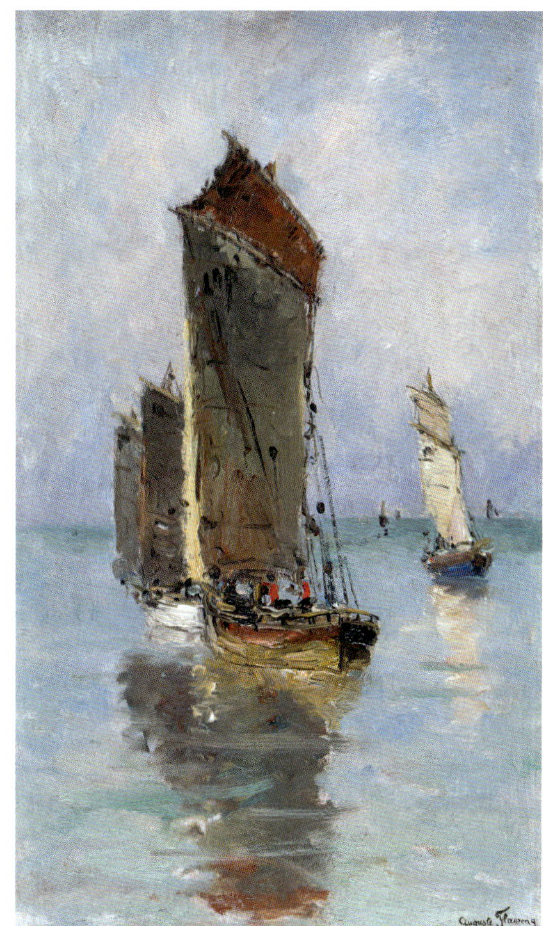

97 {cat.} – Eugène Boudin, *Voiliers* (Sailboats), 1869. Oil on wood, 9½ × 12 in. (23.9 × 30.9 cm).
Musée d'Orsay, Paris, on long-term loan to the Musée des Beaux-Arts, Caen.

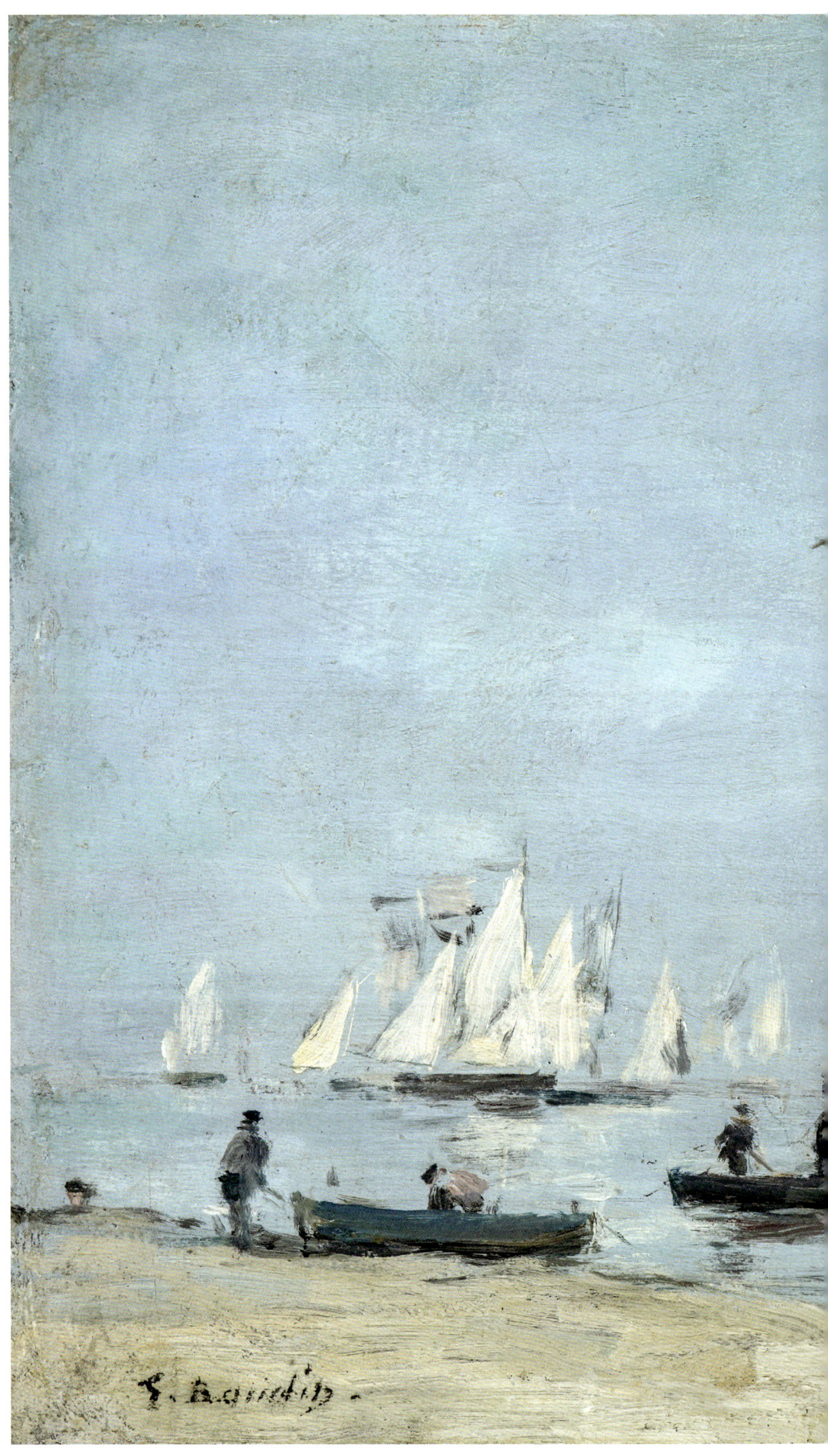

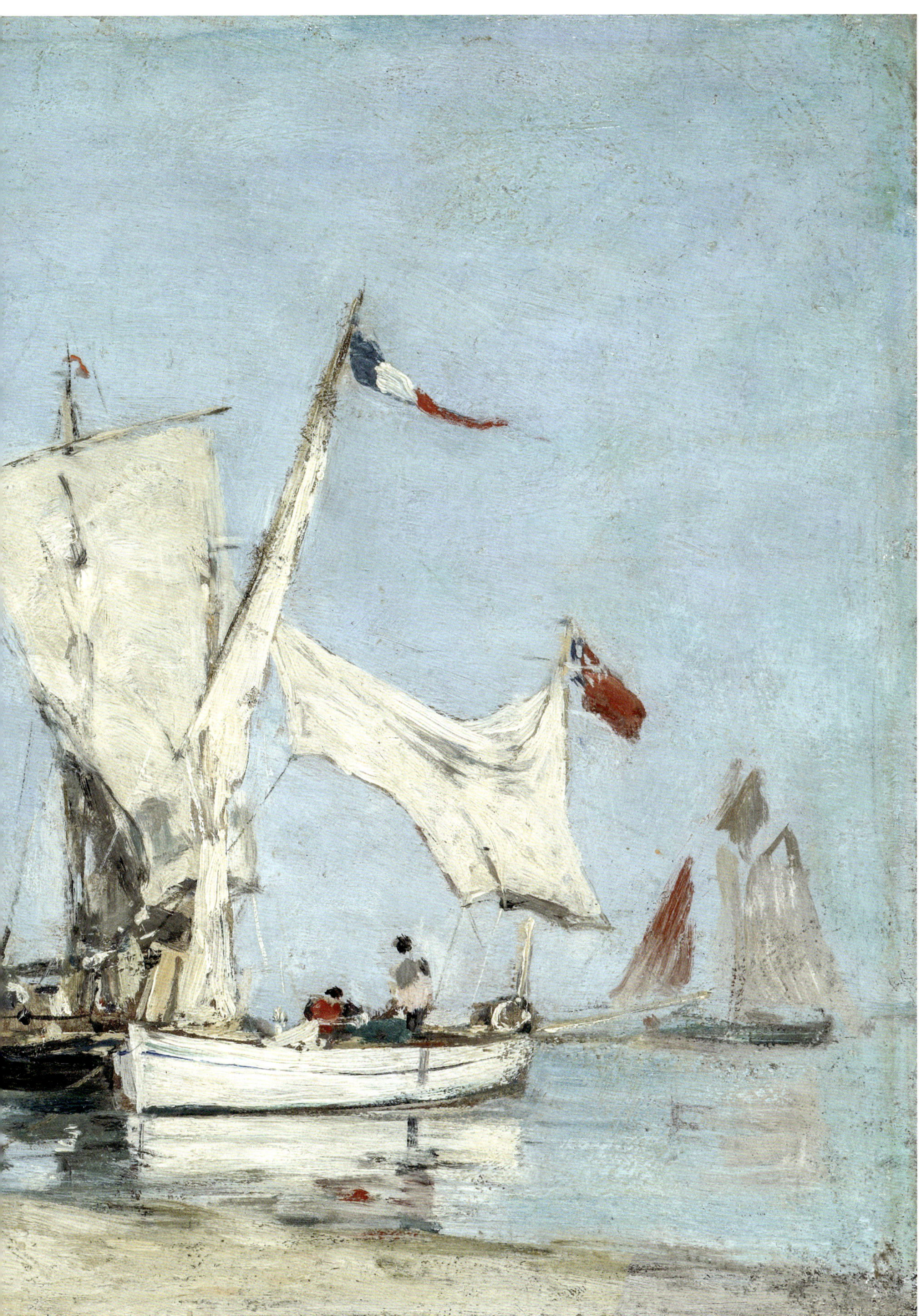

FLIGHT

In the late nineteenth century, with the Industrial Revolution, and the development of train and boat travel, the discovery of new lands became a leitmotif for many artists. Monet escaped to Belle-Île-en-Mer in search of fresh inspiration, while Gauguin left for Pont-Aven the same year. But flight was not solely artistic: Édouard Manet depicted the famous escape of convict Henri Rochefort from the penal colony on Nouméa, New Caledonia in *L'Évasion de Rochefort* (*The Escape of Rochefort*) {cat. 99}. A tribute to Géricault's *Radeau de la Méduse* (*Raft of the Medusa*; 1818–19, Musée du Louvre, Paris), the work is fascinating for the way in which the immensity of the green sea contrasts with the tiny craft transporting the fugitive toward a ship in the distance. As a result, flight by sea became a subject of artistic interest. A taste for travel and for exotic locations runs through the body of impressionist works, from Pissarro's early days in Saint Thomas, in the West Indies, in 1853, to Charles Laval and Gauguin's voyage to Martinique in 1887. But the most radical artist among them remains Gauguin, who abandoned everything—family, friends, "civilization"—for a life in Tahiti. In this regard, his *Paysage de Te Vaa* (Te Vaa landscape) {cat. 103} renewed the theme of the sea by integrating symbolist elements that brought the impressionist period to a close, and which opened up fundamental perspectives for artistic creation in the twentieth century.

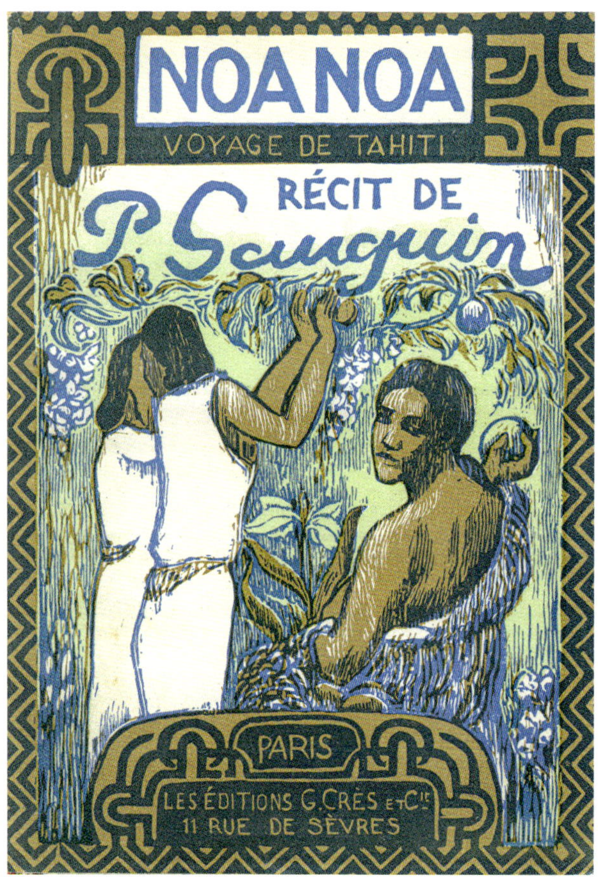

98 {cat.} – Paul Gauguin, *Noa Noa* (Paris: Les Éditions G. Crès et Cie, 1924).

99 {cat.} – Édouard Manet, *L'Évasion de Rochefort* (*The Escape of Rochefort*), 1881.
Oil on canvas, 31 × 28½ in. (79 × 72 cm). Musée d'Orsay, Paris.

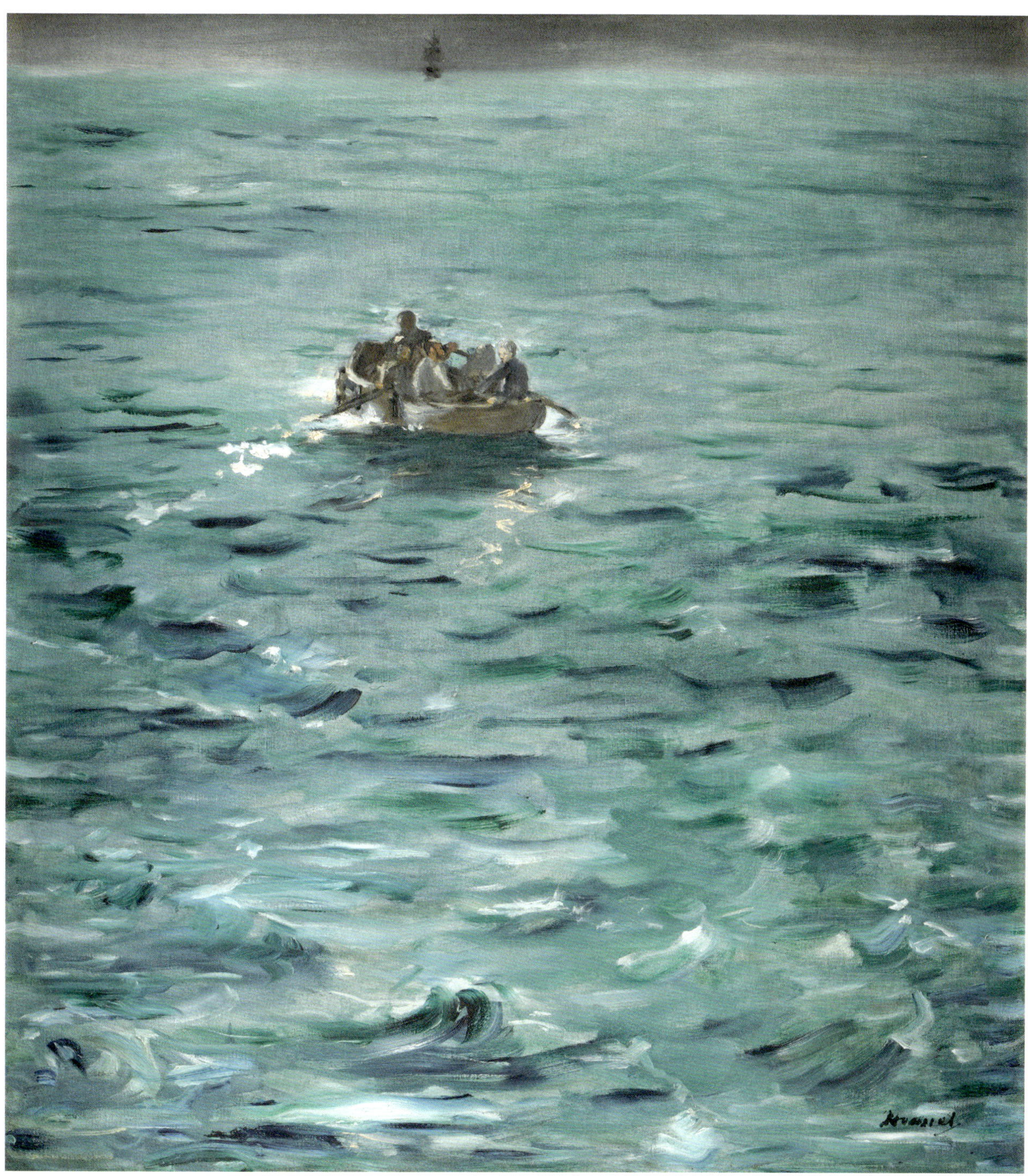

100 {fig.} – Paul Gauguin, *Noa Noa, voyage de Tahiti* (*Noa Noa: Voyage to Tahiti*), manuscript, 1893–1899. Musée d'Orsay, Paris.

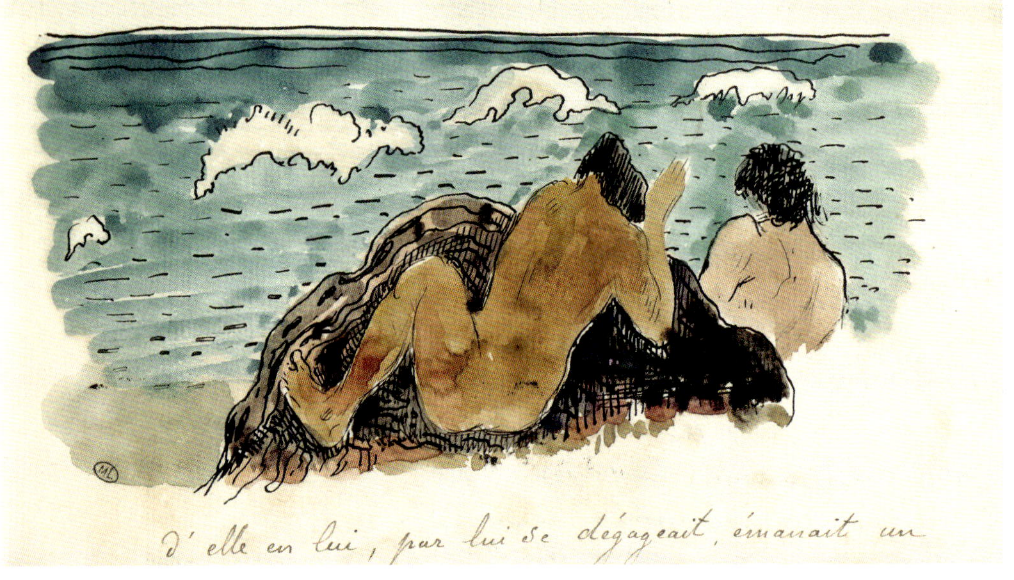

101 {cat.} – Camille Pissarro, *Cocotiers au bord de la mer, St. Thomas* (*Coconut Palms by the Sea, St. Thomas*), 1856. Oil on canvas, 10½ × 13½ in. (26.67 × 34.93 cm). Virginia Museum of Fine Arts, Richmond, VA.

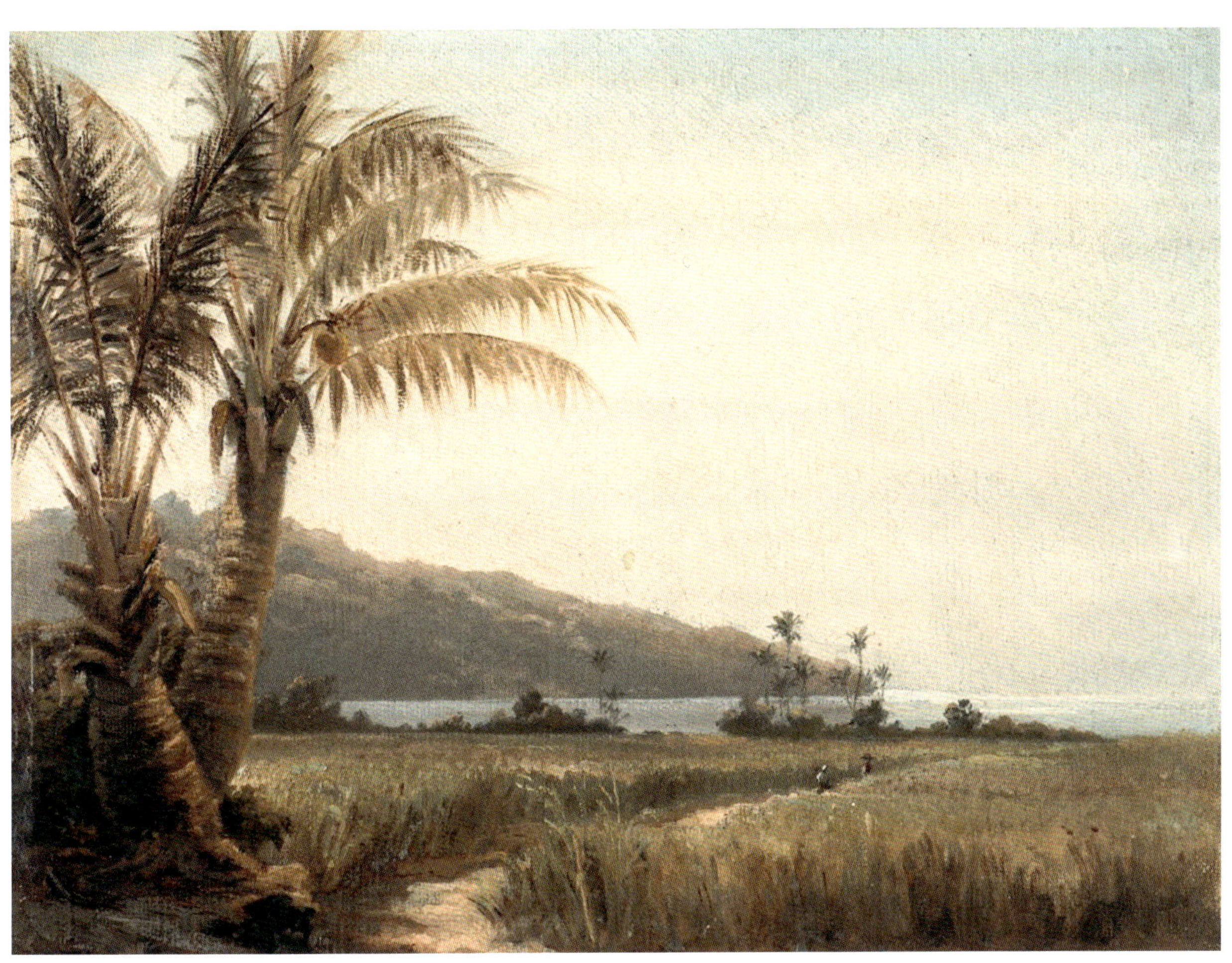

"Flight, only flight! I feel that birds are wild to tread
The floor of unknown foam, and to attain the skies!"
Stéphane Mallarmé, "Sea Breeze," *Poems*, 1887

102 (cat.) – Charles Laval, *Femmes au bord de la mer, esquisse* (Women on the shore, sketch), 1889. Oil on canvas, 2 ft. 1½ in. × 3 ft. (65 × 91.5 cm). Musée d'Orsay, Paris.

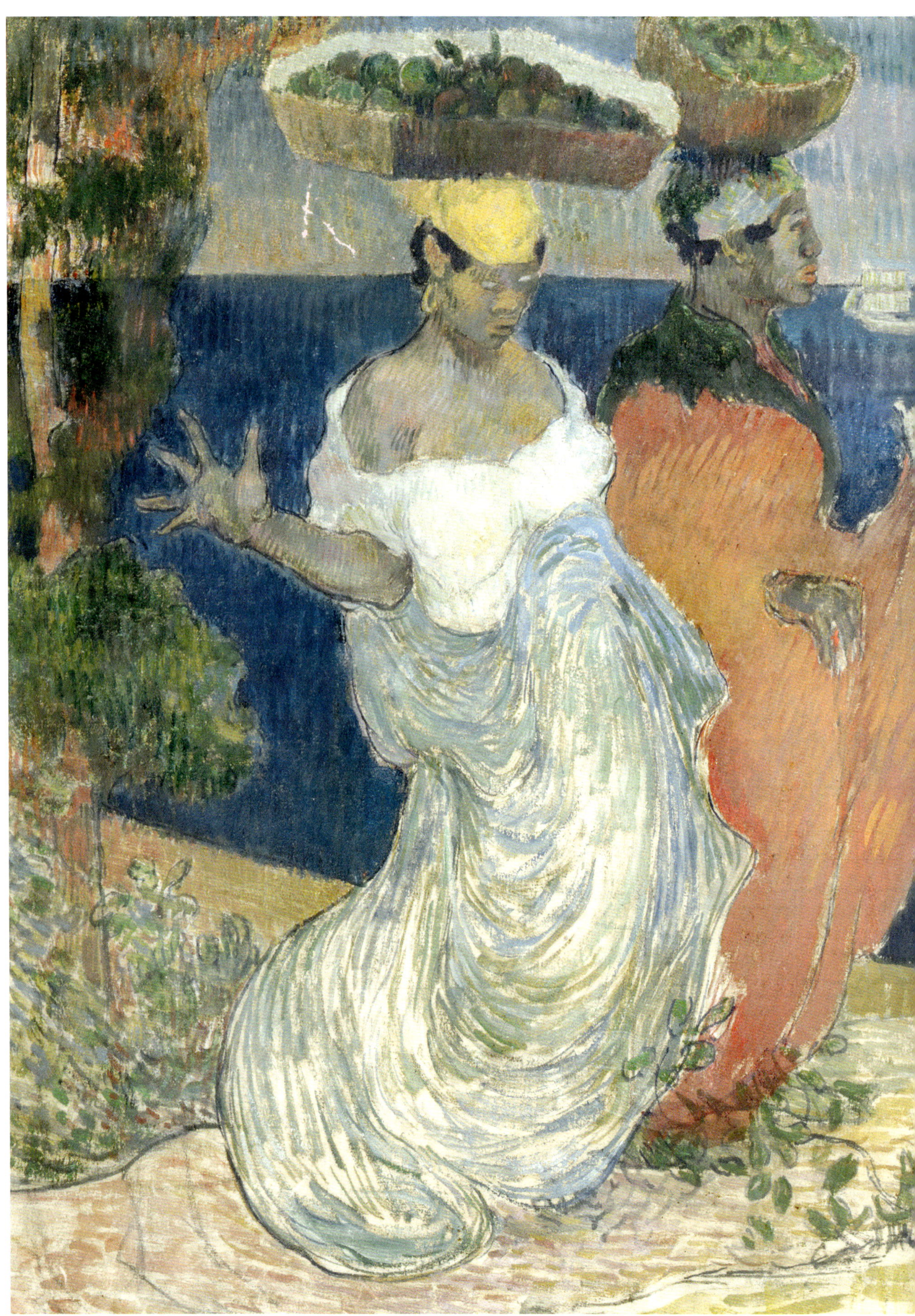

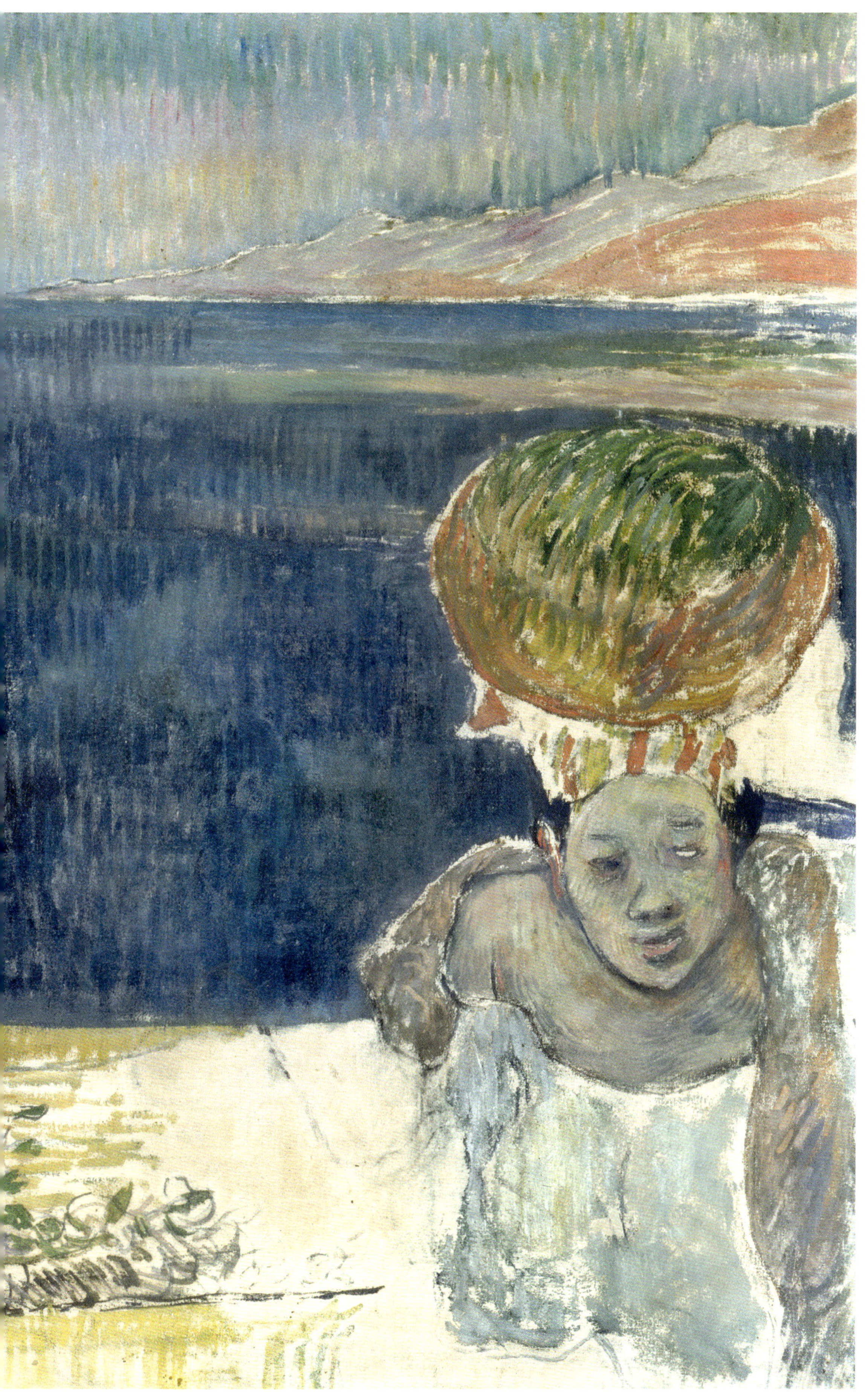

103 (cat.) – Paul Gauguin, *Paysage de Te Vaa* (Te Vaa landscape), 1896.
Oil on canvas, 18 × 29 in. (46 × 74 cm). MuMA, Le Havre.

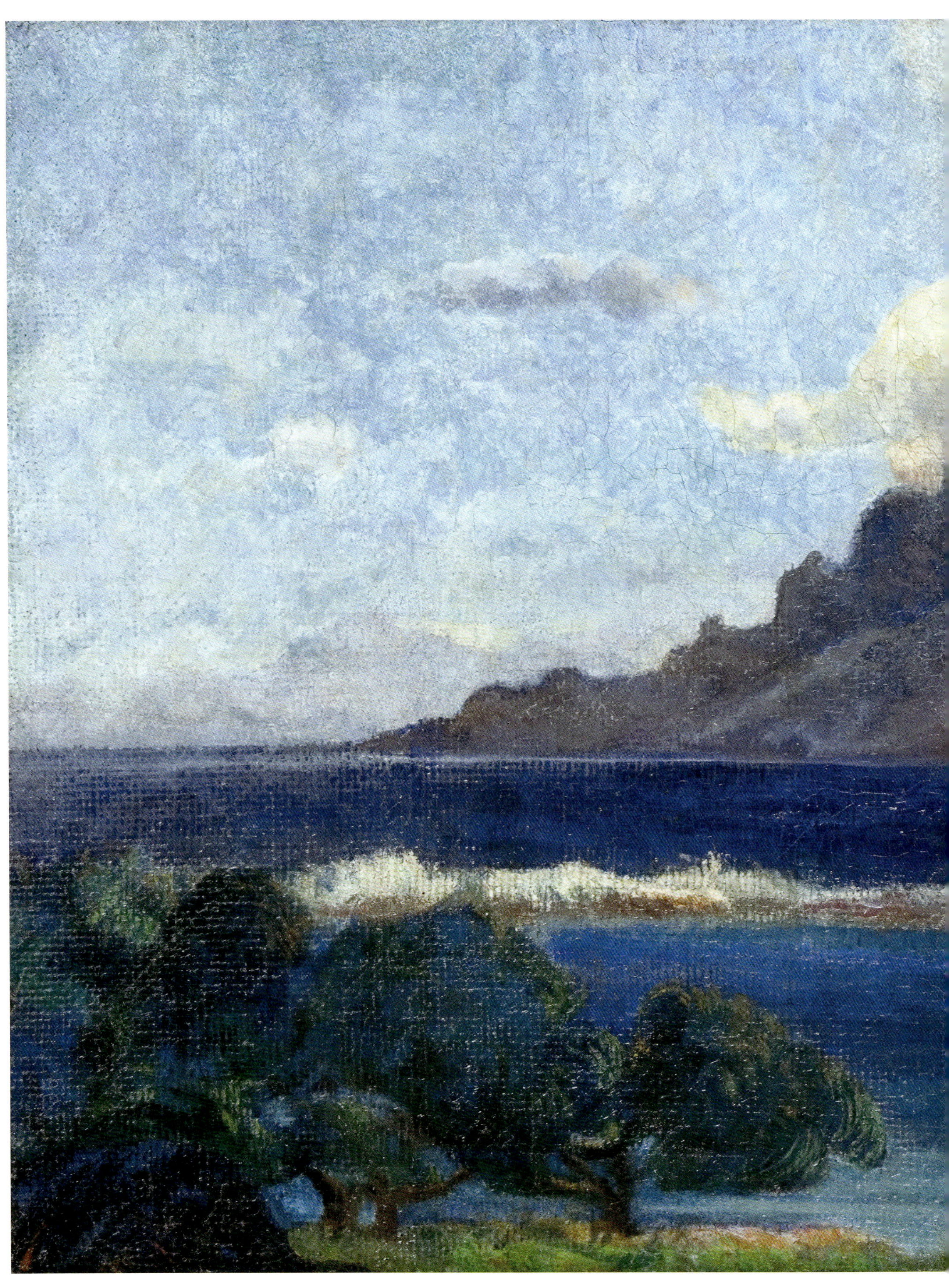

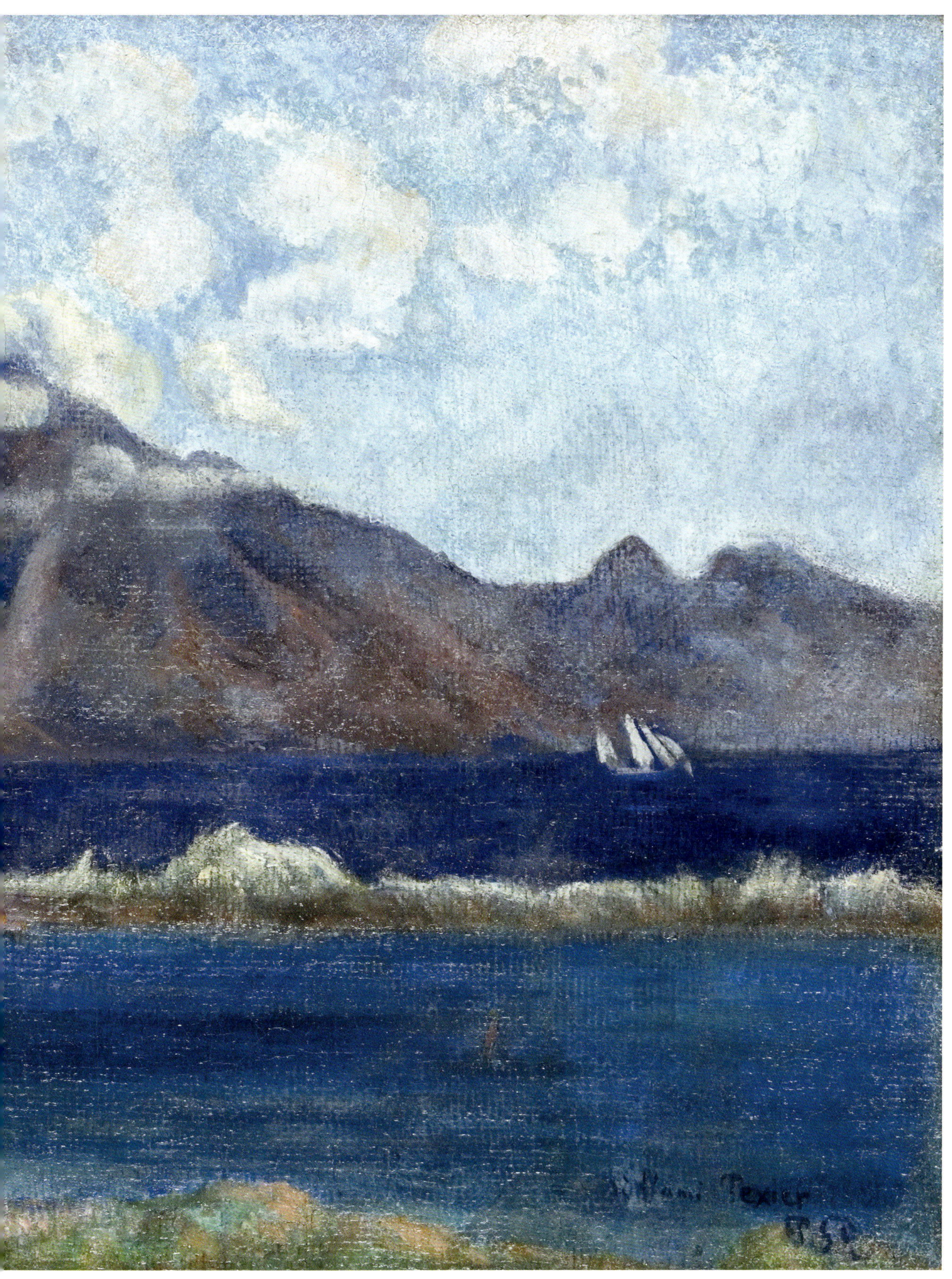

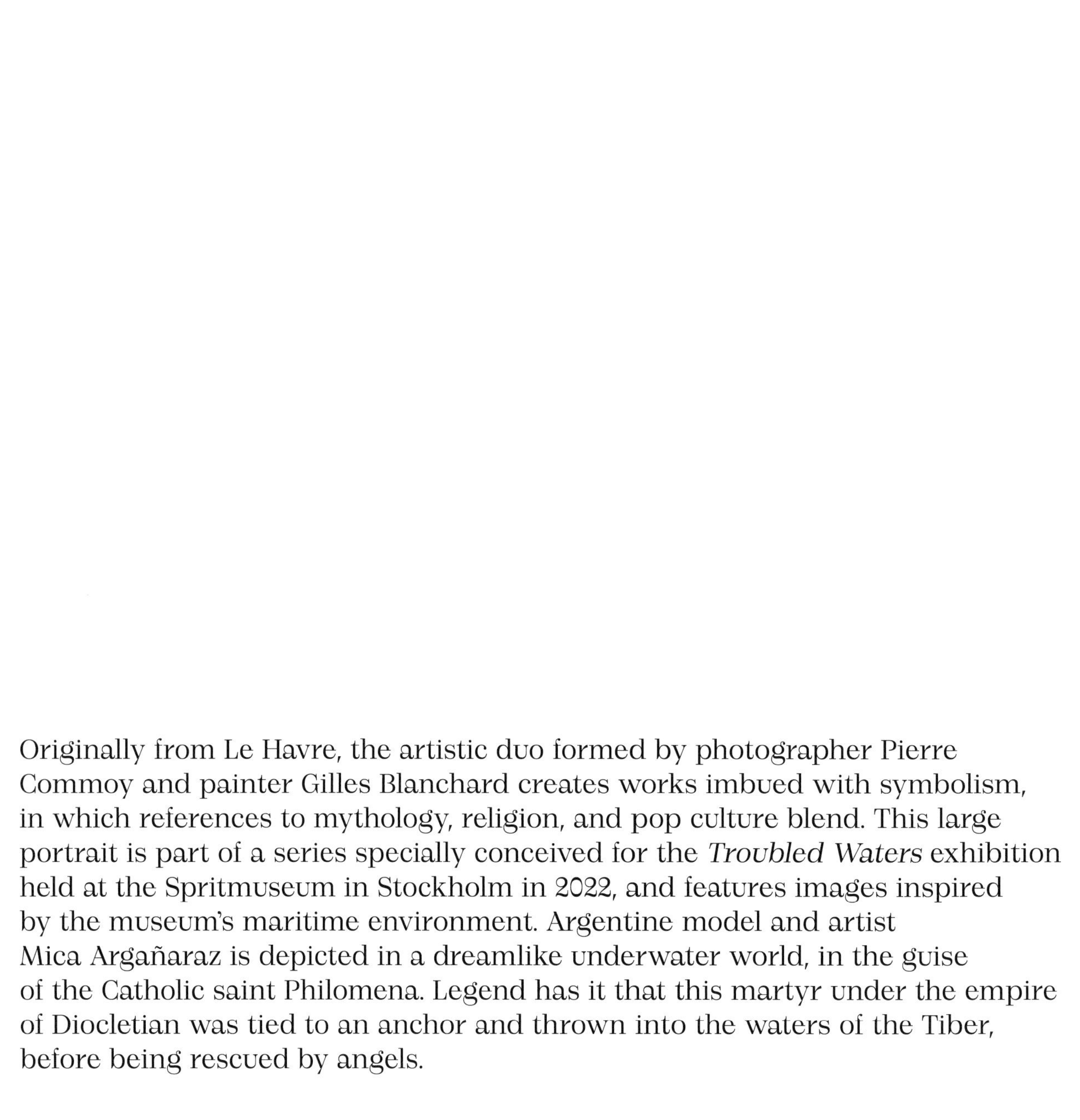

Originally from Le Havre, the artistic duo formed by photographer Pierre Commoy and painter Gilles Blanchard creates works imbued with symbolism, in which references to mythology, religion, and pop culture blend. This large portrait is part of a series specially conceived for the *Troubled Waters* exhibition held at the Spritmuseum in Stockholm in 2022, and features images inspired by the museum's maritime environment. Argentine model and artist Mica Argañaraz is depicted in a dreamlike underwater world, in the guise of the Catholic saint Philomena. Legend has it that this martyr under the empire of Diocletian was tied to an anchor and thrown into the waters of the Tiber, before being rescued by angels.

104 (cat.) – Pierre et Gilles, *Philomène (Mica Argañaraz)*, 2021.
Inkjet photograph printed on canvas and painted, 4 ft. 2 in. × 2 ft. 10 in. (127.5 × 87 cm).
Les Franciscaines, Deauville.

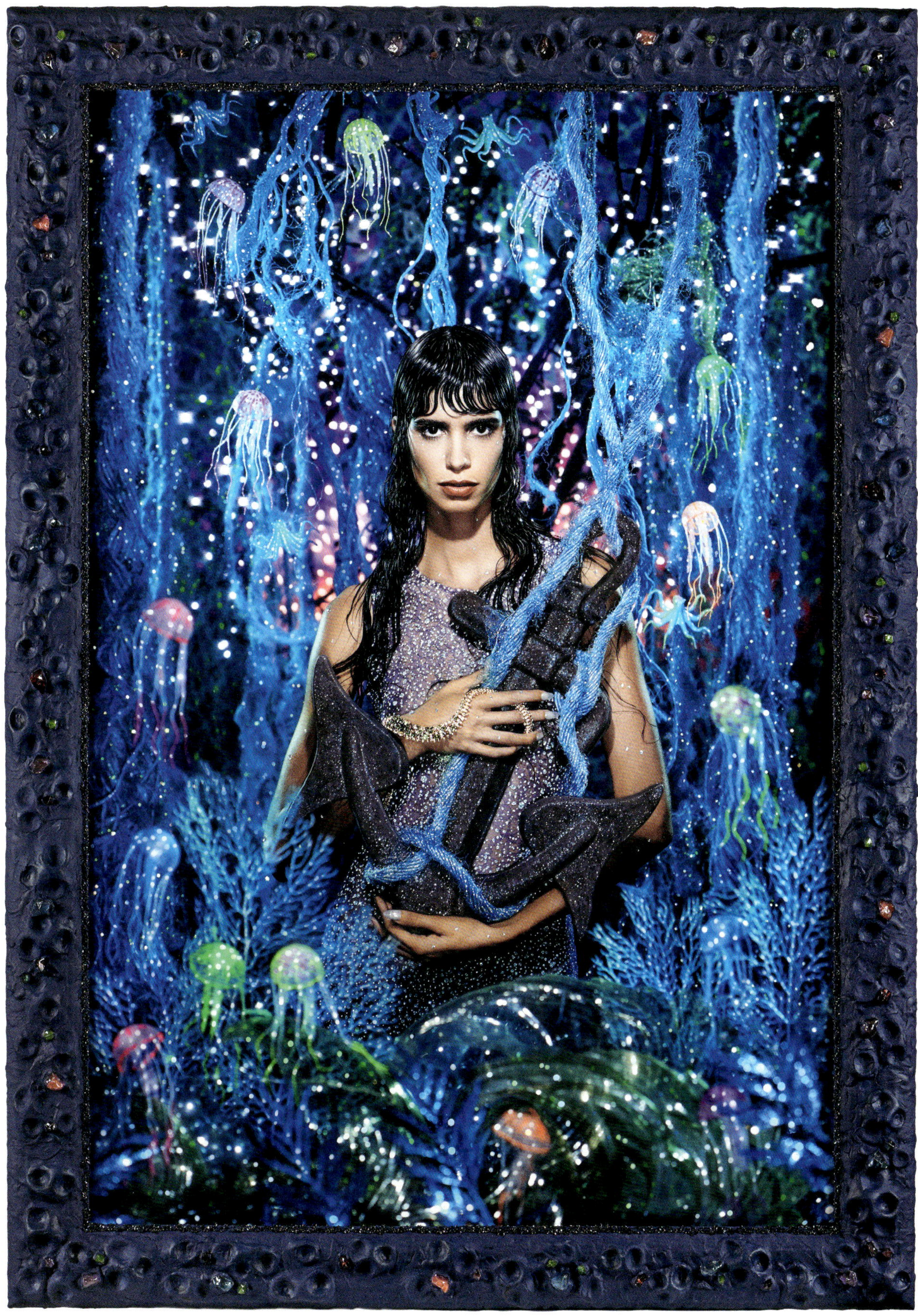

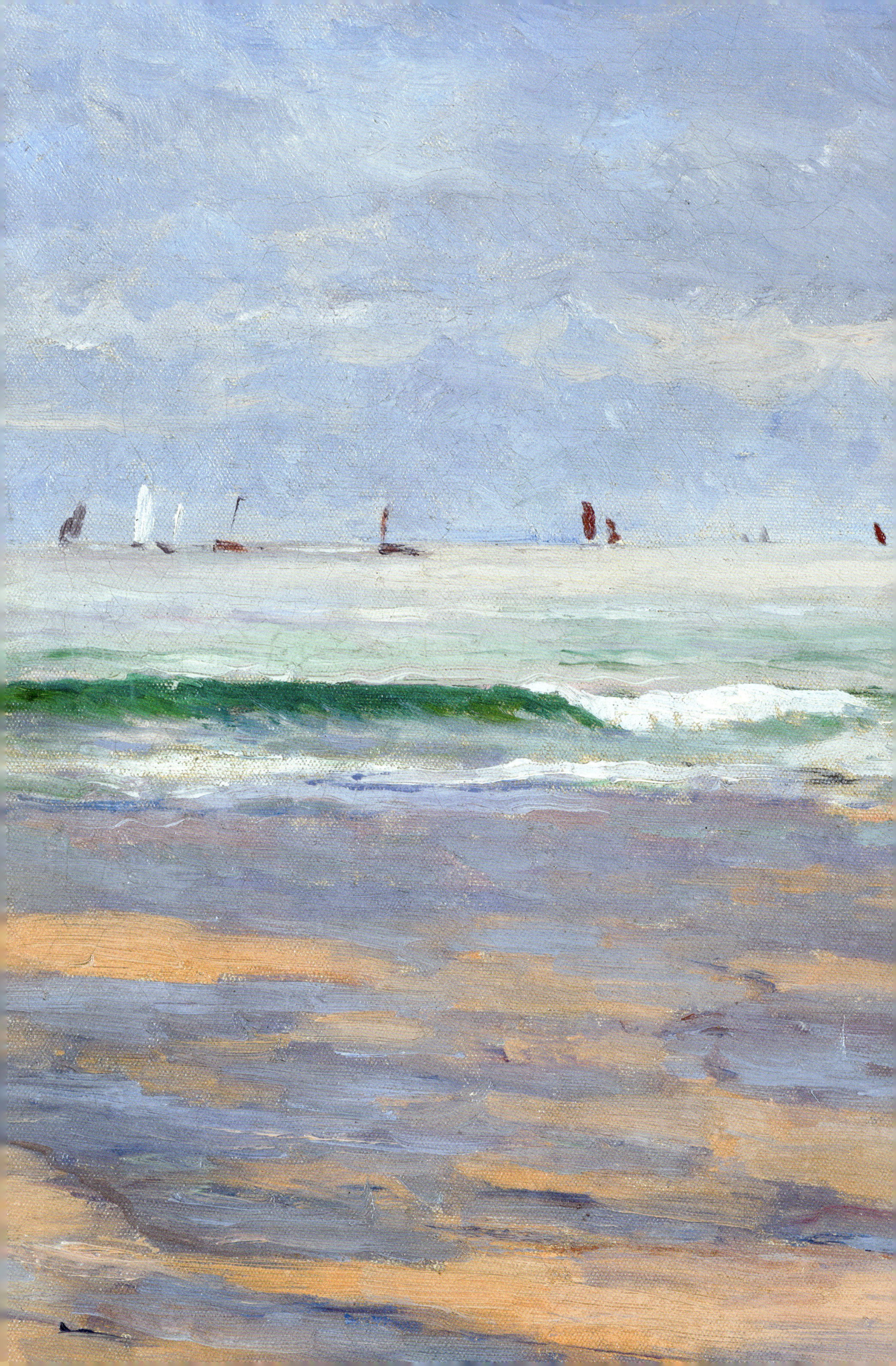

CHRONOLOGY

By Cyrille Sciama, Marie Delbarre, and Valérie Reis

1820

The Établissement des Bains de Dieppe, a sea-bathing resort, is established. The Duchess of Berry is a frequent visitor between 1824 and 1829.

1824

July 18: Eugène Boudin is born in Honfleur. His father is a sailor working on cargo ships sailing between Honfleur, Le Havre, and Rouen. His mother works as a chambermaid cleaning boats.

1825

Painter Charles Mozin discovers Trouville, marking the beginning of the town's success as a seaside resort.

1826

Painters Richard Bonington, Paul Huet, and Eugène Isabey begin traveling to Honfleur and gather at the Saint-Siméon farm.

1830

For the first time, a steamship, *Le Courrier*, is built in Le Havre, at the Augustin Normand shipyard.

1835

• The Boudin family moves to Le Havre.
• Painter Adolphe-Félix Cals participates in the Salon for the first time.

1839

May: The Compagnie des Paquebots du Finistère (Finistère Steamship Company) is founded, and the steamer *Le Morlaisien* makes its maiden voyage on July 10. Two paddle steamers then shuttle between Le Havre and Morlaix during a voyage that lasts between eighteen and twenty hours.

1840

Eugène Isabey meets Boudin in Honfleur in the 1840s, and encourages him to paint.

1841

Spring–Summer: Gustave Courbet visits Normandy. In Le Havre, he sees the ocean for the first time and recounts the experience in a letter to his parents: "We finally saw the sea, the horizonless sea—how odd for a mountain dweller. We saw the beautiful boats that sail on it. It is too inviting, one feels carried away, one would leave to see the whole world."[1]

1842

• December 6: The *Napoléon*—the first propeller-driven ship built in France, in Le Havre—is launched.
• Camille Pissarro, born in Charlotte Amalie, on Saint Thomas island, in the Danish West Indies, arrives in France at the age of twelve. He sees Le Havre's harbor for the first time. The young Pissarro will return to his native island in 1847.
• Rouen's harbor is the first to be connected to Paris by railroad. It will be followed by Le Havre in 1847, then Dieppe in 1848, and finally Marseille in 1852.

1845

The Monet family moves to Le Havre. Claude is five years old.

1846

March: Johan Barthold Jongkind leaves the Netherlands for France. He begins working in the Paris studio of painter Eugène Isabey.

1847

July: Jongkind goes to Le Havre accompanied by Isabey. It is his first trip to the Baie de Seine. He sails to Brittany on a Compagnie des Paquebots du Finistère boat. He visits Morlaix and, in all likelihood, Landerneau and Brest. Jongkind will make the same trip in 1850 and 1851. During his travels, he captures views of Étretat, Dieppe, Yport, Saint-Valery-en-Caux, Honfleur, Douarnenez, Landerneau, Brest, and Camaret-sur-Mer.

1848

Jongkind participates in the Salon de Paris for the first time with *Un port de mer* (A sea port; location unknown).

1849

Paul Gauguin and his family board a ship in Le Havre for Peru. His father dies of a ruptured aneurysm in the Strait of Magellan. His mother, Aline Gauguin, settles with her two children in Lima. In 1855, the family returns to France, to live in Orléans.

1850

• Over the next half-century, a new kind of port, inspired by those in London and Antwerp, is established in France, with structural modifications to accommodate major changes in naval and rail transport.
• Camille Corot visits Honfleur.

1851

• Marseille-based ship owner Albert Rostand creates the maritime transport company Messageries Maritimes, and signs an agreement with the French state to provide postal sea transport.
• The Macaire brothers, photographers based in Le Havre, use daguerreotypes to successfully capture the movement of waves. The images catch the attention of the Académie des Sciences.
• Cals paints on the banks of the Seine, and in Normandy and Brittany.

1852

Camille Pissarro, aged twenty-two, leaves Saint Thomas for Venezuela, accompanied by the Danish painter Fritz Melbye. His departure marks the beginning of his artistic career, despite his family's misgivings.

1853

• Napoleon III and Empress Eugénie visit Dieppe.
• Louis Hachette launches the Bibliothèque des Chemins de Fer (The railroad library), a series of works intended to keep train passengers entertained. In addition to literary classics, essays, and treatises, the series includes travel guides. Of the fourteen "guide-itineraries" published from 1853, three describe a journey to the coast, from Paris to Dieppe, Paris to Le Havre, and Rouen to Le Havre.

1 Courbet to his parents, in Howard F. Isham, *Image of the Sea: Oceanic Consciousness in the Romantic Century* (New York: Peter Lang, 2004), 307.

Maxime Maufra, *La Plage du Pouldu, rivage breton à marée basse. Finistère* (The beach at Le Pouldu, shoreline at low tide: Finistère), detail, 1891 {cat. 74}.

1854

• May–September: Courbet stays in Montpellier, where he paints the sea at Palavas {see cat. 30}. In June 1857, he returns to this coastline, and is inspired to paint new canvases.
• The Société Thermale purchases its first plots of land in Cabourg. A wooden casino is built the same year.

1855

• Jongkind paints *Le Port d'Anvers* (Port of Antwerp) {cat. 15}. In late November, he returns to the Netherlands, after nine years in the French capital, following his disappointment at not receiving a prize at the Salon, where he exhibited three views of Paris in the French section. He settles in Rotterdam, a port city that offers him varied subject matter related to the lives of sailors.
• The Pereire brothers found the Compagnie Maritime Générale in Granville.
• Boudin sells one of his landscape paintings, enabling him to leave for Brittany—the first of many trips to the region.
• October: Pissarro arrives in France. He stays with Anton Melbye, the brother of his friend Fritz and a painter himself. Until 1866, Pissarro presents himself as Melbye's student when he participates in the Salon. Anton Melbye will buy small tropical landscapes dated 1856 from the young artist {see cat. 101}, which will remain in his collection until his death in 1875.

1856

• In Le Havre, Monet meets Boudin, who takes him to Rouelles to paint outdoors.
• December: In London, Gustave Le Gray exhibits a photographic seascape for the first time: *Le Brick au clair de lune* (*Brig on the Water*) {fig. 33}. The seascapes he produces between 1856 and 1858 immediately attract the critics' attention and become some of his most famous works.

1857

Charles Baudelaire publishes *Les Fleurs du mal* (*The Flowers of Evil*). The maritime motif plays a central role, as in his famous line, "Free man, the sea is to thee ever dear!"[2]

1858

At the exhibition of the Société des Amis des Arts in Le Havre, Monet presents a painting for the first time: *Vue prise à Rouelles* (View at Rouelles; Marunuma Art Park, Asaka).

1859

• May: Monet leaves Le Havre for Paris.
• June: Boudin meets Courbet and stays with him in Honfleur.
• Boudin participates in the Salon for the first time, with *Pardon de Sainte-Anne-la-Palud* (*Pardon of Sainte-Anne-la-Palud*), which will be acquired by Le Havre's fine art museum the following year.
• Baudelaire spends a significant part of the year in Honfleur, where he meets Boudin. For the 1859 Salon, he publishes an article in his *Curiosités esthétiques* in praise of the painter.
• December 1: Doctor Joseph Olliffe and banker Armand Donon purchase the first plots of land for the construction of a new seaside resort in Deauville, under the patronage of the Duke of Morny.

1860

• April: As a result of profits from a sale organized by his friends, Jongkind returns to Paris, accompanied by Adolphe-Félix Cals, who had been dispatched to Rotterdam to protect the artist from his own excesses.
• The Bibliothèque des Chemins de Fer series is replaced by the Guides Joanne, named for the editor recruited by Hachette to direct the series. The volumes in the subseries L'Itinéraire Général de la France quickly cover all regions of the country.

1861

• Jules Michelet publishes *La Mer* (*The Sea*).
• Boudin moves to the Butte Montmartre in Paris.
• Armand Guillaumin takes classes at the Académie Suisse, where he befriends Pissarro.
• After obtaining the contract with the French state for postal services on transatlantic lines, the Pereire brothers' Compagnie Générale Maritime is renamed Compagnie Générale Transatlantique.
• The first Grand Hôtel in Cabourg is constructed. It will be rebuilt in 1907, and future guests include Marcel Proust.

1862

• Boudin spends time in Honfleur and Trouville, where he meets Jongkind in the fall.
• In Sainte-Adresse, Jongkind and Monet meet. Monet, who stays with his family, will later comment, "At home, I flaunted my new acquaintance. The name Jongkind impressed my parents and gave them confidence in my beginnings."[3]

1863

• Manet, Boudin, Jongkind, Pissarro, Cals, and Guillaumin participate in the Salon des Refusés.
• August–October: Jongkind makes his first long stay in Honfleur, accompanied by Boudin. He paints outdoors, particularly in oil on canvas. Jongkind will return to Honfleur in the summers of 1864 and 1865—his last trip to Normandy.

1864

• Monet paints his first seascapes in Sainte-Adresse and Honfleur: *Le Phare de l'Hospice* (Hospice lighthouse; Kunsthaus, Zurich).
• Manet paints *Le Kearsarge à Boulogne* (*The "Kearsarge" at Boulogne*; The Metropolitan Museum of Art, New York). This Union warship used during the American Civil War sank the Confederate ship *Alabama* off the coast of Cherbourg several weeks earlier.
• The Compagnie Générale Transatlantique inaugurates a route between Le Havre and New York with the paddle steamer *Washington*, measuring 346 feet (106 meters) in length and weighing 3500 tons (3200 metric tons). The *France*—the first liner to bear the name—is added to the route the same year.

2 Charles Baudelaire, "Man and the Sea," *Baudelaire: The Flowers of Evil*, trans. Cyril Scott (London: Elkin Mathews, 1909).
3 Claude Monet quoted in Marc Elder, *À Giverny, chez Claude Monet* (Paris: Éditions Mille et Une Nuits, 2010).

1865

• Monet exhibits for the first time at the official Salon. He presents two seascapes: *La Pointe de la Hève à marée basse* (*La Pointe de la Hève at Low Tide*; 1865, Kimbell Art Museum, Fort Worth, TX) and *L'Embouchure de la Seine à Honfleur* (*The Mouth of the Seine at Honfleur*; 1865, Norton Simon Museum, Pasadena, CA).
• September: Courbet discovers Trouville and paints a series of seascapes and portraits while there. He works alongside Boudin and James Abbott McNeill Whistler.
• December 6: Gauguin embarks as a pilot's apprentice aboard the three-masted *Luzitano* headed for Rio de Janeiro.

1866

• Victor Hugo publishes *Les Travailleurs de la mer* (*Toilers of the Sea*).
• Mid-September: Courbet spends a month in Deauville, accompanied by Boudin and Monet. He paints twenty-five "ocean landscapes."
• The Guides Diamant—a subseries of the Guides Joanne—are launched, providing abridged versions of the Guides Itinéraires Joanne. They focus on destinations that are easy to reach by train or boat, especially French regions that are already popular, such as Brittany, Normandy, and the Mediterranean coast, with a particular emphasis on seaside resorts.

1867

During the summer, Monet stays in Le Havre. While there, he paints *Terrasse à Sainte-Adresse* (*Garden at Sainte-Adresse*; 1867, The Metropolitan Museum of Art, New York).

1868

• Jongkind makes the etching *Le Soleil couchant, port d'Anvers* (*Sunset, Port of Antwerp*) {cat. 14}. Between 1862 and 1878, he produces twenty engravings, including this view of Antwerp's port, as well as several views of Honfleur's harbor.
• At the Salon, Monet exhibits two views of the ocean at Le Havre: *Navires sortant des jetées du Havre* (Ships leaving the jetties, Le Havre; canvas lost) and *La Jetée du Havre* (The jetty at Le Havre; 1867–1868, location unknown), both of which are praised by Émile Zola.
• Manet stays in Boulogne-sur-Mer, where he carries out several plein air studies, which he uses later for *Sur la plage à Boulogne* (*On the Beach, Boulogne-sur-Mer*; Virginia Museum of Fine Arts, Richmond, VA).

1869

• Jules Verne publishes *Vingt mille lieues sous les mers* (*Twenty Leagues Under the Sea*).
• Edgar Degas spends time in Trouville, where he paints four beach scenes (National Gallery, London).
• August–September: Courbet stays in Étretat, where he continues the series of low tide landscapes that he began in Trouville, in 1865. From late summer to spring of the following year, he paints—both outdoors and in his studio—several works featuring waves or stormy seas.

1870

• Monet spends the summer in Trouville, where he paints *L'Hôtel des Roches Noires. Trouville* (*The Hôtel des Roches Noires at Trouville*) {fig. 8}, *La Plage de Trouville* (*The Beach at Trouville*; National Gallery, London), and *Sur la plage à Trouville* (On the beach at Trouville; 1870, private collection).
• July 19: France declares war on Prussia. Monet goes to London, initially leaving his wife, Camille, and their son, Jean, under the protection of the Boudin family; they will join him later. While in London, he paints three canvases of port activity on the Thames, which illustrate his growing interest in modern industrial ports—a theme that he will develop upon his return to France.

1871

Boudin, who sought refuge in Belgium during the war, paints scenes of markets, canals, and ports, including *Port d'Anvers* (Port of Antwerp) {cat. 16}.

1872

• After spending seven years as a sailor, and traveling to Peru, Chile, the Mediterranean, the Black Sea, and the North Sea, Gauguin becomes a broker in Paris. His guardian, banker and collector Gustave Arosa, introduces him to the art world. Gauguin soon takes up painting as a hobby.
• In Le Havre, Monet paints *Impression, soleil levant* (*Impression, Sunrise*; Musée Marmottan Monet, Paris).

1873

• Manet stays in Boulogne-sur-Mer, painting *Sur la plage* (*On the Beach*; Musée d'Orsay, Paris).
• Cals buys a house in Honfleur, where he will spend the last ten years of his life.

1874

May 15: the first impressionist exhibition opens at Nadar's studio on Boulevard des Capucines in Paris.

1875

Henry Moret carries out his military service in Lorient. His regiment is commanded by Colonel La Villette, whose wife, Élodie, is a well-known seascape painter. Moret takes his first drawing lessons from painter Ernest Corroller, whom he may have met through La Villette.

1876

• Gauguin exhibits a landscape at the Salon.
• Gustave and his brother Martial Caillebotte join the Cercle de la Voile sailing club in Paris. They win many regattas. Gustave Caillebotte goes on to draw blueprints for twenty-five boats, becoming equally famous for the advances he brings to naval construction methods.
• Henry Moret enrolls at the École Nationale des Beaux-Arts in Paris, in Henri Lehmann's studio.
• Philip Wilson Steer, an adolescent with a passion for objets d'art and coin collecting, visits the Louvre.

1878

• The inaugural issue of *Yacht*—the first French sailing magazine, sponsored by Gustave Caillebotte—is published.
• Philip Wilson Steer enters the Gloucester School of Art, in the UK.

1879

Renoir stays with the family of banker Paul Bérard at the Château de Wargemont, near Dieppe. He explores the coast and paints his first seascapes.

1880

Moret and Charles Laval exhibit for the first time at the Salon.

1881

• March–April: Monet stays in Fécamp.
• Late summer: Monet travels to Sainte-Adresse and Trouville. Moret moves to Le Pouldu.
• Édouard Dantan starts spending time in Villerville.
• The young Paul Signac begins boating on the Seine. Painting and sailing will be his two great passions in life. Harbors will inspire him throughout his career {see cat. 25}; his series *Ports de France* (Ports of France), carried out between 1929 and 1931, will be the culmination of his lifelong interest in the theme and of his work as a watercolorist.

1882

• February–mid-April: Monet spends time in Dieppe and Pourville. He returns to Pourville with his family the following summer.
• July–August: Signac stays in Port-en-Bessin, where he paints *Port-en-Bessin (étude no. 5, l'avant-port)* (Port-en-Bessin [study no. 5, outer harbor]) {cat. 26}.
• Caillebotte paints *Trouville, la plage et les villas* (Trouville, beach and villas; private collection).
• Steer enters the Académie Julian in Paris.

1883

• Winter: Monet returns to Étretat for the first time since 1867.
• Summer: Renoir spends five weeks on Guernsey, where he produces forty or so drawings, prints, and paintings depicting the area around Moulin Huet Bay.
• Invited to the home of Léon Monet, Claude's brother, Pissarro stays at Les Petites Dalles, between Fécamp and Saint-Valery-en-Caux.
• Steer enters the studio of Alexandre Cabanel at the École des Beaux-Arts.
• Monet and Renoir visit the Côte d'Azur, and paint Bordighera, Monaco, and Antibes.

1884

• At the beginning of the year, Monet returns to the Mediterranean coast alone.
• Boudin purchases land in Deauville, near the dunes, and has a house built.
• Steer moves to London.

1885

• Gauguin is living in Dieppe, where he paints a series of impressionist seascapes: *Baignade à Dieppe* (*Bathing, Dieppe*; 1885, Ny Carlsberg Glyptotek, Copenhagen); *Baigneuses à Dieppe* (Bathers at Dieppe; 1885) {fig. 9}; *Le Port de Dieppe* (*Harbor Scene, Dieppe*; 1885, Manchester Art Gallery, Manchester).
• Guillaumin makes Signac's acquaintance. Signac meets Pissarro in Guillaumin's studio.
• September: Monet returns to Étretat, where he stays until February 1886. There, he meets Guy de Maupassant, who later mentions the painter's work, and that of Courbet, in *Gil Blas*: "La vie d'un paysagiste" (The life of a landscape painter), September 28, 1886.

1886

• Early in the year, the book *Par les champs et par les grèves* (*Over Strand and Field: A Record of Travel through Brittany*) is published. It recounts a trip through Brittany undertaken by Gustave Flaubert and Maxime Du Camp in 1847. Monet keeps this edition in his personal library.
• Pierre Loti publishes *Pêcheur d'Islande* (*An Iceland Fisherman*).
• Steer and his friend Walter Sickert are among the founding members of the New English Art Club, through which they both defend impressionist painting.
• April 10–May 10: Art dealer Paul Durand-Ruel holds his impressionist exhibition in New York.
• July–October: Gauguin stays in Pont-Aven, where he meets Laval. The two men soon become friends.
• August: Renoir rents a house in Saint-Briac, a small port on Brittany's Emerald Coast. The young Signac and Émile Bernard also stay in this village the same year.
• September 12: Monet arrives on Belle-Île-en-Mer, where he stays until November 25. He meets Australian painter John Peter Russell and art critic Gustave Geffroy there. He writes to his friend Gustave Caillebotte, "I had gotten used to painting the Channel, and I knew how to go about it, but the Atlantic Ocean is quite different."[4] While there, Monet carries out a series of thirty-nine paintings from nature {see cat. 68}, which will be exhibited the following year in Paris, at Georges Petit's gallery. Several other artists will follow his example and paint sites around Belle-Île, including Jean Francis Auburtin in 1894, Henri Matisse in 1896, and Maxime Maufra in 1907.

1887

April 10: Gauguin and Laval set sail from Saint-Nazaire for Panama. Their ship stops in Martinique on April 23. After failing to find work in Panama, the two men return to Martinique in June. Gauguin stays until October, while Laval extends his trip until 1888 {see cat. 102}.

4 Letter from Claude Monet to Gustave Caillebotte, October 11, 1886, quoted in Denise Delouche, *Monet à Belle-Île* (Quimper: Éditions Palantines, 2006), 78.

1888

• January–April: Monet paints in Antibes.
• In Pont-Aven, Henry Moret's studio becomes a gathering place for painters, among them Gauguin, Émile Bernard, and Laval, who has returned from Martinique.

1889

• May: Maxime Maufra discovers Pont-Aven.
• October: Gauguin stays at Marie Henry's, in Le Pouldu, near the Grand-Sables beach. Moret is nearby, in Le Bas-Pouldu, at another inn.

1890

• Octave de Champeaux is awarded the title Peintre de la Marine (official painter of the fleet).
• Gauguin stays in Le Pouldu.
• July 14: Moret meets Maufra in Pont-Aven and the two men become friends.

1891

• April 1: Gauguin sets sail from Marseille for Oceania, via the Panama Canal. He arrives in Papeete on June 9.
• Maufra spends six months in Pont-Aven before making his way to Le Pouldu.
• Guillaumin wins a large lottery prize, which enables him to leave his job with the city of Paris and devote himself to painting and travel. His first reaction is said to have been, "Great, I will be able to paint the sea!"

1893

• At the beginning of the year, Moret stays on the island of Groix, where he paints *Île de Groix, paysage côtier* (Groix island, coastal landscape) {cat. 70}.
• Guillaumin paints in Agay {see cat. 62}, where he spends winter and spring from now on.
• June 4: Gauguin leaves Tahiti. After a long stop in Nouméa, he arrives in Marseille on August 30.

1894

• February 21: Gustave Caillebotte dies. In his will, the painter leaves his collection of impressionist paintings and pastels to the French state. This bequest will be officially accepted, but only partially, in 1896.
• May–November: Gauguin makes his sixth and final trip to Pont-Aven and Le Pouldu. During an excursion to Concarneau, a fight erupts with some fishermen, leaving Gauguin with a broken ankle.

1895

• Durand-Ruel offers Moret a contract. The dealer's support provides the artist with some financial security.
• Guillaumin likely visits Belle-Île this year.
• July 3: Gauguin sets sail for Marseille. He arrives in Papeete on September 9.

1896

• The *Belem*—the last French three-masted ship still in operation—is built in Nantes.
• Georges Méliès produces two short films, which have since been lost: *Déchargement de bateaux au Havre* (*Unloading the Boat*) and *Panorama du Havre vu d'un bateau* (*Panorama of Le Havre Taken from a Boat*).

1897

• January–March: Monet returns to Pourville and paints the Gorge of the Petit Ailly, near Varengeville {see cat. 52}.
• February 9: The Caillebotte bequest is exhibited for the first time, at the Musée du Luxembourg in Paris. The collection includes many views of the Seine, and two seascapes: Monet's *Les Rochers de Belle-Île, la Côte sauvage* (Rocks on Belle-Île, Côte Sauvage) {cat. 68} and Paul Cézanne's *Le Golfe de Marseille vu de l'Estaque* (*The Bay of Marseille Seen from l'Estaque*; 1877–1879, Musée d'Orsay, Paris).
• May–July: Boudin makes his final trip to Brittany. He visits places thus far only familiar to him through the paintings of his contemporaries: Belle-Île and Pont-Aven.
• July: Moret stays on the island of Ushant, where he paints *L'Île d'Ouessant, la chaussée Keller* (Ushant island, Keller's causeway) {cat. 69}.

1899

Following successful painting sessions in Rouen in 1898, focused on views of the harbor, Pissarro travels to Varengeville in search of new motifs. Later, in 1900, he will stay in Berneval, and then in Dieppe in 1901, where he will nevertheless refrain from painting the harbor.

1901

September 10: Gauguin leaves Tahiti for the Marquesas Islands.

1902

Once again, Pissarro travels to Dieppe. This time, he explores views of the port that inspire a series of twenty-one canvases.

1903

• Summer: In Le Havre, Pissarro completes a series of depictions of Normandy harbors that he had begun during trips to Rouen and Dieppe. He stays at the Hôtel Continental, facing the jetty, from whose windows he paints more than twenty canvases of the harbor entrance, which is undergoing renovation to accommodate new, increasingly large ships {see fig. 2 and cat. 24}.

1905

Maufra stays in Le Havre. Captivated by this modern, industrial port—a stark contrast to the Breton fishing villages with which he is familiar—he carries out a series of paintings of the various boats circulating there, and in particular the large transatlantic liners {see cat. 93}.

1912

December 6: At Cinéma-Théâtre (7 Boulevard Poissonnière in Paris), the Société des Établissements Gaumont presents a film in natural colors produced using the company's Chronochrome technique. The images include shots of the beaches at Deauville and Trouville, featuring strollers and bathers, as well as the harbor at Honfleur {see cats. 7, 90, 91, 92}.

1913

Marc Elder publishes *Peuple de la mer* (The people of the sea), which receives the Prix Goncourt.

105 {cat.} – Maxime Maufra, *L'Orage* (The storm), 1892.
Graphite, gouache, and watercolor on paper, 17½ × 24½ in. (45 × 63 cm). Private collection.

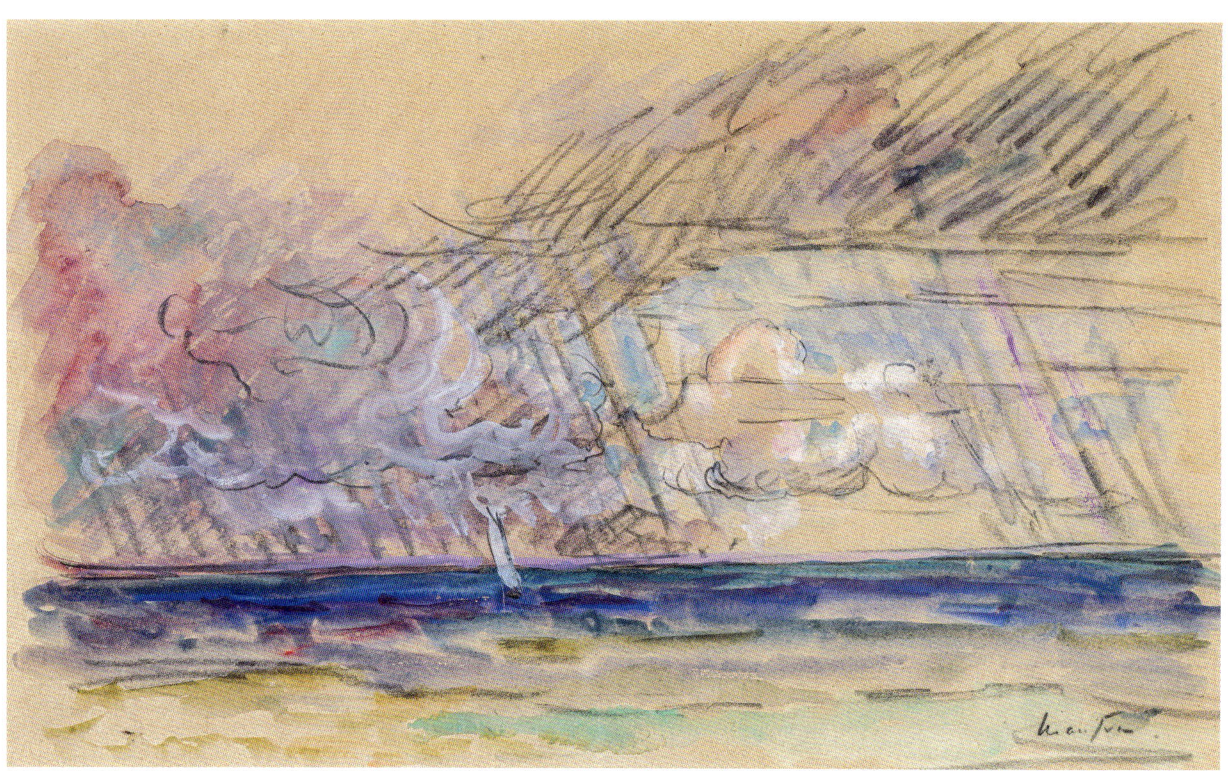

LIST OF EXHIBITED WORKS

Darren Almond (born 1971)
Fullmoon@ Dunluce, 2007.
C-print mounted on aluminum, 4 ft. 2 in. × 4 ft. 1½ in. (128 × 126 cm).
FRAC Normandie Collection, 2011.003.4 {cat. 40}.

Jean Francis Auburtin (1866–1930)
Les Pêcheries. Falaises de Pourville (Fishing grounds: Cliffs at Pourville), n.d.
Oil on canvas, 2 ft. 7 in. × 4 ft. 3 in. (78.4 × 130.4 cm).
Musée des Impressionnismes, Giverny, gift of Francine and Michel Quentin, 2019, MDIG 2019.4.1 {cat. 54}.

Jean Francis Auburtin
Varengeville. Rayons jaunes aux falaises de Mordal (Varengeville: Yellow light on the cliffs at Mordal), n.d.
Oil on board, 2 ft. 1½ in. × 3 ft. (65 × 92 cm).
Musée des Impressionnismes, Giverny, gift of Francine and Michel Quentin, 2019, MDIG 2019.1.1 {cat. 55}.

Jacques-Émile Blanche (1861–1942)
La Plage de Dieppe (The beach at Dieppe), n.d.
Oil on canvas, 19½ × 23½ in. (50 × 60 cm).
Château-Musée, Dieppe {cat. 39}.

Eugène Boudin (1824–1898)
Barques de pêche et voiliers (Fishing boats and sailboats), 1853–1859.
Oil on board, 8½ × 12½ in. (22 × 32.4 cm).
Musée d'Art Moderne André Malraux, Le Havre, B 148 {cat. 23}.

Eugène Boudin
Ciel (Sky), c. 1855–1860.
Pastel on paper, 3½ × 6½ in. (9.5 × 16.5 cm).
Private collection, through the Galerie de la Présidence, Paris {cat. 32}.

Eugène Boudin
Rivage normand (Normandy coastline), c. 1858–1869.
Pastel on gray paper, 4 × 7 in. (10 × 18 cm).
Private collection, through the Galerie de la Présidence, Paris {cat. 29}.

Eugène Boudin
La Plage (The beach), c. 1863–1866.
Pastel on paper, 10 × 16 in. (25.5 × 40.5 cm).
Private collection, through the Galerie de la Présidence, Paris {cat. 79}.

Eugène Boudin
Élégants et crinolines sur la plage (Dandies and crinolines on the beach), 1864.
Watercolor on paper, 7 × 10½ in. (18.3 × 27.1 cm).
Private collection, through the Galerie de la Présidence, Paris {cat. 78}.

Eugène Boudin
La Plage de Trouville (The beach at Trouville), 1865.
Oil on board, 10½ × 15½ in. (26.5 × 40.3 cm).
Musée d'Orsay, Paris, bequest of Eugène Béjot, 1932, RF 3663 {cat. 83}.

Eugène Boudin
Normandes étendant du linge sur la plage (Norman women drying laundry on the beach), 1865.
Oil on canvas, 18 × 24 in. (46.2 × 61.3 cm).
Musée d'Orsay, Paris, recovered at the end of World War II and entrusted to the French Musées Nationaux in 1950. History incomplete between 1933 and 1945 based on current research. If dispossession is discovered, the work will be returned to its rightful owners, MNR 192 {cat. 50}.

Eugène Boudin
Scène de plage (Beach scene), 1866.
Watercolor on paper, 5½ × 10½ in. (14.3 × 26.6 cm).
Private collection, through the Galerie de la Présidence, Paris {cat. 82}.

Eugène Boudin
La Plage de Trouville (The beach at Trouville), 1867.
Oil on wood, 12 × 19 in. (31 × 48 cm).
Musée d'Orsay, Paris, gift of Dr. Eduardo Mollard, 1961, RF 1961 27 {cat. 84}.

Eugène Boudin
La Plage (The beach), 1868.
Watercolor on paper, 6 × 10 in. (15 × 26 cm).
Private collection, through the Galerie de la Présidence, Paris {cat. 87}.

Eugène Boudin
Scène de plage (Beach scene), 1869.
Oil on panel, 7 × 12½ in. (18 × 32.5 cm).
Private collection, through the Galerie de la Présidence, Paris {cat. 85}.

Eugène Boudin
Voiliers (Sailboats), 1869.
Oil on wood, 9½ × 12 in. (23.9 × 30.9 cm).
Musée d'Orsay, Paris, on long-term loan to the Musée des Beaux-Arts, Caen, bequest of Isaac de Camondo, 1911, RF 1966 {cat. 97}.

Eugène Boudin
Port d'Anvers (Port of Antwerp), 1871.
Oil on wood, 12½ × 18 in. (31.5 × 46.5 cm).
Musée d'Orsay, Paris, gift of Max and Rosy Kaganovitch, 1973, RF 1973 10 {cat. 16}.

Eugène Boudin
Port de Camaret (Port of Camaret), 1872.
Oil on canvas, 22 × 35½ in. (55.5 × 89.5 cm).
Musée d'Orsay, Paris, on long-term loan to the Musée des Beaux-Arts, Angers, bequest of Enriqueta Alsop in the name of Dr. Eduardo Mollard, 1972, RF 1972 15 {cat. 19}.

Eugène Boudin
Lavandière près de Trouville (*Washerwoman near Trouville*), c. 1872–1876.
Oil on wood, 10 ½ × 16 in. (27.6 × 41.3 cm).
National Gallery of Art, Washington, D.C., Collection of Mr. and Mrs. Paul Mellon, 1983.1.15 {cat. 49}.

Eugène Boudin
La Poissonnerie de Trouville (The fish market in Trouville), 1875.
Oil on wood, 9½ × 14 in. (24 × 36 cm).
Musée des Impressionnismes, Giverny, gift of Christophe and Teresa Karvelis Senn, 2023, MDIG 2023.1.1 {cat. 22}.

Eugène Boudin
Berck, pêcheuses sur le rivage (Fisherwomen on the shore, Berck), 1880–1885.
Oil on panel, 5½ × 6½ in. (13.5 × 17 cm).
Private collection, through the Galerie de la Présidence, Paris {cat. 86}.

Eugène Boudin
Coucher de soleil à marée basse (Sunset at low tide), 1884.
Oil on canvas, 3 ft. 10 in. × 5 ft. 3 in. (117 × 161 cm).
Musée d'Art et d'Histoire, Saint-Lô, 2008.1.1 {cat. 46}.

Eugène Boudin
Deauville, le bassin (Deauville, the basin), 1884.
Oil on panel, 18½ × 15 in. (46.5 × 38 cm).
Musée des Impressionnismes, Giverny, acquired through the generosity of the Cercle des Mécènes du Musée des Impressionnismes Giverny, the Caisse d'Épargne Normandie, and Quadra Consultants, 2020, MDIG 2020.1.1 {cat. 12}.

Eugène Boudin
Le Bassin de l'Eure au Havre (The Eure basin at Le Havre), 1885.
Oil on canvas, 25½ × 35½ in. (65 × 90 cm).
Musée d'Art, d'Histoire et d'Archéologie, Évreux, 7859 {cat. 21}.

Eugène Boudin
Crinolines sur la plage de Villers (Crinolines on the beach at Villers), 1886.
Oil on panel, 5½ × 10½ in. (14 × 26 cm).
Private collection, through the Galerie de la Présidence, Paris {cat. 4}.

Eugène Boudin
Un grain (Squall), 1886.
Oil on canvas, 3 ft. 10 in. × 5 ft. 3 in. (117 × 160 cm).
Collection du Musée des Jacobins, Morlaix, 2011.6.1 {cat. 58}.

Eugène Boudin
Deauville, le bassin (Deauville, the basin), 1887.
Oil on panel, 10½ × 8 in. (27 × 21 cm).
Private collection {cat. 13}.

Eugène Boudin
Les Crinolines à Trouville (Crinolines at Trouville), 1889.
Oil on board, 5½ × 9 in. (14 × 22.8 cm).
Private collection, through the Galerie de la Présidence, Paris {cat. 89}.

Eugène Boudin
La Plage de Deauville (The beach at Deauville), 1893.
Oil on canvas, 20 × 29½ in. (50.5 × 74.5 cm).
Musée des Beaux-Arts, Caen, no. 217 {cat. 44}.

Eugène Boudin
La Plage de Bénerville, coucher de soleil (The beach at Bénerville, sunset), also known as *Les Vaches noires* (The Vaches Noires rocks), 1894.
Pastel on paper, 10 × 15½ in. (26 × 40 cm).
Musée des Impressionnismes, Giverny, acquired through the generosity of the Cercle des Mécènes, 2022, MDIG 2022.6.1 {cat. 34}.

Eugène Boudin
Soleil couchant sur l'estuaire de la Seine vers Honfleur (Sunset over the Seine estuary near Honfleur), n.d.
Pastel on paper, 5½ × 8½ in. (14.5 × 21.8 cm).
Musée des Impressionnismes, Giverny, acquired through the generosity of David Ummels, Guernsey, 2022, MDIG 2022.7.1 {cat. 31}.

Eugène Boudin
Sur la plage (On the beach), n.d.
Watercolor on paper, 5 × 9 in. (13 × 23.4 cm).
Private collection, through the Galerie de la Présidence, Paris {cat. 81}.

Théodore de Broutelles (1842–1933)
Paysage côtier (Coastal landscape), c. 1900.
Pastel on board, 13 × 8½ in. (33 × 22 cm).
Musée des Impressionnismes, Giverny, MDIG 2023.6.1 {cat. 36}.

Adolphe-Félix Cals (1810–1880)
Pêcheur (Fisherman), 1874.
Oil on canvas, 10 × 12 in. (26 × 31 cm).
Musée d'Orsay, Paris, on long-term loan to the Musée Eugène Boudin in Honfleur, recovered at the end of World War II and entrusted to the French Musées Nationaux in 1951. Despoiled work, current research unable to determine origin. Restitution pending identification of rightful owners, MNR 627 {cat. 43}.

Octave de Champeaux (1827–1903)
Clair de lune en mer (Moonlit sea), 1897.
Oil on canvas, 27½ × 3 ft. 3 in. (70 × 100 cm).
Musée d'Orsay, Paris, RF 1090 {cat. 37}.

Camille Corot (1796–1875)
Trouville, bateaux de pêche échoués dans le chenal (Trouville, fishing boats aground in the channel), 1875.
Oil on paper mounted on canvas, 8 × 9 in. (21 × 23.5 cm).
Musée d'Orsay, Paris, gift of Max and Rosy Kaganovitch, 1973, RF 1973 13 {cat. 17}.

Gustave Courbet (1819–1877)
Les Bords de la mer à Palavas (*The Seashore at Palavas*), c. 1854.
Oil on canvas, 23½ × 29 in. (60 × 73.5 cm).
Olivier Senn Collection, gift of Hélène Senn Foulds, 2004, Musée d'Art Moderne André Malraux, Le Havre, 2004.3.31 {cat. 30}.

Gustave Courbet
La Vague (*The Wave*), 1870.
Oil on canvas, 35 in. × 3 ft. 6 in. (88.4 × 107.2 cm).
Musée des Beaux-Arts, Orléans, 314–844 {cat. 60}.

Gustave Courbet
La Vague (*The Wave*), c. 1871–1873.
Oil on canvas, 21½ × 25½ in. (55 × 65 cm).
De Bueil & Ract-Madoux Collection, Paris {cat. 57}.

Édouard Dantan (1848–1897)
Plate à Villerville, marée basse (*Boat at Villerville, Low Tide*), October 1881.
Oil on wood, 15½ × 7½ in. (40 × 19.5 cm).
Musée des Impressionnismes, Giverny, MDIG 2019.5.1 {cat. 42}.

Charles-François Daubigny (1817–1878)
Coucher de soleil près de Villerville (*Sunset near Villerville*), c. 1876.
Oil on canvas, 2 ft. 11 in. × 4 ft. 3 in. (89 × 130 cm).
The Mesdag Collection, The Hague {cat. 35}.

Marie-Auguste Flameng (1843–1893)
Marine (Seascape), c. 1880.
Oil on wood, 15 × 11 in. (38 × 27.8 cm).
Private collection {cat. 94}.

Marie-Auguste Flameng
Marine (Seascape), c. 1880.
Oil on wood, 15 × 11 in. (38 × 27.8 cm).
Private collection {cat. 95}.

Marie-Auguste Flameng
Marine (Seascape), c. 1880.
Oil on wood, 21½ × 12½ in. (55 × 32.7 cm).
Private collection {cat. 96}.

Paul Gauguin (1848–1903)
Sur la plage de Bretagne
(On the beach in Brittany), 1889.
Oil on canvas, 23½ × 28½ in.
(60 × 73 cm).
Nasjonalmuseet for Kunst, Arkitektur og Design, Oslo, NG.M.01007 {cat. 66}.

Paul Gauguin
Paysage de Te Vaa
(Te Vaa landscape), 1896.
Oil on canvas, 18 × 29 in.
(46 × 74 cm).
Musée d'Art Moderne André Malraux, Le Havre, A 458 {cat. 103}.

Paul Gauguin
Noa Noa. Édition définitive. Bois dessinés et gravés, d'après Paul Gauguin, par Daniel de Monfreid (Noa Noa, definitive edition: Woodblock prints drawn and printed by Daniel de Monfried after Paul Gauguin).
Paris: Les Éditions G. Crès et Cie, 1924 {cat. 98}.

Paul Gauguin
Noa Noa, voyage de Tahiti
(*Noa Noa: Voyage to Tahiti*).
Stockholm: Jan Vörlag, 1947.
Facsimile of the manuscript now held in the Musée d'Orsay's collections (not reproduced).

Société des Établissements Gaumont
Deauville–Trouville: The Beach and Seafront, 1912.
Chronochrome film, 6 min. 30 sec.
GP Archives {cats. 7, 90, 91, 92}.

Armand Guillaumin (1841–1927)
Rocher à la pointe de la Baumette
(Rock at Pointe de la Baumette), 1893.
Oil on canvas, 13 × 18 in.
(33 × 46 cm).
Wallraf-Richartz Museum & Fondation Corboud, Cologne, Dep. FC 559 {cat. 62}.

Armand Guillaumin
Rochers sur la côte bretonne
(Rocks off the coast of Brittany), c. 1895.
Oil on canvas, 23½ × 29 in.
(60 × 73.5 cm).
Musée d'Art et d'Archéologie, Guéret, 78.5.28 {cat. 71}.

Johan Barthold Jongkind (1819–1891)
Le Port d'Anvers (Port of Antwerp), 1855.
Oil on canvas, 2 ft. 8 in. × 3 ft. 6 in.
(82 × 107 cm).
Musée d'Orsay, Paris, on long-term loan to the Musée des Beaux-Arts, Rennes, work recovered at the end of World War II and entrusted to the French Musées Nationaux in 1950. History incomplete between 1933 and 1945 based on current research. If dispossession is discovered, the work will be returned to its rightful owners, MNR 499 {cat. 15}.

Johan Barthold Jongkind
Le Soleil couchant, port d'Anvers
(*Sunset, Port of Antwerp*), 1868.
Etching, 14½ × 22 in. (37 × 56 cm).
Musée des Impressionnismes, Giverny, MDIG 2023.3.2 {cat. 14}.

Charles Laval (1861–1894)
Femmes au bord de la mer, esquisse (Women on the shore, sketch), 1889.
Oil on canvas, 2 ft. 1½ in. × 3 ft.
(65 × 91.5 cm).
Musée d'Orsay, Paris, RF 2001 11 {cat. 102}.

Édouard Manet (1832–1883)
L'Évasion de Rochefort
(*The Escape of Rochefort*), 1881.
Oil on canvas, 31 × 28½ in.
(79 × 72 cm).
Musée d'Orsay, Paris, RF 1984 158 {cat. 99}.

Alexandre Marcette (1853–1929)
En route. Bateaux sur la mer du Nord (En route: Boats on the North Sea), n.d.
Gouache on paper on canvas, 26½ × 37½ in. (67 × 95 cm).
Musée d'Orsay, Paris, RF 1979 36 {cat. 59}.

Maxime Maufra (1861–1918)
La Plage du Pouldu, rivage breton à marée basse. Finistère
(The beach at Le Pouldu, shoreline at low tide: Finistère), 1891.
Oil on canvas, 16 × 22½ in.
(41.2 × 57.2 cm).
Musée des Impressionnismes, Giverny, MDIG 2023.7.1 {cat. 74}.

Maxime Maufra
L'Orage (The storm), 1892.
Graphite, gouache, and watercolor on paper, 17½ × 24½ in.
(45 × 63 cm).
Private collection {cat. 105}.

Maxime Maufra
Effet de lune (Moonlight), 1899.
Oil on canvas, 18½ × 21½ in.
(46.6 × 55.4 cm).
Musée des Beaux-Arts, Reims, 907.19.173 {cat. 38}.

Maxime Maufra
Rochers au soleil couchant; L'Anse du port Lonnec
(Rocks at sunset: The cove at Port Lonnec), 1899.
Oil on canvas, 21½ × 28½ in.
(54.1 × 73.1 cm).
Musée des Beaux-Arts, Reims, 907.19.175 {cat. 75}.

Maxime Maufra
Côte de Goulphar (The coast at Goulphar), 1900.
Oil on canvas, 25½ × 32 in.
(65.5 × 81 cm).
Musée des Beaux-Arts, Rennes, 1952.4.3 {cat. 61}.

Maxime Maufra
La Tempête à Quiberon
(Gale in Quiberon), 1900.
Oil on canvas, 2 ft. 8 in. × 3 ft. 3 in.
(81.2 × 100 cm).
Musée des Beaux-Arts, Reims, 907.19.181 {cat. 63}.

Maxime Maufra
Le Bateau à la côte; Morgat
(Grounded boat at Morgat), 1902.
Oil on canvas, 2 ft. 8 in. × 3 ft. 3 in.
(81.5 × 100 cm).
Musée d'Art Moderne André Malraux, Le Havre, A 478 {cat. 64}.

Maxime Maufra
Transatlantique sortant du port
(Transatlantic liner leaving port), 1905.
Oil on canvas, 25½ × 32 in.
(65.5 × 81 cm).
Musée d'Art Moderne André Malraux, Le Havre, A 476 {cat. 93}.

Maxime Maufra
Entrée du port de Port Goulphar, Belle-Île-en-Mer (*Entrance to the Port on Port-Goulphar, Belle-Île-en-Mer*), 1909.
Oil on canvas, 20 × 25½ in.
(51 × 65.5 cm).
Carmen Thyssen-Bornemisza Collection, on long-term loan to the Museo Nacional Thyssen-Bornemisza, Madrid, CTB.1994.11 {cat. 72}.

Claude Monet (1840–1926)
Sainte-Adresse, 1867.
Oil on canvas, 22½ × 31½ in.
(57 × 80 cm).
National Gallery of Art, Washington, D.C., gift of Catherine Gamble Curran and family, in honor of the fiftieth anniversary of the National Gallery of Art, 1990.59.1 {cat. 48}.

Claude Monet
Falaises à Pourville
(*Cliffs at Pourville*), 1882.
Oil on canvas, 1 ft. 11½ in. × 3 ft. 3 in.
(60 × 100 cm).
National Gallery of Art,
Washington, D.C., Collection
of Mr. and Mrs. Paul Mellon,
1985.64.27 {cat. 53}.

Claude Monet
Les Rochers à Pourville, marée basse (*The Rocks at Pourville, Low Tide*), 1882.
Oil on canvas, 25½ × 31 in.
(64.3 × 78.7 cm).
Memorial Art Gallery, Rochester,
NY, 1939.22 {cat. 47}.

Claude Monet
Marée basse aux Petites Dalles
(*Low Tide at Les Petites Dalles*),
1884.
Oil on canvas, 23½ × 28½ in.
(60 × 73 cm).
Hasso Plattner Collection,
MB-Mon-16 {cat. 45}.

Claude Monet
Les Rochers de Belle-Île, la Côte sauvage (Rocks on Belle-Île, Côte Sauvage), 1886.
Oil on canvas, 25½ × 32 in.
(65.5 × 81.5 cm).
Musée d'Orsay, Paris, bequest
of Gustave Caillebotte, 1894
{cat. 68}.

Claude Monet
La Pointe du Petit Ailly
(*The Pointe du Petit Ailly*), 1897.
Oil on canvas, 29 × 36½ in.
(73.5 × 92.7 cm).
Nahmad Collection, CM55165
{cat. 52}.

Henry Moret (1856–1913)
Gros temps à Doëlan
(Rough weather at Doëlan), n.d.
Oil on canvas, 31½ × 23½ in.
(80 × 60 cm).
Musée des Beaux-Arts, La Cohue,
Vannes, 33.6.1 {cat. 67}.

Henry Moret
L'Île d'Ouessant, la chaussée Keller (Ushant island, Keller's causeway), 1897.
Oil on canvas, 23½ × 28½ in.
(60 × 73 cm).
Musée Lambinet, Versailles,
91.9.39 {cat. 69}.

Henry Moret
Île de Groix, paysage côtier
(Groix island, coastal landscape),
c. 1893.
Oil on canvas, 3 ft. × 2 ft. 1 in.
(92 × 64 cm).
Musée de la Compagnie des
Indes – Musée d'Art et d'Histoire
de la Ville de Lorient, Lorient, 166
{cat. 70}.

Pierre et Gilles (Pierre Commoy and Gilles Blanchard, born 1950 and 1953 respectively)
Philomène (Mica Argañaraz), 2021.
Inkjet photograph printed
on canvas and painted,
4 ft. 2 in. × 2 ft. 10 in. (127.5 × 87 cm).
Les Franciscaines, Deauville,
2022.7.1 {cat. 104}.

Camille Pissarro (1830–1903)
Cocotiers au bord de la mer, St. Thomas (*Coconut Palms by the Sea, St. Thomas*), 1856.
Oil on canvas, 10½ × 13½ in.
(26.67 × 34.93 cm).
Virginia Museum of Fine Arts,
Richmond, VA, Collection
of Mr. and Mrs. Paul Mellon,
83.45 {cat. 101}.

Camille Pissarro
L'Anse des pilotes. Le Havre, matin, soleil, marée montante
(*The Outer Harbour of Le Havre, Morning, Sun, Rising Tide*), 1903.
Oil on canvas, 21½ × 25½ in.
(54.5 × 65 cm).
Musée d'Art Moderne André
Malraux, Le Havre, A 495 {cat. 24}.

Pierre-Auguste Renoir (1841–1919)
Petit port (Small port), 1919.
Oil on canvas, 18 × 22 in.
(46 × 56 cm).
Musée d'Orsay, Paris, recovered
at the end of World War II
and entrusted to the French
Musées Nationaux in 1951.
History incomplete between
1933 and 1945 based on current
research. If dispossession
is discovered, the work will be
returned to its rightful owners,
MNR 840 {cat. 27}.

Paul Signac (1863–1935)
Port-en-Bessin (étude no. 5, l'avant-port) (Port-en-Bessin [study no. 5, outer harbor]), summer 1882.
Oil on canvas, 12½ × 21½ in.
(32 × 55.5 cm).
Musée des Impressionnismes,
Giverny, gift of Charlotte Hellman
Cachin, 2019, MDIG 2019.2.1
{cat. 26}.

Paul Signac
La Trinité, May 29, 1929.
Graphite and watercolor on paper,
11¼ × 17 in. (28.3 × 43 cm).
Musée des Impressionnismes,
Giverny, gift of Charlotte Hellman
Cachin, 2019, MDIG 2019.2.2
(not reproduced).

Paul Signac
Barfleur (preparatory sketch for the eponymous painting, FC 596), 1931.
India ink wash on paper,
2 ft. 4½ in. × 3 ft. (73 × 92 cm).
Musée des Impressionnismes,
Giverny, gift of Charlotte Hellman
Cachin in memory of her mother,
Françoise Cachin, 2017, MDIG
2017.1.1 {cat. 25}.

Philip Wilson Steer (1860–1942)
Jeune femme sur la plage
(*Young Woman on the Beach*),
1888.
Oil on canvas, 4 ft. 1 in. × 3 ft.
(125.5 × 92 cm).
Musée d'Orsay, Paris, gift
of Mr. Paul Rosenberg, 1927,
RF 1980 169 {cat. 77}.

INDEX OF NAMES

Page numbers in **bold** refer to illustrations

PHOTOGRAPHIC CREDITS

© Alamy Images: fig. 9; cat. 101
© All rights reserved/photo: Jean-Charles Louiset: cat. 94; cat. 95; cat. 96; cat. 105
© Darren Almond: cat. 40
© Stefano Bianchetti/Bridgeman Images: fig. 5
© Bibliothèque Nationale de France, Paris: fig. 1
© Bibliothèque Nationale de France, Paris, Dist. RMN-Grand Palais/image BNF: fig. 10; fig. 56
© Carmen Thyssen Collection: cat. 72
© Château-Musée, Dieppe: cat. 39
© Christie's Images/Bridgeman Images: fig. 3
© De Bueil & Ract-Madoux Collection, Paris: cat. 57
© Fuji Art Museum, Tokyo/ Bridgeman Images: fig. 6
© Galerie de la Présidence, Paris: cat. 4; cat. 13; cat. 29; cat. 32; cat. 78; cat. 79; cat. 81; cat. 82; cat. 85; cat. 86; cat. 87; cat. 89
© GP Archives: cat. 7; cat. 90; cat. 91; cat. 92
© Memorial Art Gallery of the University of Rochester, Rochester, NY: cat. 47
© The Mesdag Collection: cat. 35
© Ministère de la Culture – Médiathèque du Patrimoine et de la Photographie, Dist. RMN-Grand Palais/ Paul Lancrenon: fig. 20
© Ministère de la Culture – Médiathèque du Patrimoine et de la Photographie, Dist. RMN-Grand Palais/ Touring Club de France: fig. 41
© MuMa Le Havre/David Fogel: cat. 24
© MuMa Le Havre/Florian Kleinefenn: cat. 23; cat. 30; cat. 64; cat. 93; cat. 103
© MuMa Le Havre/ Charles Maslard: fig. 2
© Musée d'Art et d'Histoire, Saint-Lô/photo: P.-Y. Le Meur: cat. 46
© Musée d'Art, Histoire et Archéologie, Évreux: cat. 21
© Musée des Beaux-Arts, Caen/photo: M. Seyve: cat. 44
© Musée des Beaux-Arts, Orléans, 2023: cat. 60
© Musée des Beaux-Arts, Reims/photo: Christian Devleeschauwer: cat. 38; cat. 63; cat. 75; cover
© Musée des Beaux-Arts, Rennes, Dist. RMN-Grand Palais/Patrick Merret: cat. 15
© Musée des Beaux-Arts, Rennes/ photo: Jean-Manuel Salingue: cat. 61
© Musée des Beaux-Arts, Vannes: cat. 67
© Musée des Impressionnismes, Giverny/photo: Jean-Charles Louiset: cat. 12; cat. 14; cat. 22; cat. 26; cat. 31; cat. 34; cat. 36; cat. 42; cat. 54; cat. 55; cat. 74
© Musée des Impressionnismes, Giverny/photo: Patrice Schmidt: cat. 25
© Musée des Jacobins, Morlaix: cat. 58
© Musée Lambinet, Ville de Versailles: cat. 69
© Musée du Quai Branly – Jacques Chirac, Paris, Dist. RMN-Grand Palais/ image Musée du Quai Branly – Jacques Chirac: fig. 76; fig. 80; fig. 88
© Nahmad Collection: cat. 52
© Nasjonalmuseet/Jarre, Anne Hansteen: cat. 66
© National Gallery of Art, Washington, D.C.: cat. 48; cat. 49; cat. 53
© Pictorial Collection, Ville de Lorient: cat. 70
© Pierre et Gilles: cat. 104
© Hasso Plattner Collection: cat. 45
© Rheinisches Bildarchiv: cat. 62
© RMN-Grand Palais/ Benoît Touchard: cat. 71
© RMN-Grand Palais (Domaine de Chantilly): fig. 33
© RMN-Grand Palais (Musée d'Orsay)/Martine Beck-Coppola: cat. 97
© RMN-Grand Palais (Musée d'Orsay)/Jean-Gilles Berizzi: cat. 19
© RMN-Grand Palais (Musée d'Orsay)/Gérard Blot: fig. 100
© RMN-Grand Palais (Musée d'Orsay)/Alexis Brandt: fig. 51
© RMN-Grand Palais (Musée d'Orsay)/Adrien Didierjean: cat. 68
© RMN-Grand Palais (Musée d'Orsay)/Jean-Pierre Lagiewski: cat. 43
© RMN-Grand Palais (Musée d'Orsay)/Hervé Lewandowski: fig. 8; cat. 17; fig. 18; cat. 37; cat. 59; cat. 77; cat. 83; cat. 102; fig. 106
© RMN-Grand Palais (Musée d'Orsay)/Stéphane Maréchalle: cat. 50
© RMN-Grand Palais (Musée d'Orsay)/Mathieu Rabeau: cat. 16
© RMN-Grand Palais (Musée d'Orsay)/Franck Raux: cat. 84; cat. 99
© RMN-Grand Palais (Musée d'Orsay)/Patrice Schmidt: cat. 27; fig. 73; fig. 98
© SZ Photo/Bridgeman Images: fig. 65
© Tallandier/Bridgeman Images: fig. 11
© Victoria and Albert Museum, London, Dist. RMN-Grand Palais/image Victoria and Albert Museum: fig. 28

Cover image – Maxime Maufra, *Rochers au soleil couchant; L'Anse du port Lonnec* (Rocks at sunset: The cove at Port Lonnec), 1899. Oil on canvas, 21½ × 28½ in. (54.1 × 73.1 cm). Musée des Beaux-Arts, Reims. Photo © Manuel Cohen

Gustave Le Gray, *Le Soleil au Zénith, Normandie* (*The Sun at Its Zenith—Ocean*), detail, 1856 (fig. 28).

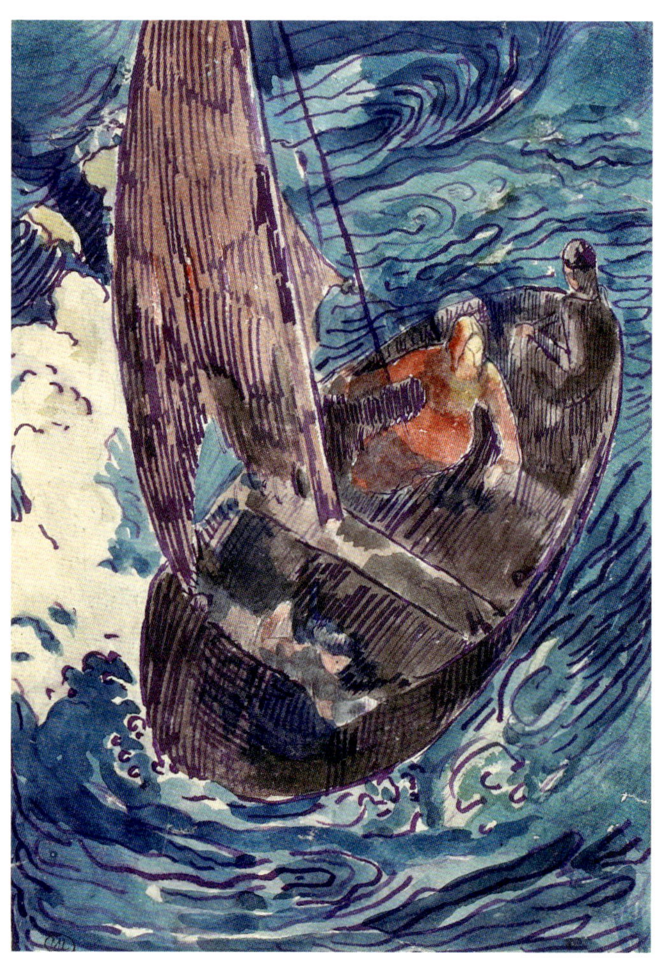

106 {fig.} – Paul Gauguin, *Noa Noa, voyage de Tahiti* (*Noa Noa: Voyage to Tahiti*), 1893–1899.
Musée d'Orsay, Paris.